MW01165675

"And thou Daniel
sealing חתם until Time's end." Daniel 12.4a

The CODE is activated!

'the last shall be first and the first last'
Matthew 20.16

Forward Text

בשנתשלושלמכ \ לגרלכלקצהימין

Daniel 12.13......................Daniel 1.1

Reversed becomes...

נימיהצקלכלרגל \ כלמלשולשתנשב

Daniel 1.1......................Daniel 12.13

...the Back Text

**The <u>end</u> of the Book of Daniel is the <u>beginning</u>
Of the hidden book of Daniel.**

"One jot or one tittle shall in no wise pass from the Law, till
all be fulfilled." Matthew 5.18

**After more than 2400 years, God is again
speaking to mankind, through the reading of His
original Hebrew Scriptures in *reverse!***

The Linear Bible Code

The Sealed Book of Daniel Revealed

The Linear Bible Code
Reading the Text Backward

Edited and Translated by Gustav Mahler

הספר הי לגר
"The Book of Wailing Belonging to the Sojourner"
Paragraph 117

"And thou Daniel shut up סתם the words and fasten up by sealing חתם the Book until Time's end." Daniel xii.4.a.

Being the translation of the Back Text
with Notes and Appendices;
translated from the
Forward Text of Daniel
Biblia Hebraica Stuttgartensia
and other Ancient Witnesses.

Edited and Translated by
Gustav Mahler
Copyrighted 2005
ISBN 0-9773032-0-9
SAN 257-2745
Also with an exhaustive

REGISTER

Of Names and Subjects in Hebrew-Aramaic-English

A MAHLER HOUSE
Publication
327 County Road 341
Dove Creek, Co. 81324
Info@mahlerhouse.com
Visit our website: Mahlerhouse.com

The Linear Bible Code

Table of Contents

Preface

This is the most important discovery in memory. It is equal to the authority and power of the Scriptures themselves.

The ability to read the text of the Hebrew Scriptures in both directions- forward and backward –is equal empirical evidence that G-d did indeed write the Text of the Book of Daniel. It becomes a second witness that G-d lives and communiates His Will to Mankind.

Reading the Masoretic Text backwards gives us the complete Book of Daniel perhaps in fulfillment of the prediction found in chapter 12.4: 'many shall go quickly and knowledge shall be multiplied.'

What then was to be sealed up? The Key of Knowledge to read the Back Text. In our scientific age where evidence is demanded in the place of Faith, G-d now gives His Evidence in the form of the Lineaer Back Text Code. Hidden in plain sight His Message has now been read and translated. It is a simple code that any one with a knowledge of Hebrew and Aramaic may read. Although it is simple it still is beyond our comprehension how to write the Book of Daniel so it may be read forward and backward.

In these latter days of Earth's existence the Book of Daniel is the book which has introduced the world to the Linear Back Text Code. When the Code is applied to the whole body of the Hebrew Scriptures we are further impressed with the foresight of G-d in the first instance. In the second instance we are astounded that other books also contain the Linear Back Text Code.

Understanding the Book of Daniel in total was reserved for the end of the world as we know it.

A Note from the Editor and Translator

I first became acquainted with Dr. Rips' Bible Code in 1999. The references in Michael Drosnin's book to reading the text backward in some instances lay dormant in my mind and the mind of Ruth Mahler until January 2004. It was at that time that she asked me to see if The Ten Commandments contained a message backwards. My first coherent experience with the Back Text began with לא תרצח "Thou shalt never murder". In the reverse חצרת אל translates "The Court of God". I was shocked by its simplicity but accuracy down to the construct state of the feminine word "Court" חצרה\חצרת!

This simple rendering grew into a huge text as I expanded in both directions from this point. I put several chapters of Exodus in one strand with spaces removed between letters and reversed them. The Ten Commandments was center stage in this long strand. I was able to parse the text into coherent words, sentences and messages with no letters remaining. This process also revealed a textual error in the Forward Text which was remedied using the duplicate text in Deuteronomy!

I next reversed Genesis chapter one. It too confirmed my experience in Exodus. I was astounded by the message as well as the Back Text itself. The pivotal point is verse 22 which reads in part:

> The Father is the fashioner of the Pure One.
> He illuminated him.
> From the days of the hills were His Chamber,
> His Angels and His Pure One;
> and he healed the Height of God.
> יוצר אב בר יפועהו מימי-במים התאו
> אלמו וברו ורף רם-אל

The Linear Bible Code

When I shared this with my brother Wayne he too was excited. He asked me to see if Daniel could be read in reverse. I was not enthusiastic about the project because I held the view that it was a book of fiction. But nevertheless I proceeded to make a lengthy strand of chapter twelve. Reluctantly I entered the text. It was not until I had gone a long way into the parsing the text did I acknowledge that Daniel too contained coherent messages reading the letters in reverse.

It is now over a year and a half since I began the Back Text of Daniel. I have gone through the long strand seven times. Each time I went through I brought more knowledge of Aramaic and Hebrew. The text has been parsed and translated and it is in a state fit for publication. I call upon all those interested to examine in detail my work. I believe whole heartedly that the Back Text of Daniel was composed anciently at the time the Forward Text was written. This is the unsealed Book of Daniel and it is the End Time.

Gustav Mahler
August 2005

A Poem Extracted From The Text

Let *God's* Beloved come into being! Paragraph 169
The Rib of the Father. Para. 158
The Pure One even His Son. Para. 125
The Hand of the Father is the Mark. Para. 146
The Mark is the Pure One. Para. 16
Thy Prince I shall prepare. Para. 126
The Pure One of Integrity; he shall be chosen, he shall be magnified.
      Para. 10
God makes tender the Poor One;
He made *him* slow *to anger.* Para. 17

Is not a people a sheep? They have wandered. Para. 73
Mankind is not seasoners of Light;
Mankind is bitter because of Light.
Give Thou O God of all of us a Plan and a Region a clod *of earth.*
      Para. 193
The Son, lo, I shall send him down. Descend thou O Seed! Para. 205
The Prince, the Mark-of-All-of-Them descended. Para. 135
The Mark fell *earthward;* he was swaddled. Para. 124
Surely My Son is the Gift of the Veil. Para. 194

The Man of Grace is a fine Gift. Para. 191
The Sufficiency of God is Distinction. Para. 216
The Mark, My Pure One, promoted My Law. Para. 193
God is with him. Para. 107
Who is above a sheep? The Noble Mark, the Passage Way of God. Para.
      102
Thou o hand of sorrow carried knowledge. Para. 219
The Pure One pulled along the people of God. Para. 233
As he wept he swallowed down his tears because they were not many.
      Para. 56
Surely for them His Witness was made to shake. Para. 242
My Only One prophesied against the *people*;
The flat of thy hand is against *them.*
And deceitful is My people. Para. 18
All of them are against Me of the Tel-City *(Jerusalem)* of the Mark.
      Para. 174
God loathes the proud ones of apostasy. Para. 241
They snorted at the Law of YAH. Para. 192
Emptiness spoke: "Dispute!

"The hand of the Tabernacle is *against* me, by the Instrument of God. Para. 177

Thou shalt despise His Son. Para. 165

The essence of My Light; but they rejected *him*. Para. 204

He is becoming sorrowful. Para. 171

In the Garden all is bitterness. Para. 40

The People smote the Upright One. Para. 43

Thou ravaged My Tender One. Para. 65

The Mark of Gentleness. Para. 67

He heaped up sorrow. Para. 73

He swallowed up the burden of a sheep. Para. 122

He was made to show grief. Para. 135

The Mark-of-All-of-Them even is swallowing the burden of a sheep. 182

The Son, lo, I shall make thee tremble. Para. 180

The Pure One of heart. Para. 186

The one grieving- he caused God pain. Para. 12

O his sobs; *they* wounded the heart. Para. 157

They pierce thee. Para. 26

The hand is His Sign. Para. 168

And of His Sign We are in awe. Para. 138

He became the Mark for God, and the Tears of God. Para. 34

Alas, the blood of the Witness falls down. Para. 107

They gazed at the Lamb of Blood. Tremble everyone! Para. 189

Grace died. Para. 163

The tears of God fell down. Para. 106

O the quivering *lip* of the Father. Para. 228

The Mark-of-All-of-Them was put to death. Para. 185

They murdered the Light with its sufficiency My Son. Para. 261

This is the Tears of God. Para. 44

I shall pour out a fullness by the injured one. Para. 173

For the Father a vessel of purity He raised thee up. Para. 143

Who worked a Wonder? Para. 97

The sufficiency of the Son. Para. 39

The Thin One with perpetual pureness.

The Father established the Ordinance of the Veil. Para. 97

A Son shall ascend; the Mark grew great. Para. 132

He shall cause to arise a sleeping *people*. Para. 196

O the Prince...of the mighty people of YAH.

Let thou give them light; move you gently. Para. 198

He giveth victory even the Living One! Para. 91

From the Assembly of Yeshua I shall feed them. Para. 155
A few he has caused to shine even the oppressed of the Father. 162
The Mark-of-All is King. Para. 35
My Son abideth. Para. 161
The Son of the Father. Para. 274

Praise you My Gift because he was made *the people's* Deliverer. 35

Compiled by Wayne Knecht

The more one understands the Forward Text of the Hebrew Scriptures the more one will understand the Back Text of Daniel. G.M.

A key to the Text

The Masoretic Text is the main source for the Back Text of Daniel. In some few cases I have modified its text. These modifications were made on the authority of the footnotes of the Biblia Hebraica Stuttgartensia, hereafter cited as BHS, as well as due to my conjecture. In all cases I have placed a line beneath the effected text. The justifications for these modifications are explained in detail in the 'NOTES' section of the book.

Out of respect for Diety the usual title is abbreviated as well as the short form of the Tetragrammaton.

In preparation at this writing is the Linear Back Text Code of the Book of Ruth and the prophet Malachi. This will be the second volume in what is projected as a series.

The
INTRODUCTION

Cracking the Linear Bible Code

What is the 'Bible Code'? In 1997 Simon and Schuster published a book called "THE BIBLE CODE" by Michael Drosnin. He wrote how Dr. Eliyahu Rips, "one of the world's leading experts in group theory, a field of mathematics that underlies quantum physics" in connection with Doron Witztum found a code in the Old Testament. In particular the code was isolated in the Torah or the five books of Moses. "To find the code, Rips eliminated all the spaces between the words, and turned the entire original Bible [Gen.-Deut.] into one continuous letter strand, 304,805 letters long."

"The computer divided the entire Bible [Gen.-Deut.]- the whole strand of 304,805 letters- into 64 rows of 4772 letters." "Rips explained that each code is a case of adding every fourth or twelfth or fiftieth letter to form a word. Skip X spaces, and another X spaces, and another X spaces, and the hidden message is spelled out....But it is more than a simple skip code. Criss-crossing the entire known text of the Bible, hidden under the original Hebrew of the Old Testament, is a complex network of words and phrases, a new revelation. There is a Bible beneath the Bible."

Michael Drosnin went on in his description. "The Bible is not only a book- it is also a computer program. It was first chiseled in stone and handwritten on a parchment roll, finally printed as a book, waiting for us to catch up with it by inventing a computer. Now it can be read as it was always intended to be read."

He said further: "The computer searches that strand of letters for names, words, and phrases hidden by the skip code."

This is not the place to explain the workings in detail of the computer search program. It is a fact that there is a code embedded in the matrix of the Hebrew text of portions of the Bible. It is a fact that many facets of the code are still unknown. "There is still a great deal no one knows about the Bible code. Rips, who knows more than anyone, says it's like a giant jigsaw puzzle with thousands of pieces, and we only have a few hundred."

There are many levels to the code. When the text is arranged in tiers of letters as previously described the code appears at times in what is described as 'crossword puzzles'. Dr. Rips is reported to have said, "It is almost certainly many more levels deep, but we do not yet have a powerful enough mathematical model to reach it...It is probably less like a crossword puzzle, and more like a hologram. We are only looking at two-dimensional arrays, and we probably should be looking in at least three dimensions, but we don't know how to."

The Sealed Book

In Mr. Dronsin's book, chapter four, entitled "THE SEALED BOOK" he mentions the two great apocalypses of the Bible, Daniel and Revelation. In Daniel an angel instructed Daniel to seal up the words of the vision until the End Time.

Mr. Drosnin asked the question "Could the Bible code be the 'sealed book'? "Had we really opened the 'sealed book'?"

Just as the Bible code is many faceted so too is the answer to his question. Yes the computer and Doron Witztum's program has opened the sealed book of Daniel. But I contend that it is only a portion of that sealed book. The major portion of the sealed book is found in another level of the code which I have called the 'Linear Bible Code'.

The Linear Bible Code

What is meant by 'linear'? The Bible code of Mr. Rips was constructed by writing out the Hebrew text in one continuous strand of letters and omitting all the spaces between the letters. This placement of the letters is linear. Therefore when I write of the Linear Code it is finding a code within this linear strand of text. In order to activate the Linear Code an additional step is necessary. This step is the reversing of the strand of letters. The first letter is now the last and the last letter is the first.

The Book of Daniel was subjected to this two phase operation by this editor. The complete text of Daniel was written out in one continuous strand with the spaces between words omitted. This is illustrated below. I have reproduced a part of the first sentence of the Book of Daniel chapter one verse one:

Daniel 1.1a

בשנתשלושלמלכותיהויקיממלכיהודה

"In the third year of the reign of Jehoikim king of Judah

The key to unlocking the Linear Code is reversing the order of the letters. This is how it looks in Hebrew.

Daniel 1.1a Reversed

הדוהיכלממיקיוהיתוכלמלשולשתנשב

The whole process resulted in one line of text running over 250 feet in length for Daniel (if the type face is 12 point).

When we jump all the way to the end of this strand we come to the end of the Book of Daniel, the last chapter the last verse. Here is the text written out without spaces:

Daniel 12.13

ואתהלכלקכצותנוחותעמדלגרללקכצהימינ

"And thou, go thou to the end and rest thou and stand
at thy allotted portion at the end of days."

Now that the strand is in place it is time to apply the
key to the Linear Code. The strand is reversed. The last part
of the book is now the first part of the sealed book; i.e.
chapter twelve is chapter one of the sealed book and chapter
one is the last chapter of the sealed book.

How does one read this reversed strand? Divide the
text into words and place spaces between them. The entire
strand can be separated into words, sentences and
paragraphs. There are no left over letters.   Here is the
beginning of the sealed book; *(please remember it is actually the last
verse of Daniel chapter 12 now written in reverse)*:

Daniel 12.13 Reversed

נימיהצקלכלרגלדמעתוחונתוצקלכלההתאו

Here is the text with the spaces between words along
with my translation:

Daniel 12.13 Reversed and Parsed

ני מיה צק לך לרגל דם עתו חון תו צק לך לה תאו

"Wailing is from YAH! Distress is for thee to tread the
blood of His Time. The Mark loathes distress for thee;
in regards to it *(Time)* is His Chamber."

This is the beginning of the sealed book of Daniel.
The text parses (is separated) with some little difficulty
from beginning to end. This is the opening of the sealed
book. What are the closing words? Again, I repeat the text
of Daniel 1:1a; I call it the Forward Text. This text is then
reversed which I call the Back Text.

The Linear Bible Code

Daniel 1.1a Forward Text

בשנתשלוללמלכותיהויקיממלכיהודה

"In the third year of the reign of Jehoakim king of Judah"

Daniel 1.1a Reversed (Back Text)

הדו היכלם מיקיו הי תו-כלם לשולש תן שב

"Give you a *joyous* shout O Palaces of His Obedient One! A lamentation of the Mark-of-All-of-Them is for the dividing into three the Jackal. Repent thou!"

The Linear Bible Code is the simplest of all codes. It does not rely upon a computer. Any student of Hebrew and Aramaic can read this linear code. It is probable that others have read it.

The Implications

This is the most important discovery in memory. It is in my estimation more significant than the computer code. It is equal to the authority and power of the Scriptures themselves.

The ability to read the text of the Hebrew Scriptures in both directions- forward and backward –is empirical evidence that a Supreme Power did indeed write the Text of the Book of Daniel.

Reading the Masoretic Text backwards (called the 'Back Text') gives us the sealed Book of Daniel in the Linear Code. The Forward Text of Daniel of course predicted the coming forth of the sealed book and its knowledge for mankind perhaps in fulfillment of the prediction found in chapter 12.4: 'many shall go quickly and knowledge shall be multiplied'. *The translation of Daniel's sealed linear code book contains more than double the material found in the forward text!*

What then was sealed up so long ago? It was not the Book of Daniel that has been available for over 2,200 years. How many people have read the Forward Text of Daniel and were perplexed by it? How many people thought the Book of Daniel was a spurious document because they believed it was once sealed and then was opened at the End of Time over 2,000 years ago? The truth is it is now open to our view. The sealed book is the Back Text of Daniel! The sealed book is also the computer code. All this taken together creates awe in the student and scholar alike.

What is the Linear Back Text Code? A very descriptive message to the Jewish Nation. How was it to be unsealed? The Key of Knowledge. This Key is empirical in its nature. In our scientific age where evidence is demanded in the place of faith the Linear Bible Code of Daniel should make everyone stand still and ponder its implications. Hidden in plain sight all these centuries was a Message. It has now been read. It is a simple code but within its simplicity is found a message for our day. Who so long ago could have written a book forward and a second book twice its length in content read backward?

The wonder is amplified three fold when it is realized that other portions of the Hebrew Scriptures also contains the linear back text code.

The universal understanding of the sealed Book of Daniel was reserved for the end of the world as is plainly recorded in Daniel 12.4.

The Book of Daniel is a Jewish book. The Linear Back Text is a Jewish book. It is a fact, borne out by its own text, that it belongs to the Jew of the Diaspora. The opening sentence of the Back Text reads "Wailing is from YAH." In chapter seven verse nineteen the Back Text records the name of this book of 'Wailing'.

Daniel 7.19b

הספר הי לגר

"The Book of Wailing belongs to the sojourner."

This is repeated in 7.7c.

For thousands of years the Jewish Nation has lived as sojourners among the nations of the world. There was a time when they had their kingdom under David and Solomon. A 'sojourner' during that epoch had a very different meaning; non-Israelites living among them!

Zionism was a catalyst to restore the kingdom of Israel. However, the restoration is far from complete. The 'Book of Wailing' has come forth during this epoch just in time to assist in the restoration of Israel. Millions of Israelites still live among the nations. The reality of its revealment and translation in this century speaking to the Jew must be considered the highest priority.

The Characteristics of the Linear Code of Daniel

This Linear Bible Code is the simplest and is the most accessible of the codes. It is also the most dramatic and awesome. Although Dr. Rips' and Mr. Witztum's computer code breaking is impressive it does not reveal knowledge in large blocks of material like the Linear Code which is composed of complete sentences, paragraphs and whole sections of coherent subject matter.

The decoding process in principle was a simple exercise but because this editor was acting alone the actual parsing and translation was difficult. I was a pioneer in new territory. I believe that there has not been anything quite like it in a long time. The discovery of the Dead Sea Scrolls sixty years ago is not an exception. All those documents (sacred and secular) had spaces between the words. The task before me was many times more challenging but I had many resources from which to draw. I consider this huge task of parsing and translation of the Back Text of Daniel as a work in progress. In years to come others will perhaps parse portions differently and in that process my work will either be vindicated or emended but certainly not destroyed.

The parsing of the reverse strand of the text of Daniel in most places seemed inevitable. In the beginning of the process the text divided into sentences simple and compound. If this trend was to continue words could not appear in isolation. In this I was not disappointed. This is the inevitableness I am talking about. Futhermore, I had to start at the beginning if I hoped to decipher correctly the text. At first I jumped into the middle and began parsing words and words became sentences. But reading them out of context of the whole stream of letters I could not be sure they were correct. This is difficult for modern people to appreciate. Modern languages that contain vowels and consonants cannot be encoded at length backward. The Hebrew language is exclusively written in consonants. The reader supplies the vowels. Modern Hebrew newspapers do not print the vowels. Now imagine a newspaper going one step beyond and the text has no spaces between words. Only in the most simple sentences would there be no difficulty in parsing the text in one's mind. But the Linear Back Text Code is very complex and very ancient. The imagery of metaphor alone is foreign to us. So it is true that the first words and sentences I encountered did change when I started at the beginning. All the letters of the preceeding strand had to be accounted for. This is the nature of working with an ancient and unfamiliar text.

Scholars and philologists alike point out that the oldest portions of the Hebrew Scriptures were first written without spaces between words. The ability to parse mentally such a text as Exodus or Joshua must depend then on knowledge of all the vocabulary found in a given book and the grammar and syntax too. The parsing of the Linear Back Text Code of Daniel was a huge challenge and I had to grow in knowledge to accomplish it.

The unsealed Book of Daniel as might be expected does add to our knowledge of language and grammar and syntax. Writing a book in the 'Forward Text' with spaces between words accompanied with the vowels is a huge aid to the student.

The Linear Back Text Code is a fact and who ever composed the Forward Text had to be very selective in its words, syntax and spelling. Viewed as a whole it seems a miracle of composition. Could it have been composed in a world without the computer? In my mind no human could have accomplished this feat without a computer and perhaps even today it is impossible. Viewed as a whole the Forward Text and the Back Text fold in on each other to create a circular ribbon of text; together they keep going on infinitely.

I have already mentioned that the Linear Back Text Code increases our knowledge of ancient Hebrew and the Aramaic languages by its use of vocabulary, syntax and grammar. Many are the sentences that read in the biblical syntax: verb, subject and object. But because of the needs of the Back Text Code there are also many sentences that do not conform to the norm. We find the syntax after this manner: subject, verb and object. Modern English follows this form of writing sentences.

I have found new words in the Back Text some of which are easy to give an etymology and some that are translated by conjecture only. Although this may alarm some it is a fact that portions of the Hebrew Scriptures also contain these exact characteristics. There are quite a number of Hebrew words in the Forward Text of some books that are read by conjecture.

In the Forward Text vocabulary all verbs do not appear in every conjugation. It is expected that a new book would continue to fill out the possible paradigms. Grammarians will be thrilled by the Back Text because many verbs are in paradigms new to lexicons.

There are some words only defined from modern Hebrew! In some instances there were groups of letters that could only make sense as words by using a Modern Hebrew dictionary! What is the implication for this fact? Is it not a witness to the fact that the writer of the Linear Bible Code knew in advance our language and used where necessary our modern words? I believe this. If one believes in future prophecy as contained in the Bible why believe that our modern words would remain unknown as well?

The Book of Daniel is composed in two languages, Biblical Hebrew and Biblical Aramaic. The Hebrew text comprises chapter one, chapter 2 verses 1-4a and chapters 8-12. The Aramaic text is found to begin with chapter 2.4b and concludes with chapter 7.28. The Back Text parses into words and translates nicely through these sections without interruption; see Paragraphs 108\109 and 256\257. I see a design in composing Daniel and this supplies another piece of evidence.

Another characteristic of the Back Text is the truncation of words. By this, I usually mean defective spelling of words. This is a known characteristic in the Forward Text. Words are not always spelled out fully consonant by consonant. An example is found in Paragraph 274 of the Back Text. The word translated 'Palaces' היכלם is the plural masculine of היכל . The truncation is the loss of the 'yod' between the 'lamed' and 'mem' (לִַם). When this text is printed with vowels a small dot called HIREQ would be placed below the 'lamed'. This example can be multiplied many times in the Forward Text of the Hebrew Scriptures. One example is the spelling of 'Jerusalem'. It is spelled at times fully ירושלים but in some places it is spelled defectively just like 'Palaces' in the Linear Back Text Code, ירושלם.

It is a fact that the Masoretic Text contains errors in spelling. Due to the sacredness of each letter no editor has felt he had the authority to supply the correction. The text of the Bible long ago was 'fixed' in place errors included. However scholars were not prohibited from writing about these errors. In some printings of the Scriptures these errors were 'set' with extended vowels or in the margin in what is called *Qere* (what is read) and *Ketib* (what is written).

Now the reality of the Linear Back Text Code of Daniel gives us pause over these misspellings. The reason for misspelling a word in the Forward Text of Daniel is mostly due to the needs of the Back Text. Just one letter can change the meaning of a sentence in the Back Text. One wrong letter can also make a mess of the Back Text rendering that portion incoherent. The fact of the matter is that parsing the Back Text is a proof of the accuracy of the Masoretic Text. *If there are unintentional errors in the Masoretic Text the parsing of the Back Text strand will verify them*. I have come across a number of these unintentional errors and by fixing them the parsing of the Back Text proceeds.

The student and scholar alike will note with interest those places where the Back Text demands emendation. In these places the Masoretic Text was in error *accidentally*. In all cases these emendations brought into balance both texts. In the present printing of the Back Text I have underlined these emendations. The accompanying Notes explain fully these emendations and their implications.

It is remarkable that given the length and complexity of the Back Text there are so few truncated words. It is usually the case then that one finds the Back Text written out fully just as the Forward Text of the Hebrew Scriptures.

The Back Text of Daniel contains words that are not used in any portion of the Hebrew Scriptures except the Book of Daniel. A few examples are instructive in explaining this statement. The word רה appears only in Daniel out of all the books of the Hebrew Scriptures. It appears in this spelling once in chapter 4.6. It appears in two other permutations in chapter 2. Now in the Linear Back Text Code this word is used 7times (Paragraphs 22, 233, 261, 265, 269, 270).

The Linear Back Text Code contains other words unique to the Book of Daniel. A partial list includes בות 'to pass the night', Daniel 6.19; ית the mark of the accusative; דחל 'to fear', 'to make afraid'; the interjection אלו; חוא 'to shew, to declare'; רשם to 'inscribe, sign'; and זן 'kind'. A more full list is found in Appendix 'A'.

The implication of this sharing of words may be interpreted to mean that the author of the Forward Text of Daniel is the author of the Back Text. He uses the same vocabulary at various times.

The Back Text is part poetry and part prose. Some of the poetry is discernibly written in Parallelism and other forms.

The Back Text also contains many place names and personal names. Some are new such as 'Jachesahan', 'Jaihan' and 'Joez'; some are evidently old in origin, 'Jareb', 'Ham', 'Hennom', 'Seneh' and 'Gabriel'; and a few are of the present age, 'Belarus', 'Janet and Keith' and 'Sunni' .

The Text is in part made up of short exclamatory statements in a matrix of long developed themes. One short theme that appears quickly and may be looked upon as appearing in isolation concerns the 'Sunni' in Paragraph 222. "The Sunni waveth! A Banner fluttered!"

An example of a long development spaced out over the full length of the book is introduced at the outset of the Back Text in the enigmatic name/title 'the Mark', (see Paragraph 1). The further one reads in the Back Text the more one discovers about 'the Mark' until at the very end his identity is fully revealed. After God Himself the 'Mark' is the center of the sealed book.

There are other parts of the unsealed text that are more fully developed. One such section is contained in Paragraphs 233 through 238. The main theme is the Passover.

Some of the text is clearly divided into sections. These divisions are titled such as "<u>A Lamentation</u>" in Paragraph 199 and concludes in Paragraph 201. Paragraph 202 comprises another document entitled "<u>The Wail of the Gift of the Veil</u>" There are other ways of dividing the text into subsections. One such way is the repeating of the word י which I translate "O the wailing!" (see Paragraphs 211, 213, 216 and 217)

Most of the sections and subsections are without title. Their appearance is somewhat disconcerting to us who are used to everything nicely packaged. They just run on together endlessly. (If the shorter sections in the books of the prophets were without identification the same effect would be experienced.)

The Back Text of Daniel is at times prophetic. There is one theme that runs like a thread throughout the book. It is God working through His Son among the children of Israel. This 'Son' has a number of titles. Some of these titles are: Pure One; the Thin One; the Poor One; The Mark; The Mark-of-All-of-Them; the Tears of God; the Instrument of God; Gift of the Veil and Messiah. In one place he is called by name "Yeshua" a derivative of Joshua and is variously translated 'God is help' or 'savior'. This name rendered in Greek in the New Testament is 'Jesus'.

The continuous thread that illuminates the 'Son' of God is similar to the references to the Messiah found scattered throughout the Hebrew Scriptures. There are some who count 300 references to the Messiah. These are at times only a part of a sentence; (see Genesis 49.10) "the scepter shall not depart from Judah nor a lawgiver from between his feet **until Shiloh come**." At other times a complete sentence is the reference as in Numbers 24.17 "there shall come a star out of Jacob and a scepter shall rise out of Israel and destroy all the children of Sheth." There are other references that are multiple sentences in length such as Isaiah 9.6-7 and chapter 53 which is 12 verses in length.

The references in the Linear Back Text Code of Daniel follows this same pattern. Here in one book are all these same characteristics, the short phrase, the full sentence and the multiple sentences. I have assembled these references to the 'Mark' the 'Son' of God and they reveal a distinct pattern. This pattern I have artificially divided into eight headings and subheadings. The first I call the 'prophecy' of his coming. The second I call **'The Birth and Mission of the Pure One'**, which is subdivided into **'The Son Comes and His Birth is Recounted'**, **'He Taught the People'**, **'The High Garden and Betrayal'**, and **'The Death of the Upright One, the Mark'**. The other divisions read **"His Descent into Sheol to Crush it'**, **'The Ascension, the Fall of the City and Silence'** and **'The Descent of the Pure One and Judgment Day'**. These titles are derived from the subjects of the quotations.

The Back Text of Daniel is a book for the Jew of the Diaspora and it presents the Plan of God for His people. The Messiah by any other name is central to this Plan. The understanding of this Plan is paramount if the Jewish People is to honour God and find their place in His Kingdom. The Back Text records the urgency the people of God felt over this issue. In the text reference Daniel 4.18a (Paragraph 193) we read in part "give thou O God of all of us a Plan and a Region, a clod *of earth!*" This is repeated with effect in Daniel 4.9 (Paragraph 200). Because this urgent plea is only now published to the world from the unsealed book one can easily state its application: The End Time. Less then sixty years ago there was no State of Israel. Truly the people of Israel called out 'give thou O God of all of us a Plan and a Region, a clod *of earth!*"

The Back Text of Daniel is written in the first person. Most of the Text is written so G-d is speaking directly to the Reader. Furthermore, the first person plural is noted in some few places (Paragraphs 88 and 89).

At the conclusion of 'The Introduction' I have assembled this Plan and entitled it 'A Psalm of Daniel' which follows loosely Psalm 77 and 118 in their scheme. It must be kept in mind that all the references to the Messiah/the Mark are not listed in this construct called 'A Psalm of Daniel'.

The Computer Bible Code and the Linear Back Text Code

Heretofore I have described some of the differences between the two codes. They appear mutually exclusive on the surface. The one needs a computer and finds words in an artificial array diagonally, horizontally, reversed and in clear text. Some times these words are found through skips between letters. The second code, the Linear Back Text Code, does not need a computer. Anyone with a knowledge of Hebrew and Aramaic can parse the text and translate it. There are no skipped letters. All the letters are connected. Some people refuse to call this a 'Code' at all.

There are similarities between the two codes. This is as it should be because codes share commonalities. The two do not tell a story sequentially. Past and Future events overlap. This is stated in Mr. Drosnin's book on page 174. The Linear Back Text of Daniel does indeed contain information past and future. The close proximity of the two might seem disconcerting. Paragraph 23 speaks about 'the region of My Witness shall shine on account of his aid'. The very next sentence plunges us back to the time of Noah! "And the bosom spoke; the mouth of Noah he loosened among My Altar Shovels; he ruled them." Proceeding right on the text jumps to the days of Moses and the Law (Paragraphs 24 and 25). The next Paragraph (26) seems to then describe certain events in the Garden of Eden. The key players are God and a man referred to as 'the Gift of Knowledge' as well as another being called the Adversary and those who followed after him and who 'magnified the Adversary of the Father of the Gift.'

Paragraph 27 refers to another subject and it is not anchored in any time line. Paragraphs 28 and 29 record a war with Put and the Kinfolk of God. Banners waved, fortresses were emptied of peoples and employed in the army were mercenary forces. And then at the end of this paragraph is a sentence that I translate 'A winding *staircase* resembled his Issue.' Is this not a reference to the Double Helix of the DNA code?

The next paragraph (30) jumps forward in time when it records "The Mark shall cause himself to come. They shall come and they shall cause themselves to enter 'The Delight of God.'"

The text continues in future tense and a future that still is unfulfilled. "And the Mark shall remove afar off the Greatness of Terror." The people who were divorced showed 'My saved ones disobedience'. 'Death shall be increased'. 'But *the Mark* magnified his own gift and he shall cast them down; and the Mark shall utterly hammer the Adversary against whom the Mark shook the Debt of the Mark. All rottenness he shall remove." The early reference to the Adversary in the Garden and his worshippers had a purpose. The future acts of the Mark shall deal with all of them.

The Text looks backwards into history only to set the stage for future events. Moses and Noah are praised for what they did and what they shall yet do. For instance Paragraph 134 records "I shall cause Noah to be circumcised. He shall make abundant the Region of Messiah." Kingdoms are destroyed; Visions and Tokens, Signs and secrets, wonders and mysteries are presented. One has only to read through the Register to see the wealth of imagery and wonderment found in this Book.

Another characteristic the two codes share is their revealment all at once. It is a fact that the Linear Back Text Code of Daniel has been revealed all at once. However, the computer Code should also be revealed all at once. "According to Rips, the whole Bible code has to be written at once, in a single flash." However the primer that will reveal it to us as that single flash remains illusive.

The computer code was created by the 'encoder' writes Mr. Drosnin, (page 174). The Linear Back Text Code refers to him as "Y-H the Enabler" יה יוכל.

When I read the paper 'Equidistant Letter Sequences in the Book of Genesis' I was struck by another very important similarity between the Linear and the Computer codes. A sure sign of design compared to randomness is the convergence of like words. When the words 'hammer' and 'anvil' intersect in the computer code or 'chair' and 'table' or 'rain' and 'umbrella' this evidence leans toward design. Now in the Linear Back Text Code the very same concept is played out time after time. Some few examples will illustrate this point.

The Linear Bible Code

In Daniel 10.7 we read backwards these words:
ואבחה בו חרבי which I translate "and the slaughter among him is of My Sword". All these words belong together especially 'Sword' and 'slaughter'. The next sentence is a follow up to this imagery: ומה ילעה לפני לד which I translate "and o how it swallows up to the corner of Lydda." The idea of a sword swallowing up anything is excellent when one realizes that the act of swallowing is figurative for destroying. The usual verb for this figure is בלע but here in the Back Text the synonym לוע is used.

In Daniel 4.33a Back Text we have the verb 'stagger' appropriately describing the effects of 'pure wine': נוע ביין בר "He staggered with pure wine".

In Daniel 1.6a,5b Back Text we note a more integral set of subjects that have the ring of the true.

הדו היין במם הב יה יוכל
Give you a *joyous* shout! The wine of the hills give thou! YAH is the Enabler.
מה ינפלו דמעים תצקם
How the juices flow down; thou poured them out.

Paragraph 69 is filled with related things: an ark, vessel, ship's hold, watercourse and sea of passage. This is an excellent example of convergence of words.

One final example is a complete 'Lamentation' found in Daniel 2.21:

וני מי כח
And a lamentation. Who is strong?
לא תם כח בהי
There is no perfection of strength within a lamentation.

נוי כלם מיקהם
A lamentation has wounded their obedience;

ווני כלמה דעהם זו אין דע
and a lamentation has wounded their knowledge.

אן שהם אוה
Sorrow is the Gem of Lust.

The Length of the Text

A unique characteristic of the Linear Back Text Code is that it contains more than twice the information of the Forward Text. How is it possible that the same number of letters written backwards double the content? There are two main reasons.

The first reason why the Back Text contains so much information is because of the large names and words found in the Forward Text. Here is a list of some of the more lengthy names and words:

יהויקים 'Yehoiakim'
נבוכדנאצר 'Nebuchadnezzar'
הפרתמים 'princes'
בלטשאצר 'Belteshazzar'
משרוקיתא 'pipe'
פסנתרין 'harp'?
שדרך מישך ועבד נגו 'Shadrach, Meshach and Abed- Nego'
חרטמים 'magicians'

In the Back Text there are very few words equaling the length of these words. The Back Text is characterized by simple two and three lettered verbs and three and four letter nouns. There are verbs longer due to the Hithpael or Hiphel and plural nouns are one or two letters longer; nonetheless they are infrequent.

The Linear Bible Code

A sample of the compactness of the Back Text is the reading of 'Shadrach, Meshach and Abed-Nego' backward. Whereas we read three names and one consonant in Biblical Aramaic (and in English) the Back Text parses into eight Aramaic words. In translation these eight words become fifteen English words!

Daniel 3.31 The Names Reversed
 וגנדבעוכשימכרדש
Shadrach, Meshach and Abed-Nego
Back Text Parsed
וגן דב עו כשי מכר דש
Back Text Translated
"And the Garden of the Bear of Ruin as a gift of value he trampled."

In Conclusion

When the Angel of the Lord instructed Daniel to seal up the vision-book he obeyed. It was not to be opened until the End of Time. Many peoples have been perplexed over this instruction because the Book of Daniel with its visions have been available for over 2,200 years. The truth of the matter is at last before us. The sealed book is contained within the known Book of Daniel. And it has remained hidden in plain sight all these millennia. The key to unlocking the sealed book is knowledge of the Linear Back Text Code.

The unsealed book is written to the Jewish Nation in the Diaspora. It reveals God Plan for His people in response to their prayer 'Give Thou O God of all of us a Plan and a Region, a clod *of earth*!' The Plan revolves around a man chosen of God. He is called many titles in this book; 'My Son the Gift of the Veil', 'the Pure One of My Nest', 'the

Mark-of-All-of-Them' and 'Our Beloved' to list a few. He is called 'Yeshua' as a proper name.

The two parts of the Book of Daniel, the Forward Text and the Linear Back Text Code taken together are incendiary in nature. We have reached the terminator dividing Former Time and the End Time.

Gustav Mahler
August 2005

A Psalm of Daniel*

In the 'Book of Wailing' the principal character is 'the Mark'. He goes by a number of names whether it is 'the Thin One', the 'Weak One' or the 'Pure One'. He is also called by G-d His 'first born son'. All these titles fold in on each other to reveal his character. The 'Book of Wailing' has many subsidiary themes. Some of these refer to ancient history and some of them are current in our own day. But the cleverness of the Author of the Linear Back Text Code is such that the over arching message of a universal Redeemer who acts on behalf of the Creator is certain. I have extracted many of the elements referring to this Redeemer and assembled them into one coherent chronological account.

The student of the forward text of the TANACH (Old Testament) realizes that scattered throughout its books are references to Israel's Redeemer or Messiah. It has been the practice to assemble those portions and present them as a whole. In that spirit I have assembled some of the key elements from the Linear Back Text Code of Daniel. They are scattered throughout its text. Some times they are only short declarative sentences; other times they are lengthy exposition. They naturally fall into three categories. This First Section is 'Prophecy'. We read of the coming 'Pure One', the 'Mark' whom G-d selected to come to earth to facilitate the redemption of Israel if not the whole World.

The Second category comprises *'The Birth and Mission of the Pure One'*. This is subdivided into several sections beginning with his birth and then proceeding through his teaching phase and then his experience in the 'High Garden' and his betrayal into the hands of the Enemy. The subsection entitled *'The Death of the Upright One, the Mark'* of the 'Pure One' brings to an end the 'Mark's' earthly life. The conclusion of Section Two describes his immediate career after his death: his descent into Sheol to crush it.

The Third Section is entitled *'The Descent of the Pure One and Judgment Day'*. The Father has sent His Son back to the earth. It is a day of redemption and fire. Israel is restored to its home while the Enemy and his followers are dealt with severely. In the end all is peace and contentment.

It is hoped that this artificial assembly of a selection of key elements in the Back Text of Daniel will bring to the attention of everyone one purpose of the Code. It is a strong witness for the redemptive power of Y-H, the G-d of Israel and of the whole world.

---

*Although this 'Psalm' is artificial it follows the two great Psalms in the 'Books of Psalms' in the TANACH (Old Testament). These are Psalm 77 and Psalm 118. The first recount is a lesson in history from Jacob until the kingdom of David. In between the dealings of G-d with His people is recounted. In the latter Psalm which some see as Messianic in nature uses an artificial device to present isolated ideas into one coherent whole.

SECTION I: PROPHECY

He *the Instrument of the Father* shall prophesy
And he shall cause wailing to be wounded.
"Set thou the rampart and the Tel-City!
"Draw near O Y-H!
"And the Pure One purified himself and he fed them.
"The Son abideth and his efficient Wisdom.
"…the Favour of the Oppressed came even the Son." Para. 178

A Lamentation
Y-H established the Sabbath
And the Pure One volunteered
And they of the affliction shall become his Debt;
He shall take it away with Innocence.
Where was he strengthened?
Come forth Err when he feedeth My Portion.
This is food: the Utterance of the Witness.
And the firebolt is removed afar off.

And I shall pour out a fullness by the injured one. 175

And the Son, lo, I shall send him down. "Descend thou O Seed!" A
burden he set at the time and the Mark-of-All wounded it because he
caused the Abyss to totter. When it happened they died. O the lament
of the Pure One. Their Pure One is like Y-H. 205

The Pure One of Integrity he shall be chosen.
He shall be magnified! Be thou astonished!
He shall walk the waste place and he spoke
But they answered:
"A weak light is stitching together profaneness."
They have severed Eternity; they shall weep. 10

Who worked a wonder?
The Thin One with perpetual pureness.
The Father established the Ordinance of the Veil.
And He set *it* beside Mash;
He made the Mouth and the Height the sufficiency of mankind. 97

And the measure of the Nest is with the Pure One even His Son.
Lo, and a Name *G-d* established;
He shall work extraordinarily a Wonder of Y-H. 125

The Pure One shall exterminate sorrow rightly so.
It shall be he shall pulverize and pull *it* down.
The Hand of Knowledge leadeth to a watering hole its travelers. 115

A Sign and Distress was against *the Adversary*.
Sufficient are his weak ones.
And *he shall be* against the coverts of the Mark *Y-H'S* Pure One.
The Mark is the Pure One;
The Mark shall contend with him [the Adversary]. 16

Out of the obedience of the Instrument I shall cut off the Shadow by an
utterance. O the wailing from a wild goat! I shall feed them the favour
of the oppressed and the Son. 227

The Mark became wretched. 106

Let thou O Death turn aside the knee of the Pure Mark,
And thou shalt totter the Mark.

The Linear Bible Code

The Hand shall be purified; he fed them Desire.
Did the Terrible One repeat the Song?
"Thy posterity scattered the Gift of Y-H
"And lest *there be* the Cloud and the Light of His Daughter
"They snorted at the Law of Y-H." 192
But instead give Thou O G-d of all of us a Plan and a region, a clod *of earth!* The Son of Light spread it about; it shineth forth! And I G-d shall lay bare everything of the Mark. They pushed away the Region of the Dominion of Gentleness. From Y-H is myrrh. And the Mark, My Pure One, promoted My Law. He pushed away the hand of sorrow from Me. Surely his firebolt shall sparkle because Mankind is not seasoners of Light; *Mankind* is bitter because of Light. 193

A lamp scattered even the sufficiency of Y-H
And lest they hide the light of His Daughter
He shall begin the Mystery of Y-H. And *they said:*;
"Underneath give Thou O G-d of all of us a Plan and a region, a clod *of earth.*
"The Son of Light, let him scatter it; let him shine."
I thy G-d shall lay bare the Stone Cutter, the Mark. 200

The flames of the Mark proposed a plan for the people
of Emptiness. 14

The flame of the Father of Hope He made to flicker; and it shall feed them the Favour of the Oppressed and the Son. 212 for the Lamp is more than Appetite. 222

I shall feed them forever even the pure. 231

To Me is a fisherman; I shall make exceeding white the Poor One. 99

Your Creator awoke and He caused to purge Death because of the Earth; the Fire of Dew is in her from the Gift of the Thin One of the region. The Hand itself is judged. Surely My Son is the Gift of the Veil. 194

Is not the Mark-of-All-of-Them to be pounded to powder?
My Pure One is among the valleys;
He is becoming sorrowful. 171
The Instrument shall be hidden; thou oppressed the Witness;
And he caused thee to shake. 244

The Linear Bible Code

The Living One increased the Witness. 253
The Witness shall be salted; salting Reproach he weakened the
haughtiness of the region and Reproach. 258

The Faint One shall consume a fullness of the Firebolts of the Law. O
the greatness of the Thin One.
He was brought low; the Bosom of EL.
Lo, Desire, Desire belongs to the Instrument.
Brought low is His Witness.
My Remnant shall swallow thee
And its pride is a dreadful salt. 240

SECTION II:
THE BIRTH AND MISSION OF THE PURE ONE

The Son Comes And His Birth is Recounted

The region of the Chamber *of Desire* I shall approach. It is smitten in
front of Ravage the Foe. I shall send a Son; he shall see enough of this.
What is the Terrible Thing? All faithlessness! Surely for them sis the
Favour of the Oppressed and the Son of Heart. 206

Oh Noble Lady of thy chamber give thou birth to a proud *son* to enter a
stone and he shall be made poor. Lo, his is Precept, the Wine of Desire.
48b

A Runner I shall send to the Daughter, the Bowman of Y-H. 202

The Mark fell *earthward.*
He was swaddled. 124

A Lamentation
G-d sent a messenger and food at the days of Power;
Therefore Affliction howled. 173
This is the Dew, the Gift of *G-d's* Token.
All of them are against Me of the Tel-City of the Mark.
Cause you to see the Rib of the Father!
Surely he made a caressing gesture.
But they refused. "Return thou to Me!
"Enjoy you the life of plenty of the sojourner of the coast.
"Increase you life! The Poor One is here;
"He causeth a daughter to show grief;

"This My Thin One makes fat G-d!"
My heart struggles.
Praise thou the Bosom!
It feedeth them light of the Nest that the Thin One of the Mist
acquired. 175

The Favour of the oppressed,
The Son of Will came. O the lament!
He, My Thin One, was made to descend and his pure Token with him.
Thou and reproach he shall swallow up.
Alas, I did not wound the Jackal. 164
Alas, he was tossed about;
And alas, I was inflamed;
But I fed them at the Light.
The vomitus of the fathers is as bitterness.
With a thumb the Spirit of G-d he made a writing:
"Thou shalt despise His Son."
O the wailing! And the perfect Jackal journeyed to thee;
He fed them a measure of cold out of Lust;
He did not waver; he caused Me to tremble. 165

He Taught The People

And he came; the Favour of the Oppressed came;
The Son fed them and the daughter. 170

Did not the perfection of strength, His Strength, rebuke them?
171

The Mark came. They beheld the Rib of the Father.
He made a loving gesture surely; but they denied his strength.
The G-d of the region sojourned.
The Gift was weakened even it became old,
But *G-d* was pleased with the Robe of the Pure One. 158

He pledged a dwelling. Para. 22
The Perfect Garner is Prince of Power.
O Hand! I shall feed them from the Veil.
He raised up *perfect* Desire
And the Hand We shall support. *He said*:
"I shall bring in the Knowledge of G-d." 147

The Linear Bible Code

God loathes the proud ones of apostasy.
He shall not set the mark "Greatness" upon them;
Surely for them belongs a lament;
And a community is for wailing.
The rain of Grace shall scatter about strength;
The Oceans of the Strength of EL are for Man.
The Instrument fed them; haughtiness of Lust was made loathsome.
He has fed from the Veil at the region of the *harvest* heap. 241

My Only One prophesied against *the people;*
and deceitful is My people.
And desire shall be trampled as far as G-d allows it.
Indignation is it not for *them*? 18

The Pure One of the appointed time undeservedly erred because he
never bent. 70

The Hand of Integrity holds dominion;
It extended g-dward; it fed them;
It fed them a measure of My Nest. It raised up appetite. 148

Who is above a sheep? The Noble Mark, the Passageway of G-d. 102

The Passover shall come, the Passageway of Time from G-d. O G-d the
tears of the oppressed!
The Pure One of the Appointed Time is a vessel. He shall discourse. The
Pure One pulled along the people of G-d. O the tears! 233

The Passover of the Abode of the Shepherd was drowsy. They were
drowsy at the Discourse of Distinction.
I shall cause the Passover to dangle with the Pure One of the people of
G-d. O the tears! He shall be removed; he shall be made low by Thy
Voice. Give Thou Desire! Was it not for the Instrument to discourse the
mire? He would increase them.
"And it shall come to pass thou shalt pant. All of them shall form a scab
at the Discourse of Distinction; they shall become drowsy. The
Instrument shall brood; the Passover of the Abode of the Shepherd shll
be drowsy. 234
I am humbled. Now is the Passover of G-d.
He discourses. He rinsed thee clean and wailing bowed.

The Instrument of Y-H discoursed but to the sojourner he spake incoherently.
The Instrument prophesied of the Age of Brightness of Power *and* My Knowledge. 238
Because a scholar has fed them somnolence he is brought low. 213

"They abhoreth My Seraph, all of them.
"Poverty is to make them filthy, a garment of trembling.
"And now, wailing even shall be revealed;
"It shall tremble at the Father of Species.
"He who is their Light has been made poor;
"He is made clean by washing.
"The Seraph, the Mark-of-All-of-Them is poor. 54

"The Mark shall never fall!
        Thou didst tremble; they boasted." 55

Whosoever is a lamp of the Assembly of the Stout One is worthy of the knowledge of his Father. 104

The Mark explored the dwellings of the teeth of the Eagle;
Oh his sobs; *they* wounded his heart. 157

Every king belongs to thee O Mark!
From the Assembly of Yeshua he fed them
And give thou *to* My lions. 155

Who is the Pure One? Who to Me is Grace?
But they refused the Hand of Desire. 41

The High Garden and Betrayal

Who is the Seraph with Him?
His first born son.
He set all of them free; but a friend of His Sheep shall swallow *him* up.
In the Garden *the Adversary* wounded even a seed.
The Pilgrim-Feast is My Gift.
The Adversary poured out his abomination.
He perceived an odour from the Emptiness.
Take you a measure of Lust!
Who is the Pure One?
With the words of Shem *G-d* made him lofty.

The Linear Bible Code

The Pure One wept; He maketh tender the Poor One;
He made *him* slow *to anger.* 17

Shifting reproach Sheol ran at the Mark-of-All. 108

He entered the High Garden and he vomited;
He shook; he repented.
Quivering *of lip* his Father fed them.
At the time of judgment he allowed himself to be sick.
They shall become the measure of frivolity.
Our G-d of the Shout even put down the Mark. 143

In the Garden is the Mark exposed;
This is the Mark, he ran with the rebellion
Thy Witness belonged to it. 36

G-d reproved the Mark of Blood. 62

Our Son purified himself. Jacha' is the Pure One of Desire, the
Valiant One. 133
And the Pure One purified himself.
And surely to circumcise them the heart the Voice is with all of them.
172

The Death of the Upright One, the Mark

And *the people* smote the Upright One who is the Favour of the Measure
of His Seed. 43

The Mark-of-All-of-Them even is swallowing the burden of a sheep: the
burden is a Gift of the Law.
Have thou dominion and let thou govern.
I shall cut off Ruin. 182

Who is the Lamp? They dimmed *it!*
Who is the Lamp? Voice and Heart!
Alas, the blood of the Witness falls down; Chael is worthy.
Eminencyand the Light of Desire
caused the fire of My Desire to flicker toward *the people.*
G-d is with him. *He said:* "O G-d of my ruin let it be now."

The Remover is against the Light of Desire; he caused My Words to wander;
a Shoah passed over...107 And he shall mark the multitude.
Let it happen! And the Remover is against the Light of New Desire; thou
carried away *My Words*. 108

The Adversary swallowed up Grace; he beat *it* to pieces; and knowledge journeyed. He twisted Grace out of shape. 64

Thou ravaged My Tender One.
O a species of vanity!
It withdrew My Name;
The Moon shriveled. 65

The Spear is the Spirit of Wickedness
And from Cain the Wicked One wounded the Mark-of-All-of-Them. 113

They pierced thee;
They magnified the Adversary of the Father of the Gift. 26

Who is the Thin One of Y-H? Shall I raise him up or wailing?
I shall raise thee up, they who casteth down My Light! 264

I shall change the Mark-of-All-of-Them.
I shall magnify the Mark.
Perversity conceived the hand of thy trembling; it changed not.
They were drowsy, as Knowledge of the Mark-of-All-of-Them was put
to death. He fed them the favour of the oppressed and the Son. 185
The Man of Grace is a fine Gift but a friend surely why did he thrust
away his hand? 191

The Hand of the Father was obedient. The blood belongs to His
Shadow. 216

"Because the Poor One of a mother was given a knighthood
"A Son was decked out *in finery*;
"With her was the Mark of Blood." 56

The Adversary of Desire prevailed over His [G-d's] Sheep
And the blood of the children of the Father of the Palate he cast
Down *to the ground*.

The Linear Bible Code

O the lament of his G-d. 103
O the quivering *lip* of the Father. 228
The heart caused Thy Voice to tremble together with the thin ones of
the Ark of the Chamber of Desire. 224

I shall burn them; Grace died. 163
My Grace is swallowing up. 171
Our Pure One was made to slumber. 38

Kings of Strength have acted foolishly, every one of them;
They murdered the Light with its sufficiency the favour of the
oppressed One, My Son. 261

The Mouth was created; it died as all things;
The Moon died with him.
But the Palate was with his G-d;
Lo, the blood of his ruinations;
Yea, the Mark, he enabled them.
He passed over.
Where is the place he passed over?
Alas, he moved out of Time. 92
The Thin One has hidden at his own time a Delicacy even the Favour of
the Oppressed and the Son. 226

A Seraph inscribed: "A people of profanness of heart; and a Shoah. They
erred because it did not long for the words of the Witness of Y-H; *they*
exalted *their* own region." 49

His Descent into Sheol to Crush it.

A lament toward the Pure One the one shutting up the Terror of the
G-d of Eminency. He left behind quaking; and he betook himself to the
Error of the Pit and the Burden of Sheol. It shall be crushed. There is no
region of dispute. He rolled away lamentation. O the pride! For them he
confined it. Para. 209

The Ascension, the Fall of the City and Silence

The Porter of My Salvation has gathered together My Altar Shovels.
He chose a Seraph who teaches their seeds.
He empowers them. 47

The Linear Bible Code

Enough! I Y-H have ascended.
They have refused Us.
A Demon of Profaneness left behind darkness. 61

Y-H journeyed; He separated the unfaithful.
What is in the palate of the Poor One?
The Desire of the Eternities.
Death bears fruit as far as My Witness
And thy Fortress among them was brought low. 271

Lamentation! Wailing! Reproach!
O the Tel-City of the Mark!
O the region of the measure of the Nest!
It refused the Gift of Desire
And the Moon abideth from it. 113
Every entrance of the Tel-City a devastating storm shall throw down
through the Hand of Y-H. 158
And the city mound of Shem is to be desolate for its reputation even it
shall be swallowed up. 45

He confounded the Tabernacle.
Alas, strength being drowsy hundreds are for bitterness.
He swept bare the *city*-heap. 159
The Burden on High is for the ruination of the Witness of Y-H.
He is brought low as he is brought low by the Voice of a Star.
Scarcely was the Sheep of God destroyed *when* Neglect ran into the
mountain with the Jackal of Lust. 161

If only the Mark could change all of them.
He came; he swallowed up the Tabernacle.
I shall cast out the Gift of Knowledge.
Sufficient is the Hand-of-Knowledge.
A few he caused to shine even the oppressed of the Father. 162

I understood but alas the Instrument of Distinction removed the
Passover. *The people* slumbered.
Toward the Gentile is the mouth of *their* judgment. 238

A Son shall ascend; the Mark grew great. Let thou pine away! 132

My Noble removed afar off the Law of My Everlastingness. 202

The Linear Bible Code

His Witness endured Lamentation. I shall salt the firebolt of the
Instrument of Heart in the Days of Power for all. He measured the
Assembly. He responded to a few. He departed; they became drowsy.
My firebolt increased, the essence of My Light; but they rejected *him*.
204

And the Pure One of Heart purified himself;
He exalted the World;
He sought thee against the fierceness of Sheol.
Transgression trembled;
He boasted of Thee O Y-H. 179

"My Sword..., he set free a generation of profaneness.
"The Light came; thou denied Desire! The Light of my G-d." 59

The Father chose to wander about.
It happened He permitted the Chamber *to be* as ruin;
He was silent.
He *permitted* the increase of the haughtiness of His Own region.
He shall weep for the Spring;
Sufficient are His Bowels. 94

SECTION III:
THE DESCENT OF THE PURE ONE AND JUDGMENT DAY

The Head came but before fire proceeded. 117
What is Our Fire, even the sufficiency of the Son.
And what did We give? Our Pure One. 39
The Head came but before Him the strength of the Pure Son proceeded.
129
On what account did My Thin One, the Levite, descend?
The Pure banner's shaft was with him. 186
With the Terror of G-d the Mark threw down all of them and the
knowledgeable ones of G-d he silenced; he swallowed up the burden of a
sheep, the burden of ivory; and Y-H passed by. 122
The Terror of G-d is the Hand of the Mark-of-All-of-Them. 136

The Hand of the Father is the Mark.
I shall direct the Gift of the people of knowledge even the Mark.
The Mark darted through the cloud-mass.
I shall hide his mother. He shall empty the Tel-City of the Dragon. 146
The Seraph is Prince.

The Linear Bible Code

The Mark-of-All-of-Them descended with battle-spoils;
He was made to show grief; they showed not grief with him.
He shall see judgment fulfilled.
Let thou grieve injustice! 135

And he shall cut down Blood and Affliction of Lust but guarding thee.
And the Father shall remove afar off His saved ones. 36
And he shall cast them down;
And the Mark shall utterly hammer the Adversary
Against whom the Mark shook the Debt of the Mark.
All rottenness he shall remove. 32
And Reproach he shall cast down
And the blood of ruin and wailing *which is* the secret of injustice.
I shall direct it. 261

Praise you My Gift because of the Old One;
He was returned and he was made *the people's* Deliverer even on account
of My People, his poor ones,
And the Mark-of-All is King;
He went out; he returned; he was returned for *them.*
He moveth to and fro on account of His sheep
And sufficient is thy dismay but he will make soft the Distress with his
tears. 35

The Lamp thrust away the cold;
It shall scatter the Adversary of the Father.
Wailing is shut off or distress journeyed;
It shall fall down;
A people passed over, lo, from the Father;
 from the sweat of a mountain;
here it shall overflow.
And for Me he fished *a people.* 105
How the Light overflows he who is a people;
It shall put to death the Idols and the wicked at the days of Despairing
of Wailing.
And the multitude of the Thin One raved;
He pruned the people of his sheep the likes of a hand. 264

The Mark-of-All, the Pure King, he crashed them into ruins.
He shall spring about *as a calf.*
Ah! Above the Sea of Burden he traveled through Time itself.
Because of the poor of the people he is strong;

He empowers them;
They are a pure acquisition.
He gazed at the fruit of perfection.
Great of strength is Thy Poor One. 260

Fortress Earth belongs to Thee. For them is highness of His Region.
Our Beloved shall swallow up the Jackal of Emptiness and the Cave of
Gloom. The Mark is the Mark-of-Salt,
The Favour of the Oppressed;
The Son-of-Salt is the Favour of the Oppressed.
The Son is the Mark-of-All.
He cut off the Wicked One. 259

And My Will is a Gift and it seweth together a Community of Will; and
in regards to it, it seweth together My Grace. I have confined shame.
And who is the Pure One? The oppressed belong to him. Who is willing
and shall move to and fro among His sheep? He became the Mark for G-
d and the Tears of G-d. And he shall make himself a lineage. 34

My Poor One shall bear fruit.
From the Isle he hastened and he corrects a certain hope.
The Weak One of thy G-d is to hasten from his Isle
And he shall boast of his Land together with Me. 272

The Pure One shall boast with Me.
He fined the Adversary on account of My enemy and on account of Y-
H. He was not lead away; he crushed the constraints. And give you a
joyous shout O Palaces of His Obedient One. The Lamentation of his
Chamber is enough. With Me is the heap of My Treasures. 273

The Lamp of the Nest is above the Tel-City of the Mark;
The Abode of the Shepherd he shall cause to bear fruit. 127
And *the Lamp* guarded thee;
It gave victory and a sufficiency of My Words. 106

The Noble One caused Me to tremble.
He caused himself distress to feed them the Favour of the Oppressed
and the Son. He swallowed the Gentleness from G-d;
Thus the Mark for Shiloh dug out the Lust of the Jackal. Lo, sorrow is
made to totter. I wept. 187

"All of them, all of them I am feeding them of the Habitation.

The Linear Bible Code

It refused the firebolt but I am salting the *harvest* heap. I shall expose
G-d as a furrow. And they have chosen the Dew.
Men are entered the Habitation of Thy Tablet the Efficient Wisdom of
G-d." 237

The Son shall see enough of the poor. They are rolled up as the heart.
The Daughter of Israel is My only one. And the Mark took hold of
sorrow. The Mark-of-All-of-Them scraped clean the coast of Moses in
regards to the Calamity of the Coast. 236

And the Pure One of the Nest is the Hand of the Father.
Ah, there is no measure of the Nest.
Thou gavest them rest. 149

Lo, the Council of the Mark!
I G-d shall awaken everyone as a Sign and Token
Even all of them to establish them wealth. 114

A Seraph bedecked all of them a prince and every skirt he set. 63

I shall make My Sons Kings the desire of the mothers of My thin ones.
272

The TEXT

Paragraph 1 Daniel 12.13-10b

ני מיה צק לך לרגל דם עתו

Wailing is from Y-H. Distress is for thee to tread the blood of His Time.

חון תו צק לך לה תאו

The Mark loathes Distress for thee; in regards to it *(Time)* is His Chamber.

השם חום ישלש תו אם שלש פלאם

HaShem is darkened. The Mark divided into three a mother; three wonders.

ימיל עי גיו

He shall cut off the ruin of his valleys.

הכח מה ירשא מיעש תו מיתאם פלא מימי-ממש

The power, what shall it permit since the Mark works from the doubling of the Wonder at the days of Memesh?

צוק שת תל ודי מת

Seth brought into straits a Tel-*City* and sufficient died.

הרס והת עמו וניב ים ילך שמה

He threw down and his people shouted. And the fruit of the Sea prowled the wasteland.

Paragraph 2 Daniel 12.10a-9b

ומי עשר לכו ני בי אלו

And who is rich? Go you! Wailing is with Me, his G-d.

מי עשר ועי שרהו

Who is rich? But Ruin has regarded him

מיברו פרצת<u>י</u>ו ונבלתיו

since his violent one<u>s</u> were chosen and his foolish ones

ורר בת יצק

and the discharge of a daughter flowed.

Paragraph 3 Daniel 12.9a

תע דע מי רבדה מי מת חום

Opinion erred; who confined her? Whosoever is the black man.

ימת סיך לא ינד כל רמאיו

Seac shall die; he shall not agitate all his bowmen.

Paragraph 4 Daniel 12.8-7d

הלאת ירח

Thou hast removed afar off the Moon.

אהמין דאה רם און

I shall roar at them. A bird of prey established Wickedness.

יבא אל ויחטם שינאו

G-d shall come and He shall make them err that they shall be hindered.

הלא לך הני לכת שד

He shall remove *them* afar off for thee; here am I to crush Havoc.

Paragraph 5 Daniel 12.7c

קם עדי צפן תו לכך

My witness established the Treasure of the Mark at the burial cave

ויצחו מידעו מדע ומלי

And they shall be dazzled since they shall know from knowledge and from Me

כמלוע הי חם עבשי

as the swallowing up of a lamentation of the bosom of My shriveled ones.

ומי-משה לאו לאמשו

And the waters of Moses are for desire for his yesternight.

Paragraph 6 Daniel 12.7b

וני מי מרי וראו הים

And wailing! Who is in rebellion? But look you to the Sea,

ימלל עם מרש אם

a people shall fade because of the poverty of a mother.

Paragraph 7 Daniel 12.7a-6b

יד בה שוב לשיא התא עם שאות

A hand is against her. Return thou to the loftiness of the Chamber. A people is in an uproar.

ואלף הצקי חם דע

And My distressed one learned the perfection of knowledge.

ראי הים מללי עם מרש אם

Look thou to the Sea; a people shall fade because of the poverty of a mother.

Paragraph 8 Daniel 12.6a-5b

יד בה שוב לשיא לרם אי

A hand is against her; return thou to loftiness to raise up a region.

וראי התפש להן הדחא

And look thou, he was made to wield *a sword*, therefore he was made to thrust.

וראי התפש להן הדחא

And look thou, he was made to wield, therefore he was made to thrust.

Paragraph 9 Daniel 12.5a

מי דם עם ירחא מי נשהנה

Who resembles the people of the Moon? Who has forgotten her?

ולאי נדין אית יאר

And toward the coast we shall cause to judge the Falcon of the Nile.

Paragraph 10 Daniel 12.4,3,2b

ותעדרה הבר תום יבר

And thou shalt pass by the Pure One of Integrity; he shall be chosen;

וטט שיצק חט דע

and filth of he who pours the error of opinion.

רפס המת חום ירב דהם

Stamping he killed the black *man*; he shall be magnified. Be thou astonished!

תסל אי י נד התאו דעו

Let thou cast up an island the heap of his chamber, his knowledge.

מלו עלם יבכו

They have severed Eternity; they shall weep.

כך מי בר היקיד צם ועי קר הר הזך

Thus, who is the Pure One? Shall he cause fasting and Ruin to set on fire the cold pure mountain?

וזה זים ילך שמה ומל

And this he proved false. He shall walk the waste place; and he spoke.

וענו "אר דל תופר חלק"

But they answered: "A weak light is stitching together profaneness."

הלאו מל ועי יחל הלאו צי

They removed afar off the Moel; and Ruin tarries. They removed afar off the Howler.

Paragraph 11 Daniel 12.2a, 1c

קיר פע תמד אי נשימם יברו

A wall groaned continuously. A region We shall set them up; they shall become pure.

רפס בבות כאצם נהל

He stamped with feet in His passing the night as He pressed them to hurry. He guided them to a rest stop.

כך מא טלמי

Thus what are My oppressors?

Paragraphs 12-13 Daniel 12.1b

איה התעבו איה התעה דע

Where did they do abominably? Where did opinion err?

יוגת ויהם התיה * אל

The one grieving even he shall roar; he caused G-d pain.

רשאה רק תע התיהו כמעי נבל

The runner permitted error. He caused Him pain like the bowels of a fool;

עד מעה לו דגה לאך ים דם עי

Yet a seed is for him; it is in want. The Sea waited on the blood of Ruin.

Paragraph 14 Daniel 12.1a; 11.45,44

איה התעבו

Where did they do abominably?

ולרז ועני או וצק דע

And for leanness and the poverty of desire even he pressed upon knowledge.

אבוש דק יבצר הלם ים

I am ashamed of the withered thing. Hither he shall make inaccessible the Sea.

יניבו נדף איל אה עטי

He caused it to be fruitful; help is driven about.Lo, My Stylus!

ומי ברם ירח הלו די

And who twisted the Month? They boasted sufficiently.

משה לה לד גא מח

He delivered for her Lud the proud, the fatling.

בא ציו נופצם וחר

His ship came scattering them and the nobleman.

זממו הלהבי-תו עם שו

The Flames of the Mark proposed a plan for the people of Emptiness.

Paragraph 15 Daniel 11.43, 42

ויד עצם במישך ומיבל ומירץ מתו

And the hand of might is against Meshach and Mebel and Meraz. They died.

דם חלך בו פס כהו בה זה ינמך מבלשם

The blood of thy fortress is against him. The flat of the hand rebuked him; it emptied here; it makes thee drowsy above Melshem;

והטיל פלה יה תא

And causing to cast out Y-H consecrated the Chamber;

למי רץ מצר אות וצרא בו די חלשיו

For who ran from the Adversary? A Sign and a Distress was against *the Adversary.* Sufficient are His weak ones.

Paragraph 16 Daniel 11.41, 40b

נום עין בתי ראש ובאו מום

The eye of My Daughter's <u>head</u> was drowsy and with lust a blemish;

ודא ודי מוטל מיה לאו ולשכי-תו ברו

and this even is enough of striking against Y-H for Lust's *sake* and against the Coverts-of-the-Mark His Pure One.

יבק הצר אב אביו

He shall brighten the Distress of the father of <u>his</u> father;

רבעו פטשוחתו צר אב אביו

his forge hammers shall make into a square the Adversary of the father of <u>his</u> father.

תו בר תו ינא בו

The Mark is the Pure One; the Mark shall contend with him.

Paragraph 17 Daniel 11.40a, 39b

מי שרף בו בכר בנו

Who is the Seraph with *G-d?* His first born son.

פצה כלם וילע רעת שיו

He set all of them free but a friend of His sheep shall swallow *him* up.

בגנה כלם ומעה חג נתי

In the Garden *the Adversary* wounded even a <u>seed</u>. The Pilgram-Feast Is My Gift.

צק תעבו ריח מבק לחו המד-או

The Adversary poured out his abomination. He perceived an odour from the Emptiness. Take you a measure of Lust.

מי בר במלי-שם הודו

Who is the Pure One? With the words of Reputation *G-d* made him lofty.

בכה בר ידיך הרש ארך

The Pure One wept; He makes tender the Poor One; He makes *him* slow *to anger*.

Paragraph 18 Daniel 11.39a, 38

נהו לאם עמי זעם ירץ במלה

Wail you for the mother of My people! Indignation moves quickly by a word.

שעו תו דם חבו

Behold you the Mark of the blood of His Bosom!

הרקי נבא בו פסך בו

My Only One prophesied against *the people*. The flat of the hand is against *them*

בהזבד בכי ויתב אוה עדי אל רשאה

when he caused weeping to be bestowed and desire shall be trampled as far as G-d allows it;

לאלו דב כי וֹנכל עמי

For its god is the 'Bear of Branding' and deceitful is My people.

זעמה לא לו

Indignation, is it not for *them?*

Paragraph 19 Daniel 11.37, 36b

לדגת ילך לעי כן יביא לה

To the fishes *My people* shall go for ruin; so he shall cause *it* to come into her

ולא לך לעו

but go thou not for ruin.

מישן תדם "חל עון"

When he shall sleep thou shalt whisper: 'Profaneness, iniquity!'

יביא לוי תבא יה לא עוה

A Levite He shall cause to come in. Let thou come O Y-H not for ruin.

תשע נה צר חני כמעז

Nine is Distinction; it fashioned My Grace as a fortress.

Paragraph 20 Daniel 11.36a, 35b

הלך דע חיל צהו תו אלף נר בדים

Knowledge of the fortress proceeded; they shone upon the Mark; a thousand of the Lamp are idle talkers.

The Linear Bible Code

יל אל אל עול אלך

A god howled; a god of injustice is thy god;

לע לדגתיו ממורתי וכלמה

He talked wildly toward his own fishes on account of My rebellious ones and reproach.

ונוצרך השע ודעו

But the Watcher over thee worketh victory and his knowledge.

מלד ועיך צק תע דע נבל לו

Out of Lod and thy ruin he poured out error; knowledge is foolish to him.

Paragraph 21 Daniel 11.35a, 34b

רר בלום הב פור צלו לשך

The discharge is held in; give thou a young bull his shade for a booth.

ים יליך שם הן מות וקלקל חב מיבר

The Sea brings Shem. Lo, Death and contemptable of bosom so he is not selected.

מה ילעו ולנו

How they shall speak wildly even to Us.

Paragraph 22 Daniel 34a, 33b

טעם רז עו רז עי מלשכה בו

He tasted the secret of Ruin; the secret of Ruin is from the Lishka among him.

מימי הזבב ויבש בה

From the days of the fly even he shall be ashamed at *the Lishka*.

בהל בו בר חבול שכן

The Pure One made haste against him; he pledged a dwelling.

Paragraph 23 Daniel 11.33a, 32

מי בר לו ניבי מעילי

Who is the Pure One? To him belongs the Fruits of My Robe

כשמו וששעו וקן חי

According as is his Name and his Opulence but the Living One is set off *from him*.

ויהל אי עדי מעותו

And the region of My Witness shall shine on account of his aid.

קל חב פי נח יתיר ביעי שרם

The voice of the Bosom is the Mouth of Noah; among My Altar Shovels he shall lead; he shall rule them.

The Linear Bible Code

Paragraph 24 Daniel 11. 31, 30b

וממושה צו קשה ונתן ודי מת

And from <u>Moses</u> a severe commandment and it was given and enough died;

הור יסה וזו עם השד

And a mountain was veiled and this is a people dealt violently with.

קמהו ללחו ודם עיו

He raised *them* up toward his Tablet and the bood of its ruin.

נם ממי-ער זו שדקתי רב

They were drowsy at the Waters-of-Excitement; this that I should crush many.

Paragraph 25 Daniel 11.30a, 29b

יבז על ענביו בשו השעו שד

They showed contempt over *their* own vineyards; they felt shame; they liberated Havoc.

וקתי רב לעם עז ובשו

I subdued many for a mighty people and they felt shame.

הא כנו מי-תך מי יצובו אבו

Lo, they set up the Waters-of-Oppression. Who shall position his freshness?

הן רח אך והן שארך היה תא לו

Lo, the Spirit surely; and lo, thy remnant, a chamber exists for it.

Paragraph 26 Daniel 11.29a, 28

בגן בא בו בו שי-דע

In the Garden he came with Him; with Him was the Gift-of-Knowledge.

ומלו צר אל בש והשעו שד

And they spoke. The Adversary of G-d felt shame and they liberated a protective spirit.

קתי רב לעו בבלול

I subdued many; they babbled in confusion.

ודגשוך רבו צר אב שי

They pierced thee; they magnified the Adversary of the Father of the Gift.

Paragraph 27 Daniel 11.27b

ודעו מל צק "דו עיך חלק תא לו ורב

And know you *that* Distress spoke: "Two is thy ruin; the chamber is
equipped for him and the multitude.

די בוך דחא נחל שלע ור"

Sufficient is thy plunder. The Torrent-Valley pushed he who spoke
incoherently and the enemy."

Paragraph 28 Daniel 11.27a, 26, 25b

מל מבבל "מי כלם המה ינשו

Mebabel spoke: "Whosoever wounded them they shall be sick.

מי ברם ילל חולפנו פוט שיו לי"

"Who made a morose noise? He howled! Sweeping on us is Put. His gift
belongs to me."

חוו "הור בשי וגב תף"

Declare you: "The Mountain is against the Gift and the locust the
timbrel."

ילך אותו בשחם

His Sign marches with the lowly-ones.

ולעו בש חיי כדמעי-אל

And they shall swallow up the shame of My Kinsfolk as the Tears of EL.

ודא מד עמו צעו לו דגלי

And this is the measure of his people, they fashioned for him My
banners.

חבה מחלם להר

He withdrew from the fortresses to the mountain.

גתי בגן הכלם

My winepress in the Garden was made a reproach.

Paragraph 29 Daniel 11.25a, 24b

ולו דגלי-חב בגנה

And for him were My Banners of the Bosom in the Garden.

כלם לעו בבלו וחך רעיו

All of them, they spoke incoherently; they babbled and the palate of his
friends.

תע דעו ויתבש חם בשחים

His opinion erred and he shamed himself. O the heat against the lowly
ones!

ירצ בם לעורו זבי מהל שוכר
He ran against them to arouse him My Issue. He weakened the mercenary.

ולל שוה זבו
A winding *staircase* resembled his issue.

Paragraph 30 Daniel 11.24a

יתבא תו באו ויתבאו "שע-אל"
The Mark shall cause himself to come. They shall come and they shall cause themselves to enter the "Delight of G-d".

רשא השע ואו בי
The Opulent One permitted *it* and Desire is With Me.

הן יד-מין משם בו הול שבי
Lo, a hand of a species from Shem is with him. The Captivity is mad.

Paragraph 31 Daniel 11.23, 22b

וגט עם במצע והלע
And the Bill of Divorcement of a people is in a bed. And *they* were made to talk incoherently;

והמרם השעי וילא תו רב חת
and they showed them, My saved ones, disobedience. And the mark shall remove afar off the Greatness of Terror.

הן מות ירב די גן מגו ורב שיו
Lo, Death shall be increased; sufficient is the Garden of its Soothsayer. But he *the Mark* magnified his own gift.

Paragraph 32 Daniel 11.22a, 21

וינפלם ופטמ יפטשה תו ער זו תו קלקל חב-תו יזחהו כל מק
And the Mark shall cast them down. And he shall utterly hammer the Adversary against whom the Mark shook the Debt of the Mark. All rottenness he shall remove.

הו לשב אבית וכלם הודו
Ah! To turn back the fathers and he wounded his dignity.

ילע נתן אל והזבנו נכל עד מעו
He shall swallow *it* down and G-d requiteth; and he caused us to ejaculate; he was crafty as far as his own seed.

Paragraph 33 Daniel 11.20, 19

המחלם בא לו
The Dream came to him:
מי פא באל ורב שי
Who is here with G-d and disputed the Gift?
מי דחא מים יבו
Who thrust from the Sea? They cried shrilly!
תו-כל מרד השג ונריב עם ונכל עד מעו אצמי-אל לפן ולשכנו
The Mark-of-All revolted *at* the sin and a people quarreled and acted crafty as far as its seed, the strong ones of G-d, to perplex and to establish it.
וצרא יזוע מלני-נף בשיו
And Distress shall shake the murmurers of Memphis by His Gift.

Paragraph 34 Daniel 11.18, 17b

ולבי שי ותפר חית לב
And My Will is a Gift and it sews together a Community of Will.
ולו תפר חני צקתי בשה
And in regards to it it sews together My Grace. I have confined Shame.
ומי בר דך לו
And who is the Pure One? The Oppressed belong to him.
מי יאל וינף בשיו
Who is willing and shall move to and fro among His sheep?
היה תו לאל ודמעת אל והתיחש
He became the Mark for G-d and the Tears of G-d. And he shall make himself a lineage.

Paragraph 35 Daniel 11.11a, 16b

הלו לנתי מישן התב והשעו ומעמי רשיו
Praise you My Gift because of the Old One. He was returned and he was made *the people's* Deliverer even on account of My people, his poor ones.
ותו-כל מלך פק תב אוב לו
And the Mark-of-All is King. He went out; he returned; he was returned for *them*.
ינף משיו ודי בהלך ויבצה צרא בדמעיו
He moved to and from on account of His sheep and sufficient is thy dismay but he will make soft the Distress with his tears.

Paragraph 36 Daniel 11.16a, 15b

וינפל דם ועני או ונוצרך

And he shall cast down Blood and Affliction of Lust but guarding thee.

וילא אב ב השעיו

And the Father shall remove afar off His saved ones.

דם על חך ניאו וירחב ממעו ודמעי-אל

Blood upon the mouth; raw is it; and it shall grow wide because of his seed even the Tears of G-d.

בגנה תו ער זו תו רץ במרי עדך לו

In the Garden the Mark was exposed. This is the Mark *who* ran with the rebellion; thy Witness belonged to it.

הללו סך פשיו

They praised the Booth of its expansiveness.

Paragraph 37 Daniel 11.15a, 14b

נופץ הכלם אביו ולשכנו נוזח

The Shatterer of all of them is his Father and toward Our Pavillion is the Remover.

די מעה לו אש-ני כמעי-קיר פי נבו

Sufficient of seed belongs to him. The fire of wailing is as the belly of the Envoy the mouth of Nebo.

בגנה כלם לעו דם עי

In the Orchard all of them swallowed down the blood of ruin.

Paragraph 38 Daniel 11.14a, 13, 12b

מי בר מה המית עב

Who is the Pure One? How he caused the destruction of the Thicket!

וברש כרב ולו דגל יחבא

And a Cherub cut *it* into pieces and to him is a Banner. It shall be withdrawn.

ובאו בי מין שם

And they shall come with Me, a species of renown.

יתע הצק לו נוש אר

The Distresser shall err; for him the Light is weak.

הנם ברנו מה די מעה ונופץ הכלם בשו זו עי אל

Our Pure One was made to slumber. How sufficient is a seed but the Shatterer of all of them shamed *the Distresser*. This is the ruin of his god.

The Sealed Book of Daniel Revealed

Paragraph 39 Daniel 11.12a, 11b

חו אבר ליפהו

The Mark I shall choose to beautify him.

ובבל מרנונו

And Babylon <u>they rebelled</u> against Us.

מה האשנו ודי בן ומה הנתנו ברנו

What is our Fire? even the Sufficiency of the Son.

מה די מעה ונופץ הכלם מעו מעם חל נואציו

What is Sufficiency? A seed! And the Shatterer wounded His Own Seed on account of a profane people the ones having dispised Him.

Paragraph 40 Daniel 11.11a, 10b

בגנה כל מר מר מחיו

In the Garden all is bitterness; bitterness of his dead ones.

הזע מד עורגתיו בשיו רבעו

He made to flow the measure of his garden terraces. His shamed ones stretched out.

פטשו אוב אבו

Paragraph 41 Daniel 11.10a, 9

מי בר מי לי חן ומהו פס-או

Who is the Pure One? Who to Me is Grace? But they refused the Hand of Desire.

<u>ה</u>רגתי ונבו ותחמד אל-אב שוב גנה כל

I <u>killed</u> even Nebo. And the Wholeness of G-d the Father return thou gardenward, all of it.

מחו כלם באב

All who died are with the Father.

Paragraph 42 Daniel 11.8, 7b

ונופץ חכל ממד מעים ינש אוה

And the Shatterer obscured more than the measure of the bowels; He weakened Desire.

ומי רץ מאבי יבש בבה זו פס כמת-דם-חיל כמעם

And whosoever ran from My Father shall shame the Gate against which is the flat of the hand. As the man of blood of the Fortress so the bowels.

The Linear Bible Code

הי כס נם עם היה לא מג וקי זחהו מהו בהשע

O the lament of the Throne! A people slumbered. There shall be no soothsayer; and Kai removed him. <u>They</u> refused at the Opulent One.
Paragraph 43 Daniel 11.7a

Paragraph 43 Daniel 11.7a

ונופק הכלם זו עם באביו ליחה לא אביו

And the Shatterer of all of them is against a people with its father. He brightened not its father.

ונכה ישר שרצן מד מעו

And *the people* smote the Upright One who is the Favour of the Measure of His Seed.

Paragraph 44 Daneil 6a

מיתע בהק

On account of the skin sore was contagious

זחם וההדל-יה והא יבם

He removed them even the Thin One of Y-H. And <u>lo</u>, the Levir!

ואיה נתן חו וער זו דמעי-אל ועו

And where was the Mark presented and exposed? (This is the Tears of G-d and Ruin).

רזה חוך רק עת-אל

Thy life has grown weak; the Time of G-d has run out.

Paragraph 45 Daniel 11.6a, 5b

ומירשים חו שעל נופק הכל

And out of the inheritors of the Mark is the fox shattering all things.

מלא אובתבגנ הכל מת בו ירב-ב-חת-ים

O the fullness of the soothsayers in the Garden! All died with him even the Chief-of-Terror-of-the-Sea.

ינש צק לו וחל-שם מבר לשמם לשמו וילע

Distress becomes weakened to him. And the City-Mound of Shem on account of the Pure One is to be desolate for its reputation; even it shall be swallowed up.

קן חיו

His Living One is set apart *from it*.

Paragraph 46 Daniel 11.5a, 4b

וירשנום ובגנה כלם

And We dispossessed them, even in the Garden, every one of them.

The Linear Bible Code

קז חי

The Living One is set apart *from it.*

ולשמר שאול שמך אל

And to protect Sheol he made thee a god.

והלא דבלם מירח אלו

Is not Diblaim above the Moon his god?

ותו-כל משת

And the Mark-of-All is above Seth.

תני כות ירח אל אלו

I set the Window of the Moon a god, his god.

מי משה תו-חור עבר אל צחתו ותו-כל מרב שת

Who is Moses? The Sign of the Hollow. God passed by His Bright Ones;
but the Mark-of-All is from the greatness of Seth.

Paragraph 47 Daniel 11.4a, 3, 2b

ודם עכו ונוצרך השע ובר לשמם לשמור

But the blood of Acco and the one preserving thee was made to save;
and the Pure One is to devastate, to preserve;

ובג כל מד מעו

and every morsel is the measure of his bowels.

נוי-תו-כל מתא לך הר יעי ורשע בו

The Habitations of the Mark-of-All are from the Chamber. To thee is
the Mountain of My Altar Shovels but the Wicked One is in it.

תק זחך ולך מלו דגר שער ישעי יעי

Pull down thy pride! And go thou circumcise it! The Porter of My
Salvation has gathered together My Altar Shovels.

ברהו סרף למיד מעהם יכלם

He chose a Seraph who teaches their seeds. He empowered them.

Paragraph 48a Daniel 11.2a, 1b

השל שד ועה נה כל

The breast is made to hand down loose. And sweep thou away every
distinction.

די גאת מאה תעו ולזו עם

Sufficient is the pride of a hundred; they erred. And they turned aside a
people.

לוקי זח מלי דמעי

Lap thou up pride; cut off My Tear;

דמה שו ירד לתח

it resembles emptiness; it fell to spread out.

The Linear Bible Code

Paragraph 48b Daniel 11.1a; 10.21, 20b

את נשבי נא ומכרש לאך ים מאיך

Thou, blow thou on Thebes! And from Cyrus he sent a messenger of the Sea from thy coast.

הלא לעי מעק זח חם דחאני או-חם

Is he not for ruin tottering complete pride? Complete Lust pushed Me.

אב-תך בם

The father of oppression is among them.

ושרה תאך לדי גא לבא אבן וירש הן הוא צו יין או

And O Noble Lady of thy chamber give thou birth to a proud *son* to enter a stone and he shall be made poor. Lo, he is Precept, the Wine of Desire.

Paragraph 49 Daniel 10.20a

סרף רשם "עם חל הלב ושאה

A Seraph inscribed: "A people of profaneness of heart and a Shoah.

תטו כי לא יתאב המלת עד-יה רם איו

They erred because it did not long for the words of the Witness of Y-H; they exalted *their* own region.

Paragraph 50 Daniel 10.19

"ינתק זחיך ינדא רב

"They shall tear away thy proud ones; *the people* shall drive away a multitude.

די הרם אוית קז חת

Because thou desired Haughtiness Terror He set apart.

הי מעו רב דך וקז חוק זח כל מול שתו

O the wail of its bowels! Great is the oppressed! And every proud bosom in front of its buttocks he set apart.

דם חבר ארית לא רם

The blood of the <u>sword</u> of lionesses never exalted his coast!

Paragraph 51 Daniel 10.18, 17

"ינק זחי ומדאה ארם כי בעגי ופס ויבהר אשנאל

"My Proud One such *the breast!* And on account of the bird of prey I shall exalt burning with My breadcake and My Palm. And Ashnael shall shine.

המש נוח כי בדם עי-אל

Noah caused the burning to be removed by the blood of Ruin of G-d.

התע מין או הזין דא מערב דל

A lustful species erred. One he caused to feed from the lowering evening

הזין דא דב על כויך יה

Another he caused to be fed *even* the Bear at Thy Window O Y-H.

Paragraph 52 Daniel 10.16, 15b

"וחך-יתר צעאל וילע יריץ

"And the Palate of Excess is Zael; and it swallows; it causes ruin.

וכף הנה ארם בי

But a Rock hither I shall exalt with Me.

נד אי דגן לדמעה

The heap of the coast he heaped up for tears;

לא הרם אוה רבד או

he never exalted Lust; he confined Lust.

יפח תף או יתפש לע עג

The Timbrel shall blow *upon* Lust. He shall lay hold of the throat of Og.

נמד אי נב די תום

The region of Nob was measured a <u>sufficiency</u> of fullness.

דכה נה ויתמלא נוה

Distinction crushed it; and distinction filled itself up.

Paragraph 53 Daniel 10.16, 15b

"צראי-נפי תתנה לא המיר בדכי מעורב דב

"The distresses of My Height *distinction* shall reckon. It did not cause a pouring out at My Oppressor at the passing by of the Bear;

ומים ילן וזח דו עיך מים

but at the Sea it remained even pride. Twice is thy ruin from the Sea.

יהת ירחא בך מעל הר קיר

The Moon shall say: 'Weep thou from beside Mount Ker!

שא תאך ניבה לי

'O the ravage of thy threshing-floor! The fruit belongs to me.'

Paragraph 54 Daniel 10.14a, 13

"תאבו סרפי כלם

"They abhor My Seraph, all of them.

<u>רש</u> לצאם שית רח

<u>Poverty</u> is to make them filthy, a garment of trembling.

וני נא וינר זע לאב מין

And now, wailing even shall be revealed; it shall tremble at the Father of Species.

The Linear Bible Code

שארהם ירש הדח

He who is their Light has been made poor; he is made clean by washing.

אלאך ימה נהום וידח או

I shall send a messenger seaward groaning and he shall thrust away Lust.

מי רשעי-דגן לדמע

Who are the Wicked Ones of Dagon to weep?

סרף תו-כלם רש

The Seraph, the Mark-of-All-of-Them, is poor.

Paragraph 55 Daniel 10.12, 11b

"כי רב דב יתאב ינא

"Because of the greatness of the Bear he is abhorred; he is hindered.

וכי רב דו עם שנך יה

And because of the greatness double is the people of Thy Tooth, O Y-H.

לא ינפל חו נעת הלו

The Mark shall never fall. Thou didst tremble, they boasted.

ני בהלך בל תא

Wailing! The product of the threshing-room disquieted thee.

תתן רש אנוש ארהם ויהן

Let thou give the poor of mankind their light and it shall be made easy.

מי כלא ינה ארי

Whosoever has withheld has suppressed My Light.

תל-אי לארם איו

The City-Mound of the region is to illuminate them of its own region.

די ערם יתדמע הזהר בד

O the sufficiency of craftiness! The isolated brightness causes itself to weep;

התאים עור בד

he caused the blind to be doubled alone.

Paragraph 56 Daniel 10.11a

"בו פי לאית חלש התעיך

"With him is the mouth of weak Laeth; he caused thee to err.

כדמע לע דמעו כי לא רם

As he wept he swallowed down his tears because there not many.

די כנא רש אם ירבד בן

Because the Poor One of a mother was given a knighthood a Son was decked out *in finery*;

The Linear Bible Code

בה תו-דם חש יאל אי נדי

with her was the Mark-of-Blood. Make thou haste! The region of My Heap is willing.

לא רם אי ודי-תו פכו

He did not exalt the region nor the hands of the Mark his vial.

Paragraph 57 Daniel 10.10, 9b

"יכר בל עין עין תו יבה

He regarded not the spring, the spring *of waters of* the Mark; it is empty.

עג נדי הן הוה צרא ינף וינפל עם

He circled My Heap; lo there is distress; it waves and a people fall.

דר ניתי יהי נאו

A Pearl of My habitations let it be his dwelling.

ויבדלו קת אי עם שכו

And they shall separate out Keith an isle with its pavilion;

וירב דל וקת אעמש או חך יתרצע אלותי

And the Thin One shall be magnified but Keith I shall carry *as a load* if perchance the Palate pierces itself of My Own Oaths.

Paragraph 58 Daniel 10.9a, 8

"חשמל ילע כפה ני דו הו

"Electrum he shall swallow down as a mouth. Wailing, twice, ah!

חכי ברא שן אל ותא זה

My Palate has created the Ivory of G-d and this Chamber.

הלד גהה ארם התאה

Lydda is set free! I shall establish her chamber.

אר או יד-בלי תרא שני-נא

O light of desire, a hand of destruction shall see the teeth of Thebes.

Paragraph 59 Daniel 10.7, 6b

"ואבחה בו חרבי

"And the slaughter among him is of My Sword

ומה ילעה לפנה לד

and o how *the sword* swallows up to the corner of Lydda.

גה דר חל בא האר מהת או אר אלי מעוי-הר שא

He set free a generation of profaneness. The Light came; thou denied Desire the Light of my G-d on account of the ruinations of Mount Ravage.

מי שנאה וארם התא

Who hated it and the lights of the Chamber?

The Linear Bible Code

יד בל לאי
The hand of Bel is toward the region.

נדין אית יאר
We shall judge the regions of the Nile.

ונום הלוק כוי רב דלו
And Luke slumbered. The windows of plenty hang low.

"קול לק ק תשחן
Thou shalt inflame the voice of Luke."

Paragraph 60 Daniel 10.6a

ני עכו יתל גרמו ויתע רז ושא יד
The wail of Acco; it deceives itself and leanness shall err and ravage of power.

יפלך ויניע קרב האר מכו
It intercedes for thee; and the approach of the Light from the *Celestial Window* causes him to waver.

ינפו שי-שרת כויתי וגוז
The Gift of the noble ones of My Windows shall scatter him.

Paragraph 61 Daniel 10.5, 4, 3b

פואם תך במי-רגח וינתם ובלדח
The Oppression is swallowing the high places of Regech and Janethom and Medebesh and Beldach.

אשיא הנה וארא ויניע חא
I shall cause a deception here. And I shall look and the Chamber he shall cause to shake.

אש-או לקדח אוהל ודג הר הנה
The Fire of Desire is to kindle the Shining One; and the fish of a mountain is here.

די עליתי יה ינאונו
Enough! I Y-H have ascended. They have refused Us.

שאר השד-חל העב
A Demon of Profaneness left behind darkness.

ראו מי רש עמו
Look you! Who is the Poor One of His people?

יבו מימי מיעבש
They cried shrilly from the days of Meabesh.

The Linear Bible Code

Paragraph 62 10.3a, 2b

תשלש תא למד עית כסא לכוס
Thou shalt divide into three parts the Chamber for the measure of
ruinations. A throne for a cup.

ויפלא אבאל ני יורש בו יתל
And Abael shall do wonderously. Lamentation is taking possession
within him; it heaps up.

כא אל תו-דם חם חל מימי מיעבש
G-d reproved the Mark-of-Blood. Profaneness grew warm from the days
of Meabesh.

Paragraph 63 Daniel 10.2a, 1; 9.27b

השלש לב את מיתייה לאי נד
The Heart divides into three parts Metai-yah at the isle of the heap.

ינא מהה מימי בהארם
He would be restrained; he refused from the days of Bah-aram.

בול הניב ורבד התא ניב
A product he made fruitful and the room of fruit he decorated

ולוד גא בצו רבדה תם-או
and proud Lydda is in the Ordinance; she decorated the perfection of
Desire.

רץ אש-טל בו משאר קן רש אל
The fire-of-dew flowed among it because of the remnant of the Nest the
poor of G-d.

אין דלה לגן רבד סרף כלם שר
There is no door into the Garden. A Seraph bedecked all of them a
prince

וכל שול שת נשב ממש
And ever skirt he set. He situated himself on the side of Mash.

Paragraph 64 Daniel 9.27a, 26b

לע כתת הצר חן והלך דע
The Adversary swallowed up Grace; he beat *it* to pieces and knowledge
journeyed.

וממש ממי-צו קש פנך לעוה חן
And out of Mash from the waters of the Ordinance he lured thy face for
he twisted Grace out of shape.

מוח בזתי בשי-עו בשה יצחו
The marrow I have despised with the gift of Ruin; among the sheep he
sprinkled it.

The Linear Bible Code

דחא עוב שמי "בר" לתירב

Thrust thou away! He hid My Name "Pureness" toward Tirab.

די בגה וחום משת

Sufficient is its food and Perfection from Dignity.

צרח נה מחלם צק דע

Eminency rored on account of a dream; it constrained knowledge.

Paragraph 65 Daniel 9.26a

ופט שבו צקו אב

And a stalemate they restored; they pressed upon the Father.

הדי גן מעת

The sufficiency of the Garden is separate of Time.

יחשי-שד קהו ריעהו

O the geneologists of the Demon! They blunted his friend.

ולני או חי שמת רכי

And toward the wail of Living Desire thou ravaged My Tender One.

מין שו מיש שמי עבש הירחא

Oa species of vanity! It withdrew My Name; the Moon shriveled.

Paragraph 66 Daniel 9.25, 24c

ומי תעה קוצב וצורח ובוחר

But who is Calamity? The Shearer and the Cleaver and the Examiner.

התן בן ובו שת

A son was made perpetual and with him is Seth.

מין שו מיש שמי

O a species of vanity!

עב-שו העבש

A cloud of emptiness was made to shrivel up.

מי עב שדי-גן חי שמד

Who hid the furrows of the living garden? The Exterminator,

עמל שורי-תו נבלו

he works the heads of cattle of the Mark! They became withered.

בושה לרב דא צם

O the shame belonging to the multitude! This is fasting.

נמלך שת ועד תום

Seth was made king and the Witness of Integrity.

Paragraph 67 Daniel 9.24b

ישד קש דק חמש לו

Fine chaff he shall destroy; wealth belongs to him.

The Linear Bible Code

איב נונו זח מת חל

The enemy, they increased pride; a fortress died.

ומי מל עקד צאי בהל ונוער פך לו תו-אט חמת חלו

And who cut off the binding? The filthy one. He acted hasty even shaking a Vial toward him, the Mark-of-Gentleness, the wrath of his profaneness.

Paragraph 68 Daniel 9.24a, 23b

עש פה אלך לכדש

URSA MAJOR is the mouth; I shall travel toward Chaldea.

קרי על עו כמעל עכת חנם

My cold is above Ruin like the treachery of Acath without cause.

יעב שם יעב שה

A species of vanity shall conceal a Name; it shall conceal a sheep.

ארם בן בהו רבד בני בו התא-תו

I shall raise up a son among *them; they* shall bind My Son. Among *them* is the Chamber of the Mark.

דו מחיך די גה לי תא בין או רב

Two of thy fatlings are enough; he healed for Me the Chamber; he discerned great desire.

Paragraph 69 Daniel 9.23a, 22

דא צי כינון חתת לח חבה

This is the Howler as he increases Terror he shall efface an Ark.

ניב כלי כשה לי תא צי

The fruit of the vessel is as a sheep; the ship's hold is Mine.

התעלא ינד רם אי

The watercourse is heaped up the height of an island;

וים-ערב די וניביו

and the Sea of Passage is enough and its <u>fruits</u>.

Paragraph 70 Daniel 9.21, 20b

בר עת חנם חע כי לא עג

The Pure One of the Appointed Time undeservedly erred because he never bent.

נף עי בפעם הלח

He sprinkled Ruin at the occurrence of the New Thing.

The Linear Bible Code

תבנו זה בית יאר רשא "לאירבג" שיא

You are building the pride of the House of the Nile. Gabriel permitted loftiness.

הוה לפת בר-בד מין-אד

It came to pass the Pure One is Separation grasped with a twist a species of vapour;

ועויה לאשד קרה לעיה לאה

and her ruin is for the Lower Region of Cold for her ruin was impatient.

Paragraph 71 Daniel 9.29a, 19b

והי ינפ לי תן חת לי פמו

And wailing! The Jackal waveth at Me Terror; toward Me was its mouth

לאר שי-ים-עת

to reveal the Gift of the Sea of Time.

אט חוית אטמ הד

A gentle sound thou breathed; I shall extend the shout!

ותמול לפתם ורב דמי-נא

And let thou cut off at Pithom and the abundance of bloods of Thebes.

דו עוך מעל עוך ריע לה

Double is thy ruin from upon thy ruin. The shout *of war* he swallowed up.

אר קנך משיך יה לאנן עם לרח את

The Light of Thy Nest is from Thy Gift O Y-H; for I shall establish a peole; for a spirit art thou.

לאה שעו הביש קהין

His Noble One is was impatient; he caused Bluntness to be shamed.

Paragraph 72 Daniel 9.19a, 18b

דאה חל-סין דאה עם שי

The Fortress-of-Siin darted through the air; the people of the Gift darted through the air.

נד אמי-בר הכים חר לעיך כינפלו נין חת

O the wandering of the mothers-of-purity! A free born man smote them for thy ruin; as the progeny of terror they fell down *earthward*.

Paragraph 73 Daniel 9.18a, 17

מי לי פם ונח נאו ניח קד צלע אליך

Who is for Me? The Mouth and Noah. They restrained the habitations of Ked the stumbling of thy gods.

The Linear Bible Code

הילע כמש אר-קן

Shall he swallow up as the Light of the Nest departs?

רש-אר יעהו ונית ממשה ארו

The Poor One of Light swept him up but the habitations through Moses are his light.

כי עין החק פעם שו כן

Because of the Eye he decreased a time of emptiness rightly so.

זא הי הלא הטה ינד אן

This is <u>wailing</u>; did he turn aside? He heaped up sorrow.

עמל ממשה כשד

The Trouble is from Moses as a Demon.

קם לער ינף ראהו וינון חת לאו

The Adversary swallowed thee; he waved; he saw it, but Terror shall increase for Lust's *sake*.

כד בעת לפת לאוני

A Jar in Time; he grasped at My Wealth.

הלא עם שה תעו

Is not a people a sheep? They have wandered.

Paragraph 74 Daniel 9.16b

ונית ביבס לך להפרח לך מעו

And the Habitations at Jebus are thine for the sprouting for thee of his seed.

מל שורי ונית

Circumcise thou My heads of cattle and the Habitations.

בא תו נוע בו

The Mark came; *Jebus* trembled at him.

וני אט חביך כשד

But the lament, gentle are thy debts as a breast.

קרה מל שורי-כרי-עם כת מח וכפא אן

The Moel met the heads of cattle of the pastures of the people. He beat fine the fatling and he subdued sorrow.

Paragraph 75 Daniel 16a, 15b

בשיך תקד צל כך ינד או נע שרון

With thy sheep let thou bow down *beneath* the shadow. Thus Lust shall flee; it tossed about the Sharon.

אטחה זהם ויכם שכל שעתו הקז חד

I shall besmear *the eyes of* Zaham but sharp Hekez shall heap up the good sense of his own time.

The Linear Bible Code

יבם ירץ מצרא מכם

He is proud; he shall run from adversity, from you.

עתא תאץ והרש אוני

Now let thou make haste and possess thou My Wealth.

Paragraph 76 Daniel 9.15a, 14, 13b

הלא ינדא התעו ולקב ונעם

Shall he not drive away they who erred even for a Kab-measure and pleasantness?

שאל והשער-שאו ישע מלך לעוני הלאה

Sheol and the Gate of its Ravage the King made for the punishments of iniquities of far away.

והיקיד ציך

And shall he cause thy ship to burn?

וני לע האיבי והערה לעהו

But the lament, it swallowed up My enemies and the bare place it swallowed down.

הי דק שי וכתם אבל יכשה לו

Lamentation is the thinness of a gift and the gold of mourning. He shall gorge himself of it.

Paragraph 77 Daniel 9.13a, 12b

ונן ועם בו

And he shall increase and a people with him.

שלו ני הלאה

They are at ease; lamentation is far away;

והיין פת-און ילח ואל

and the wine *and* the morsel of vigour his G-d shall refresh.

וני לעה אב-תא זה הערה לך תא השם

And the lamentation the Father of the Chamber shall swallow up. This is the bare place for thee, *for* the Chamber of HaShem.

תר ותבה בו

The Turtledove and the Ar<u>k</u> is within it.

תך רש אך מל שורי בה

O the oppression of the poor! Surely he circumcised My heads of cattle in it.

תשען רש אך מי-משה לך תחת התשע נא

Let thou o poor repose thyself. Surely the waters-of-Moses are for thee instead of the Nine of Thebes.

לרש האל דגה
The Tent of the Fisherman belongs to the poor.

Paragraph 78 Daniel 9.12a, 11b

ערו ני לע אי בהלו נוטף שרש-או
Lay you bare lamentation! The coast spoke incoherently; they disquieted the Root-of-Desire.
ני טפש לעוו
Lamentation is gross; they swallowed it up.
ני לע רב דרש-אוי
O the lamentation! The multitude swallowed up the one seeking My Desire;
רבד תא-מקיו ולון אט חיכם יה
The one chaining the chamber of *their* rottennesses.
And Gentleness lodged for the night your Living One Y-H.

Paragraph 79 Daniel 9.11a

לא הד בע השם תר ותבה בו
There is no joyous shout! HaShem boiled a turtledove and the Ark is with Him.
תך רש אה עב שה והלאהו
O the oppression of the poor! Alas, He hid a sheep and He removed it afar off.
ני לע כת תוך לקבע
O the lamentation! Cuth talked wildly of injury to despoil
ומשית לבלרוס וכתרות תא
And of the establishing of Belarus and the crowns of the *throne*-room.
ורב על ארש ילכו
And a multitude against Eresh shall march.

Paragraph 80 Daniel 9.10, 9b

מי איבו הוי דב עדי בו
Who is his enemy? Alas, the Bear. My Witness is against him.
ני נפל נתן רש או
Wailing! He fell down; the Poor One presented Desire.
יתרות בת כללו ני הלאה
The excesses of the Daughter they completed. Wailing is out there.
והילו קב ונעם שאלו ובו נדר
And shall they boast of the Kab-measure and the pleasantness of his G-d? But against him is a vow!

Paragraph 81 Daniel 9a, 8b

מיך תו חל סהו מי-מחר

The Mark brought low the fortress; the waters-of-tomorrow were veiled.

הוני הלא ינד אלך לון אם חרש אוני

My wealth shall not thy G-d vow *it*? Gentleness lodged for the night, the Vessel of My wealth.

תבא לו וניר שלו

Let thou come toward it and the Lamp of Shilo.

Paragraph 82 Daniel 9.8a, 7b

ני כל מלם ינף התשב ונלהו

O the lamentation! All the words he waved about he repented himself of but they shall be fulfilled.

היכבו לעם רש אם לעם במשממת חד

Shall they be rolled up for a poor people, the mother of a people by the Devastation of Sharpness,

הר שאת וצר

the Mount of Devastation and Distress?

אהלך במי-קחרה ומי-ברק

Thy tent is among the waters-of-Kachrah and the waters-of-Barak.

Paragraph 83 Daniel 9.7a, 6b

הלא רש ילך לו מל שור ויבשו ילו

Shall not the poor one journey to it? A head of cattle spoke and they dried up. They boasted;

הדו "הי שיא לה זהם ויכם ינף התשב"

they shouted: "O the lamentation! Loftiness is for her; it is *now* loathsome and it was heaped up; it is *now* shed abroad and it returns of itself."

ונלו צהי נדא כל

And they are fulfilled. Be you burned! Be thou parched! Everything is thrust away!

צרא המעל כלאו

The unfaithful are is distress; they are imprisoned.

וני תבאו וני רש וני כל מלאך משב

And o the lamentation! You shall enter *it* even the lamentation of the poor and the lamentation of every messenger of the Assembly.

ורבד רש-אם יאיבנה כי דב על או

And the poverty of a mother is spread out. The Bear is hostile toward her because he is against Desire.

The Linear Bible Code

Paragraph 84 Daniel 9.6a, 5, 4b

נע משאל וכי טפש שמם

He trembled from Sheol and because the Devastator was stupid

וכת וצם מרו "סו"

(but Cuth even he fasted) they were embittered "sixty six *days*".

ונד רמו ונעשרהו

And he heaped up his height and he was enriched of it.

וני ועוו נא טחו יתו צמי-רמש לו

And o the lamentation! And they did wrong. Now *their eyes* are
besmeared. He marked the traps of creeping things belonging to him.

Paragraph 85 Daniel 9.4a, 3b

ויבה אלד סח הות ירב הרמש ארון

And Elled will cry shrilly; he shall scrape away the desire of Jareb who
caused the Ark *of the Covenant* to move about.

ולו דגה לא הין דא אן אה רם או

And for him is a fish not a Hin-measure. This is sorrow; alas, the
haughtiness of Lust.

הדות או יה לאהו היל

Y-H, Thou hast made Lust ill. They wearied the Shining One.

הלכ פת אור פא

He boasted a bit of light here.

Paragraph 86 Daniel 9.3a, 2b

וקשו מוצב מין ונח חו הלפת שק

And his stubble was a kind of palisade. And the Mark was quiet. He
grasped with a twist sackcloth.

בלם יה לאה ינד אל אי נף תא הן תאו

Y-H held back; He was impatient. EL showed grief; alas, He shook the
Chamber, lo, His Chamber.

הן שמי עב שם לשורי-תו בר חל תו-אל מלאי-בנה

Lo, My Name, he hid the Name toward the heads of cattle of the Pure
Mark; the Fortress is the Mark-of-EL, the fullness of her son.

הי מר ילאה והי רבדה יה

Bitter Wailing! He removed it afar off; and o the lamentation, Y-H shall
confine it.

Paragraph 87 Daniel 9.2a, 1b

רשא מין שה רפס ממי-רפס

He permitted a species of sheep to foul at the waters-of-Rephes by stamping.

בית ניב לאי נדין או כלם

The House of Fruit at the coast We shall judge the desire of all of them.

לתח אתן שב מיד שך

He spread you out *as a garment*. He turned aside a thorn from a hand.

חו-כלם לע כלם

The Mark-of-All-of-Them swallowed up all of them.

הרש אי דמע רזם

The Poor One of the coast winked back a tear.

שורו שח אן בשו

His Head of cattle is lowly, strength is his shame.

Paragraph 88 Daniel 9.1a; 8.27

ירד לתח אתן

He descended to spread out out.

שב ני במני-אוה

Wailing turned against Meni-of-Lust.

ארם הלעם מות שא וכלמה

I shall arise. Death has swallowed them up *even* Ravage and Reproach.

תך אלם תא השע או

Oppression bound the Chamber; Desire gained victory.

מוק או מימי-יתיל חן וית ייהן

He derided Desire from the days it caused Grace to be mocked and Jaihan.

לאי נדין או

At the Isle We shall judge Lust.

Paragraph 89 Daniel 8.26, 25b

מי בר מים יליכנו זח המח

Who is the Pure One? At the day he caused Us to journey he removed the man;

סה תא ואוה תם ארם

He veiled the Chamber and perfect Desire. I shall arise.

אן רש ארקבהו ברעה

The sorrow of the poor I shall make it rot away by a Shepherd.

הא רם ורב שי-די

Lo, He raise up and He magnified the sufficient Gift.

The Linear Bible Code

סף אבו דם-עי

His Father ended the Blood of Ruin.

Paragraph 90 Daniel 8.25a.

מי רש רש לעו

Who is the Poor One? The Poor One they swallowed up.

מי ברת יחשיה ולשבול יד גי ובבל בו

Who is the Covenant? He causes silence and for the hanging down of the hand of My valleys and Babylon with it.

ודי יבהם רם חיל צהו

And enough! He shall be tongue-tied. He raised up anguish; they struggled.

ולך של עו

But go thou, spoil the ruin.

Paragraph 91 Daniel 8.24, 23b

מי שד קם עו

Who is Havoc? He raised up Ruin.

מי מוק עת יחשה והשע וחי

Who squeezed Time? He will make haste

לצהות יחשי-תו-אל

To order the genealogies of the Mark of EL.

פנו וחך בא לו וחכם צע

Approach you even the Palate! Come thou to him and Wisdom he fasheioned.

ותו די חן יבם

And the Mark, sufficiency of Grace, acts the Levir.

Paragraph 92 Daniel 8.23a, 22b

ומי נף זע כלמד מעים

And who is Grief? He trembled as he chastised the bowels.

יעש פה מתה כמתו כל מת ירחא בו

The Mouth was created; it died as all *things* die; the Moon died with him.

וחך באלו הן דם עיו

But the Palate was with his G-d. Lo, the blood of his ruinations;

גם תו יכלם

yea, the Mark, he enabled them.

The Linear Bible Code

עבר אהי תחת עבר אה נד מעת

He passed over; where is the place he passed over? Alas, he moved out of Time.

Paragraph 93 Daniel 8.22a, 21, 20b

ותר בשן הון ושאר הכלם האוה

And the Seeker made smooth wealth; and leaven caused the humiliation of Lust;

וינע ניב רש אהל ודגה

and the fruit of the poor tossed about the Tent and a fisherman.

נרק הונו יכל מר יעש הר יפצהו סרפו ידם

His wealth was spit upon; it empowered bitterness; it made a mountain. His Seraph parted it; he was silent.

יכלם מין רק הלע בת-יאר רש-אל

A species wounded the Thin One; the House-of-the-Nile caused the Poor One of EL to be swallowed up.

Paragraph 94 Daniel 8.20a, 19, 18

יאה צק דעו מליך מעז

Distress was appropriate. They knew thy words were from Strength.

התירח אב היה ירשא תא כעי דום

The Father chose to wander about. It happened He permitted the Chamber *to be* as ruin; He was silent.

ינה רם איו ידמע לעין די מעיו

He *permitted* the increase of the haughtiness of His Own Region. He shall weep for the Spring; sufficient are His Bowels.

יבע גיו הצראי-נפל עי תם

His Valley flowed; the distressed places of untimely birth are in complete ruin.

דר ני מעו רבד בו

A generation of wailing is from Ruin; it is confined within it.

Paragraph 95 Daniel 8.17

נוצח הצק תעליך מד

The Remover poured out of thy water courses a measure.

אנב נבה ילא רם איו

He leaped toward Nob; he removed afar off the greatness of its region.

ינף לעה לפא ויתעבנו אב בו

He moved to and fro; he spoke rashly toward here and he regarded Us an abomination. A necromancer is with him.

The Linear Bible Code

ידמע לצא אביו
He weeps at the filth of his father.

Paragraph 96 8.16, 15

האדם התא זלה נב
Shall I set up the Chamber only at Nob?

הלא ירב גר מאי וארקיו ילו
Did not the sojourner increase because of the region and *from* the arracks they howl?

אניב מאל וקע משאו
I shall make fruitful the Measure-of-EL but tear thou away its usury.

רב גה ארם
The abundance set thou free! I shall raise My Self up.

כיד גן לדמע הן הוה
He worked the Orchard for juice. Lo, it happened.

ניב השק באונו
Fruit he gave to drink with its vigour.

זח התא לאי נדין אי תא רב יהי
O the pride of the Chamber at the coast; We shall judge the coast a mighty chamber. Let it be!

Paragraph 97 Daniel 8.14, 13b

ושדקק דצנו חוא משל-או
And he who crushed Our Dance was the antelope of the Dominion of Emptiness.

מי פלא רק בבר עד
Who worked a wonder? The Thin One with perpetual pureness.

עיל ארם אי וסמ
He gave suck. I shall establish a region and spice.

רם אב צו שדק
The Father established the Ordinance of the Veil

ונתַן ממש הַעש פה ומרום די מת
And He set *it* beside Mash; He made the Mouth and the Height the sufficiency of mankind.

Paragraph 98 Daniel 8.13a

הנו זח הי חם הי דע רב דם הי
Be you easy! Thrust thou away complete lamentation, the abundance of opinion, the blood of wailing!

The Linear Bible Code

נומל פלַכ שוד קדח
The Cutter <u>judges</u> burning desolation.

ארם אי ורב דם שוד קדח
I shall establish a region but O the abundance of the blood of burning desolation!

אה עם-שא
Alas, a people of Ravage!

Paragraph 99 Daniel 8.12, 11b

והחיל צהוה תשעו הצרא תם
And the anguish make you it ruins! Make you wide complete distress;

אך לשת ועשף בדי מת הלע נתן תא בצו ושד קמנו
Howbeit, for Seth and Aseph what suffices for man Nathan swallowed up the Chamber, its mire and devastation Our adversary.

כם כל שה ודי מת
Everyone heaped up a sheep and the sufficiency of man.

המיר הון מם ולי דגה אבץ הרש
Wealth makes bitter a defect but to Me is a fisherman; I shall make exceeding white the Poor One.

Paragraph 100 Daniel 8.11a, 10

דעו מסמר תום
They knew because of the bristling of Integrity.

יבכו כהנם ואבצ הנם הצר אלף-תום
They shall weep like Hennom but I shall make exceeding white Hennom the adversary of the Chief of Integrity.

ימש האב צד על דגתו
The Father shall remove the hunter against His fisherman.

Paragraph 101 Daniel 8.9

יבעה לאו חר
He will shine toward the Desire of the Noble.

זמה לאו בגנה לארת
He planned for the Desire in the Garden to be lights.

ילד גת והרי-עצם-תח
He begat a wine-press and the mountains of Azum-Toah.

אן רק אצי מהם תח אה נמו
The exclusive strength of My oppressed ones Toah denied them; alas, they slumbered.

The Linear Bible Code

Paragraph 102 Daniel 8.8

מי משה תו חור עבר-אל

Who is above a sheep? The Noble Mark, the Passageway of G-d.

הי תחת עבר את וזח

Lamentation instead of the traversing of a ploughshare even is pride.

הן לעת והלו דג הנה

Lo, thou spoke incoherently but they praised the fish of eminency.

קהה רב שן ומצעך

The greatness of tooth he blunted and thy couch;

ודא מדע לי

and this knowledge belongs to Me.

דגהם יזע הר יפצו

Their fish was made to swim the mountain *stream*; it swam it.

Paragraph 103 Daniel 8.7b

ודי מלי-אל ליצם

And because of the Words of G-d he scorned them.

הי האלו והסמריו

O the lament of his G-d and his bristling ones.

הצר או הכיל שיו

The Adversary of Desire prevailed over His sheep.

וינפל דם עללי-אב חך

And the blood of the children of the Father of the Palate he cast down *to
the ground*.

הי האלו

O the lament of his G-d!

וינר קית שתא

And he shall reveal the vomit of the drunk.

רב שיו לי אה תא כיו

The greatness of his gift is Mine. Alas, the chamber of branding.

Paragraph 104 Daniel 8.7a, 6

ארו וחך תם חבו

His Light and the Palate is the Integrity of His Bosom.

ילא צריו לבאה

He shall remove afar off His enemies to come into her.

ינפל דם עית יאר רשא

He shall let fall the blood of the ruinations of the Nile. He shall permit
it.

The Linear Bible Code

מי נר קהל-עבל יאה דע אביו

Whsoever is a lamp of the Assembly of the Stout One is worthy of the knowledge of his Father.

Paragraph 105 Daniel 8.5, 4b

ויניע ני בת וזח נר קר

But wailing shall cause the house to totter but the Lamp shall thrust away the cold;

יפצהו צר אב

it shall scatter him, the Adversary of the Father.

עגון ני או צרא הלך ינפל

Wailing is shut off or distress journeyed; it shall fall down.

עבר עם הן מאב מיזע הר

A people passed over, lo, from the Father, from the sweat of the mountain.

יפץ הנה וניב יתי יהי נא

Here it shall overflow and fruit from the Jettite let it be now!

ולי דגהו

And for Me he fished *a people*.

Paragraph 106 Daniel 8.4a, 3b

ונצרך השע ודי מלי

And *the Lamp* guarded thee; it gave victory and a sufficiency of My Words.

צמני או וינפלו דמעי-אל

Desire made Me fast and the Tears-of-G-d fell down.

תו יחלך והב גגן הנו פצו

The Mark became wretched but give thou his Garden! Be you easy! Overflow you!

המיל יאהת

He caused the worthies to be circumcised.

איתי ארהן רח-אב

My Falcon is their light, the Spirit of the Father.

Paragraph 107 Daniel 8.3a, 2b

הלעה הבג הותי נשה נמה

Has she swallowed the food of My engulfing ruin? She is sick; she is drowsy.

הבג תח אה ותוה בג

O the food of Toah, alas, even the food he labeled.

The Linear Bible Code

מי נר קהו מי נר קול ולב

Who is the Lamp? They dimmed *it*. Who is the Lamp? Voice and Heart!

אה ינפל דם עד חאל יאה

Alas, the Blood of the Witness falls down; Chael is worthy.

נה והאר-או יניע אש אוי לו אל בו

Eminency the Light of Desire caused the fire of My Desire to flicker toward *the people*. G-d is with him.

"אל עיתי יהי נא"

He cried out: "O G-d of my ruin let it be now!"

נוזח בהאר-או הנים המלי

The Remover is against the Light of Desire; he caused My Words to wander.

עבר שאה ריב הנש ושבי נא

A Shoah passed over, the strife of Hannesh and the captivity of Thebes.

Paragraph 108 Daniel 8.2a, 1b

ויתא רב יהי

And he shall mark the multitude. Let it be.

ונוזח בהאר-או הלח תביל

And the Remover is against the Light of New Desire; thou carrest away *My Words*.

אה ארן הירחא לאי נד ינא

Alas, the Barque of the Moon; toward the region of the *harvest*-heap it is restrained; the Barque is removed afar off.

ילא הארן נוזח כלמה

The Barque is removed afar off *by* the Remover. O the reproach!

רק שאל בחו-כל

Sheol ran at the Mark-of-All.

Paragraph 109 Daniel 8.1a; 7.28, 27b

מל שולעם "תנש בת רט ניב לב

The one dividing into three parts said: "The Daughter shall be ill. The fruit of appetite shall tremble.

אתלמו ילענו נחשי-יויז

I shall break it open; the roots of Javeez shall become Wormwood.

וינן להב יין ויער אי

And the flame of wine shall increase and the forest of the region.

גש לאי נד הנא

A clod *of earth* for the region of the heap was restrained.

אתלם יד אפו סהך דענו עם

I shall break into pieces power then Our Knowledge shall cover thee O people.

תשינו חלף-יה לאי נטל"

You shall sharpen the knife of Y-H at the region of burden."

Paragraph 110 Daniel 7.27a, 26b

שלכו ומלע חו כלם

The Mark traveled and swallows up all of them.

התו-כלם נין וילע יאי-דק מעלת ביה

The Mark-of-All-of-Them endures and he shall swallow down the substances of the Veil; the levels *of Heaven* are with Y-H.

יאים שלך חו-חת תו-כלם יד אתו ברו

He shall terrify thy error. The Mark-of-Terror is the Mark-of-All-of-Them, the Hand of His Pure Sign.

אן טל שוה תו-כלם

The Wealth of Dew resembles the Mark-of-All-of-Them.

ואפום דע הדבו הלו

And o the failure of opinion! They plodded on; they boasted:

"הדם-שה לנו דע"

"The Blood of a Sheep is for us knowledge."

Paragraph 111 Daniel 7.26a, 25b

הי

A Lamentation

הנטל שו-בת

The Vanity-of-a-Daughter was lifted up.

יאן ידו נד עגל

His hand encountered a heap of ear-rings.

פון יד-עון

The Hand-of-Iniquity was perplexed.

דע דעה די בן

Knowledge it learned because of the Son;

ובהיתיו תד

And I emptied it out; o the thanksgiving!

וני נמז

And wailing was emptied.

Paragraph 112 Daniel 7.25a, 24c

הי

A Lamentation

נשה לרב סיו

Toward the greatness of His Sheep He forgot.

אל ביניו ילע יש יד-קל וללם

G-d is with he who causes it to increase. He shall swallow down the substance of the swift hand and He twisted them.

יאיל עד צל

The Witness shall lengthen the shadow.

ני למו לפש

Wailing is for them to scatter.

Paragraph 113 Daniel 7.24b

הי ני כלמה

Lamentation! Wailing! Reproach!

תל-תו אי-מד קן

O the Tel-Cit of the Mark! O the region of the measure of the Nest!

מאן שי-אוה

It refused the Gift-of-Desire.

ונוה ירחא מו קין רח-און

And the Moon abided. From it is the Spear of the Spirit of Wickedness.

ומקין יכלם הרשע התו-כלם

And from Cain the Wicked One wounded the Mark-of-All-of-Them.

הנם רשע אי-נר

The Wicked One made drowsy the region of the Lamp.

Paragraph 114 Daniel 7.24a, 23b

קוה נקד תו הן שוד-תו

The sheep raiser waited for the Mark, lo, the Council-of-the-Mark.

אער אל כל כאת ואת וכלם לכנם אן

I G-d shall awaken everyone as a Sign and a Token even all of them to establish them wealth.

שת יד אער אבאו התא יעי-בר

Set thou the hand! I shall awaken *them*. I shall enter the Chamber of the *Altar* Shovels of the Pure One;

וכל מאת יעי-בר אתו

and each hundred of the Shovels of the Pure One is His Sign.

Paragraph 115 Daniel 7.23a, 22, 21b

יחרם אן כן
He shall exterminate sorrow rightly so.

יש ידק ונסח
It shall be he shall pulverize and pull *it* down.

הא חוך לם והטמא נמזו
Ah! Injury is for them and the unclean they are sucked out.

ני
A Lamentation
נוי לעיש ידק לב-הי
My Flock is at the Constellation of the Great Bear; it shall crush the will of lamentation.

אן יד ואים
Vigour is the hand and terrible.

ויקי תעה תא
And be thou obedient! The Chamber erred.

יד-דע נוהל הלכיו
The Hand-of-Knowledge leadeth to a watering-hole its travelers.

Paragraph 116 Daniel 7.21a, 20b

ני
A Lamentation
שי דק מעב דק הדב
A thin gift from a thin cloud was made to glide *overhead*.

ענך "דא נר קיתי"
It answered thee: "This is the Lamp I have been waiting for."

והה זח התר בחן מבר הו זחו
But alas, the pride of the Explorer scrutinizes because of the Pure One. Ah, his pride!

נבר בר ללם ממף והלני
The Pure One purified himself; he grasped with a twist them of Memphis but he praised Me.

ני
A Lamentation
עון כד אן רק
The perversity of a jar is sorrow altogether.

Paragraph 117 Daniel 7.20a, 19b

ותלת הי מדק נם
And thou heaped up wailing out of the drowsy dust.

The Linear Bible Code

ולפנות קלס יד

But to turn way Derision is a hand.

ירחא והששאר ביד רשע אין רק לעו

The Moon and Leaven are in the hand of the Wicked One. There is none surely for overturning.

"הספר הי לגר"

"The Book of Wailing Belongs to the Sojourner."

בא ראש וקדם הלך אש

The Head came but before fire proceeded.

חן ידה ירף טול זר

The Grace of Its Hand shall heal; it lengthened the Crown.

פיד הי נש

Wailing is exhausted *and* sick.

Paragraph 118 Daniel 7.19a, 18b

הרית יה ליחד

The Mountain of Y-H is for unity;

נוה לכנם

the abode of the Shepherd is to establish them.

הי נש חו הי דאתי עי

O the Wailing! The Mark is sick. O the Wailing! My bird of prey is Ruin.

ברא חו יח

The Mark created Jeah.

לע אב צי לחיבץ

The Father swallowed up the Howler at Tibaz.

ני דא אים לעם לע דע ואם

O the Wailing! This is a terrible thing for a people! It swallowed up knowledge and a mother.

לע דע את וכלם

It swallowed up knowledge of the Token even all of them.

Paragraph 119 Daniel 7.18a

נון סחי וני נוי לעי

Offscouring increased and wailing; My Habitation is for ruin.

שי-דק את וכל מנו לבקיו

The Gift-of-the-Veil is a Token and all of its kind is for its emptiness.

Paragraph 120 Daniel 7.17, 16b

אער אן מנומו קיניך

I shall awaken strength because thy spears are drowsy.

The Linear Bible Code

למה עבר אעבר אנין אי

Why should I indeed pass by? I shall increase the region.

דאת בר ברא תוי

The Bird of Prey of Pureness My Mark created.

תן ילא ינן עד

The Jackal shall be removed afar off. The Witness shall endure.

Paragraph 121 Daniel 7.16a, 15, 14c

והי אי למרשף ויל

And lamentation of the coast is for kindling *of fire* so howl thou!

רם או הנד לך לע הנם

Lust rose up and it was heaped up. Go thou, swallow up Hennom.

אעבא אבי צי ואים אקנם

I shall make fat my Father. The howler and the coasts I shall acquire.

דחל עת רק ינן להב יש ארי וזח

Time makes afraid, moreover the flame it increases the substance of My Flame and pride;

והנדן או גבל אי נד

But shall We judge Lust? The boundary of the coast is a heap.

הן אי חורתי רכת אל

Lo, the coast! I have drilled a delicacy of a god.

Paragraph 122 Daniel 7.14b

בחתת אל ידה תו כלם

With the Terror of G-d the Mark threw down all of them

והדעי-אל ידם לע נטל שה נטל שן

and the knowledgeable ones of G-d he silenced. He swallowed up the burden of a sheep, the burden of Ivory.

וחלף יה לא ינשל אי

And Y-H passed by. They cleared not the coast.

מא אים מעל כו וכלמו רקיו נטל שבי

What is the Terrible Thing beside the aperture *in the wall?* even his spitters who wounded the burden of a captive.

Paragraph 123 Daniel 7.14a, 13, 12b

הי

A Lamentation

הלו יה וברק

Praise you Y-H and lightning.

The Linear Bible Code

היה ומד קו

It came and the measure of a line.

הטם אים

The Terrible Thing stretched them out *a line*

ויקית עד עוה והה חא שנא

And thou obeyed as far as overturning. But alas, the Chamber he hated.

רבך אים שינן עם-עו

The Terrible Thing mixed *a drink offering* that he might increase a people of overturning.

ראו אילי לי וזח בתי

See you My Strength is My Own and the pride of My Daughter.

והה זח נדע וונמז דע נוה לתב יהי

And alas pride, it is made known and knowledge of the Abide of the Shepherd was sucked out for the return. Let it happen.

Paragraph 124 Daniel 7.12a, 11b

ני

A Lamentation

יחב הכר און והנט לש וידעה אתו

He shall embrace the Pasture of Sorrow; and the lion was made to stretch out; and he will know its Sign.

יחרש או אש את דקי לתב יהי

He shall be silent if perchance fire together with My Veil is to return. Let it happen.

והמש גד בו

And he took good fortune with him.

הוא תו יחתל

The Mark fell *earthward*; he was swaddled.

יט קיד דעתיו הה זח הללם

Let Kaid turn aside his opinions. Alas pride, he praised them.

מאן רק יד את בר בר-איל

He refused only the Hand of the Pure One, the Pure One of Strength.

מלק נמן יד אבתיו

He nipped off *his head*; he was reckoned the hand of his fathers.

Paragraph 125 Daniel 7.11a, 10, 9c

הה זחו חי פני

Alas, they thrust away the Living Being of My Face!

The Linear Bible Code

רפסו בתי-אן ידנו מוקי-יה

The Houses-of-Sorrow stamped with feet; the mockers of Y-H shall be judged

ומד קן בבר וברו

and the measure of the Nest is <u>with</u> the Pure One even His Son.

הן ושם שית יפלא פלא-יה

Lo, and a Name *G-d* established; he shall work extraordinarily a Wonder of Y-H.

ומדק נם קף נוד גן

And on account of the Thin One an Ape was drowsy; he wandered the Garden.

רון יד רהן קל דרו

The Instrument conquered Rohan the voice of his generation.

Paragraph 126 Daniel 7.9b

ניה ולגל גר

O her wailing! even for the dung of the Sojourner.

וני דני בי בש

And wailing! My judgment is with Me. Be thou ashamed!

הי סרך אקן

O the wailing! Thy Prince I shall prepare.

רם עכה ראש רעש תכה ורוח גל

Accah rose up; he left behind a shaking; and a billowing wind is her injury.

שובל בת ינים

The flowing skirt of a daughter he makes to droop.

ויקית עו וימרנו

And thou obeyed o Ruin; but he embittered Us.

Paragraph 127 Daniel 7.9a, 8b

סרך יד דעתי וההזח נבר בר

Thy Prince is the Instrument of My Knowledge. But was he made proud? The Pure One purified himself.

ללם ממף ואד אן רקב אנשא

He twisted them at Memphis and the Vapour of rotten On I hate.

יניע כן יניעו לאוה

He caused wavering rightly; they wavered at Lust.

ימד מן מור קע תא

He measured a portion. The Stallion of the Chamber procured *food*.

אתים דק אי

I shall perfect the Thin One of the region.

The Linear Bible Code

נר-קן מתל-תו נוה יניב

The Lamp of the Nest is above the Tel-City of the Mark; the Abode of the Shepherd he shall cause to bear fruit.

Paragraph 128 Daniel 7.8a, 7c

תקלס הר יעז ירחא נר קול או אי

Thou mocketh the Mountain. The Moon signaled the Lamp the voice of desire of the coast.

נרק בתי והלכת שמה לרש עני

My House was weakened. And thou went, O Appalment, toward the poor of the affliction.

נרק והים דם יד אתו יחל כזמה ינשם אי

He was weakened; the bloody hand discomforted him; it defiled as wickedness. The region pants.

היה "ספר הי לגר"

It appeared: "The Book of Wailing belongs to the Sojourner."

Paragraph 129 Daniel 7.7b

בא ראש וההקדמו הלך אן בר בר

The Head came but before Him the strength of the Pure One proceeded.

הלל זר פי-דן ינשו

He praised the Crown the Mouth of Judgment. They shall be ill.

אר יתיא פי-קת וינת

Light shall outrun the mouth of Keith and Janet.

מי אוה לי חד

Who desired Me? Sharpness.

Paragraph 130 Daniel 7.7a, 6b

הי

A Lamentation

עי בר הוי חור או

O the ruin of the Pure One! Alas, the Pit of Lust!

אילי לי וזח בתי

My Ram is Mine and the pride of My Daughter.

והה זח הנדר תאב הלבי הי

But alas, the pride of the vow the lion longed for is a lamentation.

נטל שואת ויחל ני שאר העב

O the Burden of Vanities! And wailing waited; the Darkness remained.

ראו הי בגל עפו

They beheld wailing within the heap; they are darkened.

The Linear Bible Code

עי דע בר

O the ruin of pure knowledge!

Paragraph 131 Daniel 7.6a, 5b

אני פגה לו רמן כירח אור אותי

I am an early fig to him; a pomegranate like the Moon, the Light of My Token.

והה זה הנדר תאב אי גש

And alas, the pride of the vow; the coast longed for a clod *of earth.*

רש בי לך אים וקהל נירם אנכו

The poor is with Me. Go thou terrible one and assemble thou the rows of untilled earth. I shall smite it.

Paragraph 131 Daniel 7.5a, 4b

הי

A Lamentation

נש ניב המף

The fruit of Memphis is sick.

בן יעל עתל תו תמק

A son shall ascend; The Mark grew great; let thou pine away.

הד חרט שלו

O the shout of the engraving tool of Shilo!

בדלה ים דה נינת ירחא

It divided the Sea; this is the offspring of the Moon.

הוי חור או הלבי

Ah! The Noble of Desire of My Will.

הי שנא בבל ותם יקה שן אך

O the wailing! Babylon hated *him.* But Integrity shall dull the tooth surely.

ני לגר לעו

O the lament of the Sojourner; he swallowed it down.

אער אן מחליטנו

I shall lay bare On because she covers Us over *with secrecy.*

Paragraph 133 Daniel 7.4a, 3, 2b

הי

A Lamentation

פג וטיר מי דד עתי

An unripe fig and a hedged place. Who is the Beloved of My Time?

The Linear Bible Code

והה זחה לרש ניד

But alas, she pushed at the Poor One of quivering *lips*.

ני

A Lamentation

פג והיראך אתי

An unripe fig and is thy fear Me?

מדק אדן מאד

Because of the Thin One I shall judge exceedingly.

ני

A Lamentation

נשא מי נמן קלס

A Prince. Who was apportioned derision?

נבר ברנו יחע בר-או אבר

Our Son purified himself. Jacha' is the Pure One of Desire, the Valiant One.

Paragraph 134 Daniel 7.2a, 1; 6.29b

אמיל נח יגם אי-משיח

I shall cause Noah to be circumcised. He shall make abundant the Region of Messiah.

ורע בר או ראו איליל ם

And the pure companion of Desire they beheld. I shall make them howl.

עיו זח בתי והה זח רם או

His ruin is the pride of My Daughter and alas pride elevated Lust.

לאי נד הנד רם אן

At the region of the heap he was made to toss about; sorrow rose up.

ילם שאר בת כאם לחני דאב

He yelled at them, the remnant of the Daughter; as a mother toward My Grace he became faint.

הבך שם לע השארי וזח

Shem was made to weep. My Remnant spoke wildly even of pride;

והוזח מלח לאי נד לבב

and the pride of the salt of the coast. It grieved the heart;

כלם רץ שאל בל "הדחת נשב אי"

it wounded the runner. Bel asked: "Hast thou thrust away the habited coast?"

Paragraph 135 Daniel 6.29a, 28

סרף שר וכת וכלם בושו

A Seraph is Prince but Cuth and all of them felt shame.

The Linear Bible Code

ירד תו-כלם בחלצה הנד לא ינדו אתו

The Mark-of-All-of-Them descended with battle spoils; he was made to show grief; they showed not grief with him.

ירא דין מלא ינד לביזי-שיד

He shall see judgment fulfilled. He showed grief toward the scorners of the White Washer.

אער אב ואים שב

I the Father shall awaken. And the Terrible One turned back.

ני המתו

O the wailing! He executed him.

ני תאדב עול

O the wailing! Let thou grieve o injustice!

צמו בזי-שם

The scorners of Shem fasted.

Paragraph 136 Daniel 6.27b

אפוס דע הנטל שו לב

Knowledge ends the burden of the emptiness of heart.

חתת-אל יד התו-כלם

The Terror-of-G-d is the Hand of the Mark-of-All-of-Them.

וני מלע למיקוא יח אה לא או

And wailing is swallowing up toward the company of Jeah. Alas, there is no Desire.

הי

A Lamentation

דל אי נד יד

The Door of the Isle the Hand shook.

הה לא מד קנמן

Alas, there is no measure of cinnamon.

יל חד וני עא "זנוה לי"

The sharp one howled and the wail of Gae: "Fornication belongs to me."

תו-כלם נטל שלך בי דם עט

The Mark-of-All-of-Them bore thy fault. With Me is the blood of the pen.

Paragraph 137 Daniel 6.27a, 26, 25c

מי שי מדק נם

Who is the Gift from the Veil? His is drowsy.

The Linear Bible Code

אגש ינוך מלש
I shall draw near. He shall be smitten because of strength.

אער אלך בנ ירא די דא
I thy G-d shall awaken the Son; he shall see this sufficiency;

ינשלו אי
He shall clear it away *and* the region.

מא אים מעלך לב-חך
How terrible a thing is thy treacherous act o heart of oppression!

אכלם שו ירד ני
I shall wound Emptiness; wailing shall wander restlessly.

דאבו קדה נוה ימר גלך
They fainted *for* spice; *for* a pasture. Thy rejoicing becomes bitter.

Paragraph 138 Daniel 6.25b

ואתו יראנו
And of his Sign We are in awe.

הבו טל שיד דע אב
Give you the Dew which is the Instrument of the Knowledge of the Father.

גתי ער אלו טמא לון
The wine presses of the Adversary his G-d he made unclean; he passed the night *there*.

והי שנונו הי נבנו נאו מר
And o the wailing! They changed Us.
O the wailing! it bore Us fruit; they *the fruit* hindered Bitterness.

Paragraph 139 Daniel 6.25a, 24c

אחו ירא בגל
His Sign he feared when it billowed.

ולא ינד יד-יה
And the Hand of Y-H waved not about;

וצר קול כאי דך לא אי רב
But o the distress of noise like an oppressed isle; not a mighty isle.

גוי תיהו אכלם רם או הה לאבן
The nation of Taihu I shall wound; he raised up Lust; alas, toward the stone.

Paragraph 140 Daniel 6.24b

מי יד הב חך תשה
Who is the Hand? Set thou the gums thou who lendeth.

The Linear Bible Code

אלל בחלך ואב גן-מלא ינד
It has gotten thee worthlessness by greed and the Father of Garden-of-Fullness shall show grief.

קסהו אב-גן מהק סנה לרמא
The Father of the Garden cut him off; He utterly destroyed Seneh for the bowman.

לא ינד לו יה ולעב
Y-H wavered not toward it nor toward the Darkness.

אט אי גש אכלם
O the Gentleness of the Isle, a clod *of earth*; I shall feed them.

Paragraph 141 Daniel 6.24a, 23, 22b

ני דאב תד בע אל
O the wailing! Ted became faint; God swelled up.

הלו בח אכלם כי מד קפט
O that Boach had fed them when a measure curdled.

וילת חך נשהו כזיהום
And thou howled; the Palate lended him the likes of contamination.

דקי דל בקלך ינול בח אלו אתו
My Veil is thinned by thy voice. Boach is made filthy; lo his sign.

יראם פר גס והך אלם
Al ill-manner bull put them in fear but is it like being tongue tied?

חלש יה לאי יחני
The Weak One of Y-H is a the isle; may he show Me favour.

על אכל מל מלל מאכל ממעל אי נד
Against the food supply he spoke; he withered the food because of the treachery of the region of the *harvest* heap.

Paragraph 142 Daniel 6.22a, 21b

ני דא אתו יראו מך תו בזי-שלל
O the wailing! This is *G-d's* Sign: They shall see; the Mark diminished the spoils of plunder.

כי הארי-רת בהל חלף התן אידך
Because of the Lights-of-the-Law he hastened to passing away of the Jackal of thy Calamity.

הלא אי חאה לאדב על אי-נד
Is it not for the coast of Chaah to grieve over the region of the heap?

לא ינד לרם או
He shall not grieve at the height of desire.

אך לם הנע קע זבי

Surely for them he was shaken; he pulled down Zabai.

Paragraph 143 Daniel 6.21a, 20, 19, 18b

צע לקב לא י נד

G-d fashioned a vessel for the coast of the *harvest* heap;

לאב גלה בר קמך

for the Father a vessel of purity He raised thee up;

ולזא אתו "ירא יד-אב גלה להבתה

and for this His Sign is: "The Hand of the Father shall behold the vessel of its own flame.

בוא הגן בם וקיא רפרף שב

"He entered the High Garden and he vomited; he shook; he repented.

אכלם ניד אביהו

"Quivering *of lip* his Father fed them.

לעת דן התנש ויהו מד קל

"At the time of judgment he allowed himself to be sick. And they shall become a measure of frivolity."

ענה אלנו הד וחו

Our G-d of the <u>Shout</u> put down even the Mark.

טח בו הלך יה לאכלם

Ted is with him. Y-H journeyed to feed them;

לזא ני דא לאי נד בו בצאן

for this is wailing; this is the coast of the heap with Him among the flock.

שח-אל יד-יה ונבר בר

The Column of G-d is the Hand of Y-H.

Paragraph 144 Daniel 6.18a, 17b

תקז עב והתקז עב אכל

Tekez of the Darkness even Tekez of the cloud mass ate *food*.

מה מת חוא בג מפל עתם שוא

What is a man to declare food when beans are consumed of Ravage?

דחן באתי ח°הו   כן בזי-שי-או הארי-דח

Of millet I have brought <u>emptiness</u>. Thus are the scorners of the Gift of Desire the Lights of the Law.

בהל חלף התן אידך

He hastened the passing away of the Jackal of thy Calamity.

הלא לאי נד לרם או

He removed afar off to an island a heap against the height of appetite.

The Linear Bible Code

אך לם הנע אתו ירא

Surely for them he was shaken; his Sign fear thou!

יד-אב גל ומר

The Hand-of-the-Father is a heap and bitterness.

Paragraph 145 Daniel 6.17a, 16b

ולא ינדו יתיהו רמא אכלם

But they shall never show grief; they shall set a mark on the bowman. I shall enable them.

ני דאב

O the wailing of the faint!

הי נשא לאל

O the lamentation of the deceiver toward G-d.

מיק הי אכלם יד מיקו

Lamentation mocked; I shall wound the hand that mocked Him.

רס אל כיד סרף

Crush Thou O G-d the likes of the hand of the Serpent

ויד מל תדיד אכל מעד אכל

and the hand of the cutter; it loves food ever since *there was* food.

מלן ירם או אכל מלע ושגרה

Lodging for the night he exalted pleasure of food. Swallowing even the young of her *herd.*

כלא אי רב גן

He shut up the region, the greatness of the Garden.

Paragraph 146 Daniel 6.16a, 15, 14b

יד אב התו לצהל רדת שם-אוה אשם שי לעם דע והחו

The Hand of the Father is the Mark. To make shine the Dominion of Shem-Avah I shall direct the Gift of the people of knowledge even the Mark.

בזי שלל בשמל אי

My booty he plundered among the kingdom of the coast.

נדל עוי הולע שאב אי

My ruin is laid low. The father of the coast was made to speak rashly.

גש עם שא חל

Draw near o people of the Ravage of the Tel-City!

מי דך אכלם

Who is oppressed? I shall feed them.

ני דאה חו עב

O the wailing! The Mark darted through the cloud mass.

The Linear Bible Code

אעב אמו יבה תל-תנין

I shall hid his mother. He shall empty the Tel-City of the Dragon.

Paragraph 147 Daniel 6.14a, 13c

מזו תם שר יד ארס אלע ומעט אכלם

The perfect Garner is Prince of Power. I shall crush! I shall swallow up! But a few, I shall feed them

כי לעם שאל

because for a people is Sheol.

דוהי יד אתו לגי-נב

Be thou unwell O Hand! His Sign is toward the valleys of Nob.

נם יד לאי-נד

Be thou drowsy O Hand toward the region of the heap.

יד אכלם מדק

O Hand feed them from the Veil!

ני רם או וננן יד "אבא דעת אל"

And the Hand We shall support. *He said:* "I shall enter the Knowledge of G-d."

יד סרף ויד מת דכא תל-מאב

The hand of a serpent and a hand of a man crushed the Tel-City of Moab.

Paragraph 148 Daniel 6.14b

יציר מאו אך למה נע אתו ירא בו

He shall besiege his hundred surely! Why did His Sign totter? Fear thou at it!

גל אמרתי "אך למך נם נהל"

Rejoice thou! I have said: "Surely is Lamech; he slumbered; he is refreshed."

ני תל-תנים

A Lament of the Tel-City of Jackals

וידע שן אוה לאל

And the Tooth knoweth appetite against G-d;

כנם העבי ידשן אלך

As My Thicket slumbered thy god is fattened.

יד-תם שרר סא אלה אכלם * אכלם מד קני רם או

The Hand of Integrity holds dominion; it extends godward; it fed them; * it fed them a measure of My Nest; it raised up appetite.

Paragraph 149 Daniel 6.13a, 12, 11b

וב*ר קן יד-אב

And the Pure One of the Nest is the Hand of the Father.

הה לא מד קן נחתם ואעבל אי נדל

Ah, there is no measure of the Nest. Thou gavest them rest but I shall strip the leaves of the region; it is brought low.

וחך שהו ושגרה

And the mouth of his sheep and its offspring.

כלא אי רב גני דא הנד תם דק נמד

The region confined the greatness of My Garden. This is the perfect heap of the Veil measured.

בע אוה ידל בקל

Desire gushed; it is drawn up with a shout.

כהה לאם דק אדום

The thin people of Edom have grown dim

ואלצם ויה וכר בלעך רב אוה אם

but Y-H urged them even Him; and a battering-ram is thy swallowing; the haughtiness of appetite is terrible.

Paragraph 150 Daniel 6.11a, 10b

ויבה תל-תנ ינם זו מל שור ידגן התיל עב

And the Tel-City of the Jackal is emptied; it is made drowsy against which the wall he cut off; it is heaped up; he made cause to deceive the Thicket.

הלן חית פני

The Living Being of My Presence was made to pass the night

וכוה תיבל לע אבתך

And Tibal scorched the throat of thy fathers.

מי שר ידע די ידך לאי נדו

Who is the Prince? He knows enough; he shall pound at the region of his heap.

ארס או אבתך משרשו ירדא כלם

I shall crush the appetite of thy fathers; on account of its Root he shall chastise all of them.

Paragraph 151 Daniel 6.10a, 9, 8b

הנד לב ב קל כא דעת אל

The heart caused the voice to express grief. Here is the Knowledge of G-d.

יד-סרף ויד מת דכה ינשה לאל

The hand of a serpent and a hand of a man crushed he who is forgetful toward G-d.

ידאב תך משרתו ארס

The oppression of his minister is faint; I shall crush *it.*

אמיק תאך לם נעך את וירא בגל

I shall deride thy chamber for them. A Sign shall shake thee. And he shall look at the *harvest* heap.

אמרתי "אכלם כן מנהל"

I said: "I shall feed them thus leading *them* to a watering-station."

Paragraph 152 Daniel 6.8a

ני תל-תנים

A Lament of the Tel-City of the Jackals

וידע שן אוה לאלך נם

So the Tooth knows appetite; toward thy G-d he is drowsy.

ועב העבי ידל כי דר סא

And the Thicket, My Thicket he brings low because of the generation of So.

הפק תל ואך לממיקה

He made a tel-city totter but only for the mocking of it.

מיק לאת וחף ואי רבדה

He mocked at the Sign and the shore; and the coast he confined it.

אין פרד-שח-או אין גס אתו

There is no lowly mule of desire; there is no break of His Sign.

כלם יכרס לך וטעי תאי

He wounded Icarus for thee and the lost ones of My Chamber.

Paragraph 153 Daniel 6.8a, 7, 6b

יחני מל על אכם משו

May He show me favour. He cut off more than food because of vanity.

ירד הלן ירם אנך ואכל מלע ושגר

He laid low; he was made to spend the night; he rose up; he enjoyed a life of plenty of Thee and of food swallowing down even the young *of a beast.*

הנלא אין פרד-שח-או

He obtained nothing of the lowly mule of desire.

איך רסני-דאה

Remarkable are the jaws of the kite.

הלאת דביה ולע הן חך שה

Thou removed afar off Dabeah; then the palate of a sheep swallowed them up.

נהל אל עלך הנד לאי נד לחך

G-d guilded to a watering-station. Over there is the heap *of harvest* for the coast of Nod is thy table.

Paragraph 154 Daniel 6.6a, 5b

שהנאל ידני רם

Shahanael judged Me on High.

אכלא אי רב גני

I shall lock the region of the abundance of My Garden.

דא יה ולעת חכת שה אל

This is Y-H and thou spoke incoherently; thou awaited the Sheep of G-d.

התיחשו ולשלכו

They did genealogy themselves but to cast it forth.

אוה נמי המיד לב קלך החך שה

O Desire, be thou drowsy! He made measurement of the heart of thy voice, the palate of a sheep.

Paragraph 155 Daniel 6.5a, 4b

לני לכי אלה

Spend thou the night! Go thou forth o goddess!

תיחשו הלע

She shall do genealogy but it is swallowed up.

לכו אתו כלם דצם

At the Window of His Token all of them he makes to leap.

לא ינד לה חך שה לה

He shall not show grief toward *the goddess*. The palate of a sheep is against her.

לעני עבו והאין פרד-שח-או איך

For the affliction is his Thicket. But is there no lowly mule of desire of thy region?

רס נדא אתו

Crush thou; thrust him aside.

כל מלך לך התו מקהלת ישע אכלם והב אריתי

Every king belongs to thee o Mark. From the Assembly of Yeshua he fed them and give thou to My lions.

The Linear Bible Code

חור יד לב קלך

The hollow of the hand is the will of thy voice.

Paragraph 156 Daniel 6.4a, 3, 2b

אין פרד-שח-או איך

There is no lowly mule of desire of thy region.

רס לע חץ

Crush thou; swallow thou up the arrow.

נתם אוה הן דל אי

He gave them Desire, lo, the Thin One of the region.

נד ני דא קזן אוה לאל

Wailing fled. This is the beginning of desire for G-d.

אכלם ואמעטן והלני בהי ני

I shall feed *the men;* but I shall diminish *the women.* And they praised Me in lamentation *and* wailing.

לא אין פרד-שח-אן

No, there is no lowly mule of sorrow.

והליד נוה נמד חל אי-נד ידא

And he begat a pasture; it was measured. The fortress of the Island Heap he shall thrust aside.

תלת ני כרסן והנם אל עו אתו

Thou trifled with wailing as a halter and the G-d of Ruin made His Token slumber.

Paragraph 157 Daniel 6.2a, 1; 5.30b

כל מלך בנו

Every king is His son.

הלי דני רשעו האם

The ones praising My Judgment judged as guilty the mother.

אין פרד-שח-אל אתו

There is no lowly mule of G-d with him.

כלם לעם יקהו שו

All of them of the people shall be blunted of Emptiness.

ירד מד קר פש ני

The measure of a spider's web descended; it scattered wailing.

תר תו נית שני-נשר בכאתו כלם לב

The Mark explored the dwellings of the teeth of the Eagle. O his sobs; *they* wounded the heart.

קאי-דם שו ירד איד שך

Those vomiting the blood of Emptiness are bringing down the Calamity of the Thicket.

Paragraph 158 Daniel 5.30a, 29b

אכלם רק שאל

He fed them a fragment of Sheol.

בלימ קא יליל בה

When he wrapped the vomitus he howled at her.

בא תו כל מבא-תל חטיל שאוה ליד-יה

The Mark came. Every entrance of the Tel-City a devastating storm shall throw down through the Hand of Y-H.

ולעו זרך הוה ראו צלע-אב

They have swallowed up thy stranger. It happened they beheld the Rib of the Father.

הדיד אכן ומהו אנו

He made a loving gesture but they denied his strength.

גר אל אי נדל ושי בלה ורצא של-בר

The G-d of the region sojourned. The Gift was weakened even it became old but He was pleased with the Robe of the Pure One.

Paragraph 159 Daniel 5.29a, 28, 27, 26

מאני דאב סרף ויד

In comparison to My Strength the serpent is weak and the hand.

מלת בי היו כתו כל מת

Thou spoke with Me. They became beaten down every man.

סיר פס רף ריס

A thorn in the sole of the foot he plucked out.

חת חכת שה ואין זא מבהת ליקת לקת המל שה וכתו

Fear is a hook *in the jaw* of a sheep; but this is nothing, for thou acted purely to obey o Lekeith having circumcised a sheep even the likes of the Mark.

כלם אהל אה נם אן מאת למר שפה נד

He confounded the Tabernacle. Alas, strength being drowsy hundreds are for bitterness. He swept bare the *city*-heap.

Paragraph 160 Daniel 5.25, 24, 23b

ני סרף ולקת

The Lament of the Seraph and Lekeith

The Linear Bible Code

אן מאן ממי שר

Sorrow above sorrow is more than the waters-of-the-Prince.

יד-אב תך הנד ומי-שר הנד אב תכו

The Instrument-of-the-Father *is in* the midst of the heap *of waters* and the waters-of-the-Prince are the heap of the Father *in* its midst.

אדי-יד אסף חיל שיה

The midsts of the Instrument the strength of her sheep gathered.

ומד קן מני

But the measure of the Nest is My portion.

דאבת רדה אל הלכת חר-אל כוה

Thou languished. G-d rules! Thou o Noble of G-d walked the *celestial* Window.

די בכת משני-דאה לאלו

Sufficient are the sobs from the teeth of the Eagle toward his god.

תחב שני-עדי אלי

Thou shalt love the teeth of My Witness his G-d.

Paragraph 161 Daniel 5.23a, 22

ני עם שאל

O the Lament of the people of Sheol!

וני זח אל ידא

But the lament of pride G-d removeth!

נבא ואעא אל גר פא

He prophesied. And I shall make the god of the stranger err here.

שחן אב-הד ואף סכי-הלאל

He inflamed the Father of the Shout and the anger of the Booths of Hallel

ונוה בני תשאר מח

but My Son abideth; let thou leave behind a fatling.

כת נחלו כת לגש

Crush thou his inheritance! Crush thou to a clod.

כי נבר בר התן או

Because the Pure One purified himself cause thou to set Desire!

כי מד קויתי ההתיב יד-אי

Because the measure I waited for shall I make the Hand of the region prominent?

נא מלות ממורת האי

Now are the words above bitter things of the region.

משא רם לעות עד-יה

The Burden on High is for the ruination of the Witness of Y-H.

The Linear Bible Code

נדל כידל בקל ככב

He is brought low as he is brought low by the Voice of a Star.

בל תלף שה אל רצא של בהר בההתן או

Scarcely was the Sheep of G-d destroyed *when* Neglect ran into the mountain with the Jackal of Lust.

Paragraph 162 Daniel 5.21b

הי לעם

A Lamentation of a People

יקה יה בצי ידנם

My White One obeyed Y-H; he shall judge them.

לוא שנא תו כלם

If only the Mark could change all of them.

בא ילע אהל אטיל שי-דע

He came; he swallowed up the Tabernacle. I shall cast out the Gift-of-Knowledge;

די יד-דע עבט צי

Sufficient is the Hand of Knowledge; it took in pledge the howler.

המש גא ימש לטם והן

Pride was completely removed. It had enveloped *men* and *women*.

ומעט יניר ותך אב

but a few he caused to shine even the oppressed of the Father.

שע הר ודם אי

Deliver Thou the Mountain and the blood of the region!

Paragraph 163 Daniel 5.21a, 20, 19b

דרע מעויו שאתו

An arm above His ruin is His Devastation.

יחם עה בבל ודי רט

He became hot; Babylon erred and a sufficiency of terror.

אשן אי-נב נמו הנמו

I shall sharpen the coast of Nob; they are drowsy; they were made drowsy.

ידע הה רקי והתו-כלם

He knew, alas, My Thin One even the Mark-of-All-of-Them.

אסרפן מת חן ההד זה לתף

I shall burn them; Grace died. Is this shout for the timbrel?

קת החור והבבל מר ידך ולי פשם

Keith is a free man and Babylon is the bitterness of thy hand; but for me it scattered them.

The Linear Bible Code

הוה אבצהו היד

It shall happen I shall make him white, the Hand.

ומירם הוה אבצהו היד ואחם

And because he shall be raised up it shall happen I shall whiten him, the Hand and I shall be hot.

הוה אבצהו היד ולטק אוה

It shall happen I shall make him white, the Hand even to erase Lust.

אבצהו היד-יה ומדק נם

I shall make him white, the Hand-of-Y-H and so the Thin One slumbered not.

Paragraph 164 Daniel 5.19a, 18

ני לחדון יעא זו והאי נשל

Wailing is for Chadon; he shall writhe. This and the coast he left empty.

ואי מא אים מעל כה לב הי

And the coast, what a terrible thing is treachery. Thus is the heart of lamentation.

ידא תו ברן מוכו

The Mark pushed away Beren; he humbled him.

בא רצן דך בן לב

The Favour of the Oppressed, the Son of Will came.

הי

O the Lament!

הרד הוא רקי ואתו ברו

He, My Thin One, was made to descend and his Pure Token with him.

את וכלמא ילע אה לא אכלם התן

Thou and reproach he shall swallow up; alas, I did not wound the Jackal.

Paragraph 165 Daniel 5.17

אה נעד ואה ארשף ואכלם לאר

Alas, he was tossed about; and alas, I was inflamed but I fed them at the Light.

קא אבת כמר

The vomitus of the fathers is as bitterness.

בבהן רח-אל כתיב "תבז בנו"

With a thumb of the Spirit of G-d he made a writing: "Thou shalt despise His Son."

ני והלך לך תנ חם אכלם מד קר מאו

O the wailing! And the perfect Jackal journeyed to thee; he fed them a measure of cold out of Lust.

לא ינד הנעני

He did not waver; he caused Me to tremble.

Paragraph 166 Daniel 5.16, 15b

דאב טל שתא-חו

The Dew of the Chamber of the Mark languished.

כל מבא תל-תוך ראו צלע-אב

All entering the Tel-City of Thy Mark saw the Rib-of-the-Father.

הדי דא-כן ומהו

Give thou a shout! This is right. But they refused.

שב לתאנו

Return thou to Our Chamber!

גר אי נתע דוה לה

The sojourner of the region had erred. The Faint One is against her.

רשף ואר קם לאבתך

The Firebolt and the Flame he raised up against thy necromancers.

לך ותנה נעך

Go thou and recount thy trembling.

ארשם "לני רט קור שפם לני רשף לכותי דכי"

I shall inscribe: "For wailing! The spider's web of Shapham trembled. For wailing! The firebolt is at the windows of My oppressed."

לעת עם שה נאוה יוחה

At the time of a people a sheep was wanted; the one having life.

לא תלם רשף ני לה כאל

He did not deceive them. A firebold of wailing is against her as is G-d.

Paragraph 167 Daniel 5.15a, 14

וינתע דוה לה

And he shall break forth. The Faint One is against her.

רפשונו רקיה נדה הבתך

Her weak ones inflamed Us; thy daughter grieved.

יד אי פשא אימי-כח

The Hand-of-the-Region spread out the terrible ones of strength.

ימד קו לע

It measured *with* a line; it swallowed up.

הנע כוכבת חכת שה הרית יה מכחו

Venus was made to wander; thou tarried o sheep. Thou made praise to
Y-H because of His Strength.

ונתלך שו וריהן וכבני הלא חור-יד כי לעת עם שו

And We shall trifle with thee O Emptiness and their irrigation. And like
My Son the hollow of the hand is removed afar off because thou o
people swallowed down Emptiness.

Paragraph 168 Daniel 5.13, 12c

דוה ינם יבא אכלם יתיה ידדו

The people are unwell; *they are* drowsy. He came; he fed them. *G-d* shall
cause His Beloved pain.

הי

A Lamentation

יד אתו לגי-נב נם

The Hand is His Sign toward the lowlands of slumbering Nob.

ידל אי נד או

The region is brought low; a heap of Lust.

הה תנא לאי נד לרם או

Alas, he repeated for the Isle a heap for the haughtiness of Lust.

אך לם הנע אך לם מד קלעה

Surely for them he showed grief. Surely for them he measured her
curtain.

לאי-נד ני דאב הוח

At the region of the heap is a lamentation. Havach became faint.

Paragraph 169 Daniel 5.12b

היה רשף וירקתי לאי נד

A firebolt came into being and I spit at the region of the heap.

נע כר צא שט לב המש משאך

A lamb trembled. Come thou forth transgressor, the heart of Hamas,
from thy ravage.

לם ידל אי-נד בה בת חכת שה

For them the region of the heap is laid low. Among them is a
daughter.Thou tarried o sheep.

ני

A Lamentation

רט קא רשמו "נדיח אתי"

Wring thou out the vomitus! Inscribe you: "We shall cleanse thou by
rinsing!"

וחאו ני מלח רשפם

And they were wounded. O the wailing! Salt inflamed them.

ונתלך שו עד נמו

And We shall trifle with thee O Emptiness until they are drowsy.

הריתי חור יד לב קלך

I have caused to praise the hollow of the Hand, the heart of Thy Voice.

Paragraph 170 Daniel 5.12a

אכלם כו בא המיקה

The *celestial* Window fed them. He came; he caused to mock her.

ני רז גני אדשך

O the wailing! O the leanness of My Garden. I have threshed thee.

ני פש אן ימט רחב רך

O the wailing! he scattered sorrow. The broad delicate expanse is made to shake.

ובא רצן דך בן אכלם והבת

He came. The Favour of the Oppressed the Son fed them and the daughter.

חכת שה

Thou tarried o sheep.

Paragraph 171 5.11a, 10b

ני

A Lamentation

הלא תם כח כהם כחו

Did not the perfection of strength, His Strength, rebuke them?

ונתלך שא ורי

And We trifled with thee O Emptiness and irrigation.

הנכו באים ויבו "הבן יא"

They were smitten by the Terrible One and they cried shrilly: "The Son exists!"

יד קני הלא ידך תו-כלם

The Hand of My Nest, is not the Mark-of-All-of-Them to be pounded to powder?

בר בגית יאון

The Pure One is among the valleys; he is become sorrowful.

תשיל אך יויז וכן ויערך

Thou shalt make to journey just now Joez; and make thou firm even thy forest!

The Linear Bible Code

ולהבי לאיי חני מלע

And My Flame is toward My Region. My Grace is swallowing up.

Paragraph 172 Daniel 5.10a

לא כל מתרמא ואת כלם

None are above treachery even any of them.

תנע תל לע אית שם

Let Thou shake the Tel-City; swallow thou up the Hawk of Renown!

תיבל יה ונבר בר

Let Thou lead on O Y-H. And the Pure One purified himself.

ואך למילם לב קל את כלם

And surely to circumcise them the heart the Voice is with all of them.

Paragraph 173 Daniel 5.9, 8b

ני

A Lamentation

שבת שם יה ונבר בר ויהו לעני נשיהו

Y-H established the Sabbath and the Pure One volunteered and they of the affliction shall become his Debt;

יזולה בתם אי גשר

he shall take it away with Innocence. Where was he strengthened?

צא של באכל מני

Come forth Error when he feeds My Portion.

דא אכל מלה עד

This is food: the Utterance of the Witness.

והלא רשף וארק מלא בתך

And the Firebolt is removed afar off and I shall pour out a fullness by the injured one.

ני

A Lamentation

להך אל ואכל מימי-כח

G-d sent a messenger and food at the days of power.

לכן ילל עני

Therefore Affliction howled.

Paragraph 174 Daniel 5.8a, 7b

דא טל שי-אתו

This is Dew, the Gift of His Token.

כלם בי תל-תו

All of them are against Me of the Tel-City of the Mark.

The Linear Bible Code

"הראו צלע-אב

"Cause you to see the Rib of the Father

הדיה אכן" ומהו

"Surely he made a caressing gesture." But they refused.

"שב לי אנו גר אי ננו חיה

Return thou to Me! Enjoy you the life of plenty of the sojourner of the coast; increase you life.

רש פו הנדה בת

The Poor One is here. He causes a daughter to show grief.

כה רקי ידשן אל כיד לבבי"

This My Thin One makes fat G-d. My Heart stuggles."

Paragraph 175 Daniel 5.7a, 6b

מי כח לרמא ואך למה נע אי

Who is strong before the bowman? Then surely why did the region totter?

רז גו אי דשך אי

The backside of the coast was lean; he trampled thee o coast.

פש אל הלע הללי חב

A transgression G-d swallowed up. Praise thou the Bosom.

אכלם אר קן שקנא דל-אד

It feeds them light of the Nest that the Thin One of the Mist acquired.

התבכר או ניר תשמה

Desire caused itself to rise early. A Lamp; thou shalt establish it.

Paragraph 176 Daniel 5.6a, 5b

צר חי רט קו הן ולהבי-יה

The living Adversary wrung out a measuring-line; lo, then the flames of Y-H.

ני

A Lamentation

ערו יה ולעני נשיהו

They awoke Y-H and for the Poverty its Debt

יזא-כל מני דא הבתך

the assembly of all is My Portion; this is thy daughter.

יד הד יספה זח אך למו אכלם יד אלך

The Hand of the Shout shall snatch away the proud; surely for them the Hand of thy God fed them.

יהל תך יד ארי

The injured shall praise the Hand of My Light.

The Linear Bible Code

גלע את שר בגלב קלן בתך

He exposed the Prince when he shaved the pubis of thy daughter.

Paragraph 177 Daniel 5.5a, 4, 3b

ושנוא די יד נע בצאַא קף נה

And an Ape of Distinction hated sufficiently the Instrument; he staggered among <u>excrement</u>.

תעשה בא נב או אעאאל

Thou shalt succour her. The fruit of desire of Aeael came forth.

זרף אש חן אף סך

The Fire of Grace discoursed. O the anger of the Pavilion.

ואב-הד יה לאלו חב-שוא

But the Father-of-the-Shout, Y-H, is against his god the Bosom of Ravage.

רמחו יתששאה

His lance shall cause itself to make a crash.

תן חל והתל גש יה

Set thou the rampart and the Tel-City! Draw Thou near O Y-H!

ונבר בר ואכלם נוה בו יתש או

And the Pure One purified himself and he fed them. The Abode of the Flock is with him.

"מל שו "ריב יד אהל אתי ביד-אל כי הן מוק פנה יד אב-הד

Emptiness spoke: "Dispute! The hand of the Tabernacle is *against* me by the Instrument of G-d when lo, the Corner mocked the Instrument of the Father of the Shout."

Paragraph 178 Daniel 5.3a, 2b

ינאם ויתיה ני דאב

He shall prophesy and He shall cause Wailing to be wounded; it is faint.

התן חל והתל גש יה

Set thou the rampart and the Tel-City! Draw near O Y-H!

ונבר בר ואכלם נוה בן ותשיו

And the Pure One purified himself and he fed them. The Son abides and his efficient Wisdom.

"מל שו "ריב יד-אל כי הנם יה

Emptiness spoke: "Dispute thou the Instrument of God because Y-H is made drowsy."

ובא רצן דך ובן

But the Favour of the Oppressed came even the Son.

The Linear Bible Code

קף נה יד אפסך ואב-הד ינאם לה

O Ape of distinction, the Instrument brings thee to an end and the Father of the Shout prophesies of it.

Paragraph 179 Daniel 5.2a, 1; 4.34b

עט בר יתיה

The pure pen shall wound *him*.

לא רם חם מארץ אשל

He raised not up wrath from the land of the Tamarisk Tree.

בה תשאר מח

In her let thou leave behind a fatling.

אפלא לב כ קל ופלא-יה

I shall make wonderful the heart of the Voice and a wonder of Y-H.

ונבר בר לב רם חלד

And the Pure One purified himself. He exalted the World.

בעאך מרץ שאל

He sought thee against the fierceness of Sheol.

בהל פש הללך יה

Transgression trembled. He boasted of Thee O Y-H.

Paragraph 180 Daniel 4.34a, 33b

וגבן יכלה

But a gibbon endured it.

מי דון יד התחר אוטט

Who judged the Hand? He caused himself to burn the moaner.

קיה ודב עמלך ידא משכל

He vomited and the Bear of thy trouble thrust away the one bereaving the loss of a child.

מל "רדה מוח"

He said: "Marrow ruled!"

בשם רצן דך ובן הן אנעך

By the name of the Favour of the Oppressed and the Son, lo, I shall make thee tremble.

ילת פס וההריתי

Thou howled o palm. But have I caused a pregnancy?

ובנו תנק תהית וכלם יַלעו

Then His Son thou shalt suckle! Thou art desolate and all of them shall be swallowed up.

Paragraph 181 Daniel 4.33a, 32b

נוע ביין בר בר
He staggered with the pure wine of the Pure One.

וירבד הי לו
And the lamentation is bound for him.

ילעב ותיי וזו ירד הי תו
He shall jest even Taii even so Lamentation shall bring down the Mark.

כלם רקי לו
It wounded My Thin One for itself.

ילעב ותיי עדן
He shall jest even Taii of Eden.

מאנם זהב תדרב עה מהל רם איו
He shall refuse them gold. Let thou o Aih make a donation. The haughtiness of his coast was weakened.

Paragraph 182 Daniel 4.32a, 31b

הד יבא חמי
Make thou a loud noise! My wrath shall come.

יד יחיא אלו אער אירא דו אים שלי חב דב
A hand shall mark his god. I shall awaken; I shall make afraid two islands of secrecy of the Bosom of the Bear.

עה יבצ מכוני
Aih shall surpass in whiteness above My sacrificial cake.

בי שח הלך אער אירא דלך
With Me is the Lowly One. He journeyed. I shall awaken. I shall make afraid thy door.

ורד ורדם עה
And fall thou down and sleep heavily Aih!

תו-כלם ומלע נטל שה
The Mark-of-All-of-Them even is swallowing up the burden of a sheep.

נטל שי-דת
The Burden is a Gift of the Law.

רדה ותחבש אמל עי
Have thou dominion and govern. I shall cut off Ruin.

Paragraph 183 Daniel 4.31a, 30b

חל ותך רב אי לע לו
Profaneness and great oppression of the region he swallowed up for him.

בו תי יל
Against him is Tai. He howled.

The Linear Bible Code

עי ערן מות לטנא ימשל

The ruin of Eden is Death. For a basket he shall rule.

יניע רצן דך ובן

He shall toss about the Favour of the Oppressed and the Son.

הן אהים ויתצק

Lo, I shall cause discomfort and he shall constrain himself.

לו ניר פץ כי הור פט

Tillable ground belongs to him; he scattered *seed* because of Mount Put.

Paragraph 184 Daniel 4.30a, 29b

והב רני רש נכה רעש יד-דע

And give thou o poor My ringing cry! And earthquake has struck the Hand of Knowledge.

עבט צי המש גא

The howler of Hamas gave in pledge the proud one.

ימש לט מול כא ינירו תך

Secrecy shall remove the Moel here. They shall make shine oppression.

אבש עוד ירט אש

I am ashamed again; fire flickers.

נא נמו רצן דך ובן

Now slumbers the Favour of the Oppressed and the Son.

לעת פס אתל

At Time's extreme I shall heap up.

מא תעשה בה ה ננתי

How thou worketh among her! I endure.

Paragraph 185 Daniel 4.29a, 28b

אבצי ידנם לו אשנא חו-כלם

My Whiteness judges them for him. I shall change the Mark-of-All-of-them.

באי לעטי לשי דע

Come thou to My Stylus! Strengthen thou knowledge!

דנת יד-דת כי לען ופלח

Thou O Hand of Knowledge judged because of wormwood and a millstone.

יניֵן דע העב שו

Opinion caused the Cloud of Emptiness to increase.

נום עט יכל ניר ותך

The Stylus slumbered; it empowered the Lamp and the oppressed.

אבש עוֵכר דם ארב חו

I shall shame the disturber of the blood; I shall magnify the Mark.

The Linear Bible Code

יחם עון יד רטך לא שנא

Perversity conceived the hand of thy trembling; it changed not.

נמו כנמת דע תו-כלם

They were drowsy as Knowledge of the Mark-of-All-of-Them was put to death.

אכלם רצן דך ובן

He fed them the Favour of the Oppressed and the Son.

Paragraph 186 Daniel 4.28a, 27b

ני

A Lamentation

רם אכלל פן אים שן מלק אכל ממף

Haughtiness I shall complete lest the Terrible One of Tooth nip of the food supply from Memphis.

בא תל מדוע ירד לוי נס חף קח בו

He entered the Tel-City. On what account did My Thin One, the Levite, descend? The pure banner's shaft was with him.

כלמתי בל התין בהן

I wounded Bel. He caused a covering to be set in place.

אי דאת בר-לב באי האד אל

Alas, the bird of prey of the Pure One of Heart is at the Region of G-d's Mist.

Paragraph 187 Daniel 4.27a, 26, 25, 24b

הרם או אכ לם הנעהו הכלה

O the haughtiness of Lust! Surely for them he shook it; it was destroyed

מלבב יד אתו

because of the Will of the Hand of His Token.

כל מלכי הלע רשע

All My Kings the Wicked One swallowed up.

ירתני חר יתצק לאכלם רצן דך ובן

The Noble One caused Me to tremble to feed them the Favour of the Oppressed and the Son.

לע אט מאל כך תו לשלה כרא או התן

He swallowed the Gentleness from G-d. Thus the Mark for Shiloh dug out the Lust of the Jackal.

הן ינע נחם בכתי ועוק רפה-קדץ

Lo, sorrow is made to totter. I wept. But he pressed Raphah-Kedez.

Paragraph 188 Daniel 4.24a, 23b

בכי טחו כי לע רפשי

Weep thou! They besmeared *the eyes* because he swallowed up My stamping *horses*.

יכלם אך למנה

He shall reserve them surely for a time.

לא ימש נטל שי דע

He shall not remove the burden of the Gift of Knowledge.

דנת ידנם המיקך

Thou judged he who judged them. He mocked Thee.

לך חו-כלם אן לי

Go thou Mark-of-All-of-Them! Strength is Mine,

איד-יה

the Calamity of Y-H.

ושרש רק עקב שמ לו "רמא-יד"

And an exclusive Root is reward: a name for him is "Rama-Yad".

Paragraph 189 Daniel 4.23a, 22b

והנותי אב צי ידנם

And I have made the father of the howler to endure. He shall judge them.

לו אשנא חו-כלם

For him I shall change the Mark-of-All-of-Them.

באי לעטי לשי דע דנת יד-דע כי לענו פלח

Come thou to My Pen! Knead thou Knowledge. Thou judged, O Hand of Knowledge, because We swallowed down the millstone.

ינן דע העב-שא

Opinion shall increase the cloud of Emptiness.

ני עב

A Lamentation of the Cloud

צם כל אים שלטם

All fasted. The Terrible One is master of them.

ונום עט יכל ניר ותך אב

And the Pen slumbered *but not before* it empowered a lamp and the oppressed of the Father.

שעו כר-דם הו הלא רב חו

They gazed at the Lamb of Blood. Ah, he removed afar off Greatness of the Mark.

יחם עו אשן אן מן יד רט כל

Ruin becomes hot; sorrow stiffened a portion of the hand. Tremble everyone!

Paragraph 190 Daniel 4.22a, 21, 20b

ואך למי ארם לעת יֻט מיד

And surely to whom I shall raise up at the appointed time <u>let</u> <u>him</u> <u>stretch</u> <u>forth</u> from the hand.

איה איל עתר זגו אכלם

Where is the Ram of the worshipper? His grape skin I shall feed them.

ארשף הנדיהו לענו פלח

I shall inflame he who excommunicated him. We have swallowed down the millstone.

ינין דע העב שיד-דעה קלח ארב-תו

Opinion causes the cloud mass to increase. He who is the hand of opinion scorched the Abuscade of the Mark.

Paragraph 191 Daniel 4.20a

יחם עו עבט צי אים שלט

Overturning became hot. The howler gave in pledge the Terrible One; he rules.

בו ארבי

Against him is My Ambuscade.

דא את "דבש חנו לזרף ירד וסא בו וקב"

This is a sign: "Honey of his favour for a drip shall flow; and a Seah-Measure is with him and a Kab-Measure."

שא ער אביהו

O the ravage of his Father's city!

שרש רק עם-יה

O the exclusive Root of the mighty people of Y-H.

ולב חו אן לי

And Core of the Register is strength to Me.

אוד גר מאו אים שן

The firebrand of a whelp is more than the Lust of the Terrible One of Tooth.

מת חן שי דק וריע אך למה זח ידו

The Man of Grace is a fine Gift; but a friend surely, why did he thrust away his hand?

The Linear Bible Code

Paragraph 192 Daniel 4.19, 18b

אער אף וסלך נטל שוא ימשל

I shall lay bare anger and thy basket, the burden of Ravage, he shall rule.

חט מות ברך חו בר ותפק חו

Let thou O Death turn aside the knee of the Pure Mark and thou shalt totter the Mark.

ת*בר יד אכלם אוה

The Hand shall be purified; he fed them Desire.

התנא אים שיר "פץ ננך שי-יה

Did the Terrible One repeat the Song: "Thy posterity scattered the Gift-of-Y-H;

ופן עב ואר בתו יחרו דת-יה"

"and lest *there be* the Cloud and the Light of His Daughter they snort at the Law-of-Y-H."

Paragraph 193 Daniel 4.18a, 17, 16b

ותחת הב אל כלנו זם ואי גש

But instead give Thou O G-d of all of us a Plan and a Region, a clod *of earth.*

הבן-אור יפשה יפע

The Son-of-Light spread *light* about; it shines forth.

ואער אל כל התו

And I G-d shall lay bare everything of the Mark.

זחו אי משל אט מיה מור

They pushed away the region of the Dominion of Gentleness. From Y-H is myrrh.

ופק תו הברי דתי זח יד-אן לי

And the Mark, My Pure One, promoted My Law. He pushed away the hand of sorrow for Me.

אך ירעל הרשפו כי אנש לא מלחי-אר מר מאור

Surely his firebolt shall sparkle because Mankind is not seasoners of Light; *Mankind* is bitter because of Light.

Paragraph 194 Daniel 4.16a, 15b

צא שט-לב הנעך להבי

Go thou forth Revolter of the Heart! My Flame has caused thee to tremble.

לא ארשף ואמלח רצ אש-טל

I shall not kindle nor shall I season a fragment of the Fire-of-Dew.

ברם או אכלם

Nevertheless Lust I shall wound.

הנע הן להבי יה ני

Lo, the Flame-of-Y-H caused wailing to shake.

ער והדח העשכם מות שארץ

Your Creator awoke and He caused to purge Death because of the Earth.

אש-טל בה ה משי דל אי

The Fire-of-Dew is in her from the Gift of the Thin One of the Region.

נדן יד אך בני שי-דק

The Hand itself is judged. Surely My Son is the Gift of the Veil.

Paragraph 195 Daniel 4.15a

ני הלא חורי דל הכה תן-או

O the wailing! Did not My Noble, the Thin One, cause the Jackal of Lust to be scorched?

ינת עד והלא רשפני לך

He maltreated the Witness and did he not inflame Me in regards to thee?

יאל יחו כל מימי-כח לך

He was determined he should mark all the Days of Power in regards to thee.

ידל בקל כר

He shall be brought low by the voice of the he-lamb.

מא ארשף רץ אש-טל בה

How I shall ignite a fragment of the Fire-of-Dew among her.

תן או רצן דך ובן

Give thou Desire, the Favour of the Oppressed and the Son.

אך למה נאת יזח אם לח הנד

Surely why didst thou make thyself desireable? He shall remove the Mother of the Table of the *harvest* heap.

Paragraph 196 Daniel 4.14, 13b

הי לעם

A Lament for a People

יקים ישן אלף שוא ננתי אב צי

He shall cause to arise a sleeping *people*, a thousand of the Level Plain. I have increased the father of the *desert* howler.

The Linear Bible Code

ידן מלוא שונא חו-כלם

He shall judge the fullness of the one hating the Mark-of-All-of-Them.

באיל עטי לש יד אי יחנו עד

My Pen is with the Ram. The hand kneaded the coast *as dough*. They shall show the Witness favour.

ני יד תר בר

A Lament of the Hand of the Pure Turtledove

דע את לאש

Knowledge is the Token for Man.

ני שי-דק

A Lament of the Gift of the Veil

רם אם ואם גת פן ידיע תר

He exalted a mother even the mother of the wine press lest he cause the Turtledove to be timid.

זג ביה ולענו פלח

The skin of the grape is with YAH and We swallowed down the millstone.

ינין דע העב-שו הלב היתיהו

Opinion shall cause the cloud of Emptiness of the Heart to increase. I have done it.

Paragraph 197 Daniel 4.13a, 12b

יחב בל ונון שי-אש

Bel is guilty but the Gift-of-Fire endureth.

ונא נמה בבל אער אב-שע

And now Babylon is drowsy. I, the Father of Opulence, shall awaken *him*.

בהק לח אתו יחם עו

A New Thing shines: His Token! Overturning became hot.

עבט צי אים שלט

The howler gave in pledge the Terrible One; he rules.

בו ארבי

Against him is My Ambuscade.

Paragraph 198 Daniel 4.12a, 11b

דא את "דבש חנו לזרף ידר

This is a Token: "Honey of his favour for a drip shall flow,

וסא בו וקב"

and a Seah-Measure is with him, and a Kab-Measure."

The Linear Bible Code

שא ער אביהו

O the ravage of his Father's City!

שר שרק עם רב יה

O the Prince of the Vine Tendrils of the mighty people of Y-H!

ופן ענם איר פצו יה ותַוחתן אמת ויחדן

And lest the Soothsayers of Irradiation should break asunder Y-H even <u>he breaking apart</u> hundreds then he united them.

תהבן אור דבו

Let thou give them Light. Move you gently!

Paragraph 199 Daniel 4.11a, 10b

הי

<u>A Lamentation</u>

פעור תא יה

The Chamber of Y-H opens.

ופן עוק צק ואן לי אוד גר מאן כו לי

And lest it counsel retraint and wealth for Me a firebrand of a sojourner refused the *celestial* Window that is Mine.

חבא רק תחן אים שן משי-דק וריעו

The Thin One withdrew. Thou favourest the Terrible One of Tooth above the Gift-of-the-Veil and his companion.

Paragraph 200 Daniel 4.8a, 7, 6b

לאו יבך שם לעי שארי וזח בתי

Be you weary! Shem shall weep for the ruin of My remnant and the pride of My Daughter.

והה זח אר שבלך

But alas, a light thrust away thy flowing robe.

נ*זתי הנם ואים שיר

I <u>sprinkled</u> Hennom and the Terrible One of Song.

פץ נ*ר די יה

<u>A lamp</u> scattered <u>even</u> the sufficiency of Y-H;

ופן עבו אר בתו יחל לטח יה

And lest they hide the light of His Daughter He shall begin the Mystery of Y-H.

ותחת הב אל כלנו זם ואי גש

And *they said:* "Underneath give Thou O G-d of all of us a Plan and a Region, a clod *of earth.*

The Linear Bible Code

הבן אור יפשה יפע

"The Son of Light let him scatter it; let him shine."

אער אלך פוסל התו

I G-d shall lay bare the Stone Cutter, the Mark.

Paragraph 201 Daniel 4.8a, 6b

זחו אים שלאט

Thrust you away the Terrible One who works in secret.

מי המור ופק תו אן לי

Whosoever is the Changeling even he shook the Mark; sorrow was Mine.

אהב ראי

I shall give a Vision.

גש המור ואער אאוג בן לי אול

The Changeling gropped about and I shall lay bare Aa-Og, a son of Mine, a leading man.

אותי והה זח יבך שם לעיש ארי וזחו

O My Token! But alas, pride! Shem shall weep toward the Constellation of the Great Bear My Light but his pride.

רמא הרשפות יזח יד ימל חי וזח כל

The bowman of the firebolts shall thrust aside the hand that would cut off the living and the pride of all.

סנא אל זר לכוכב

G-d lifted up an Alien to a Star.

Paragraph 202 Daniel 4.6a, 5b

ני שי-דק

The Wail of the Gift-of-the-Veil

ני הלא חורי דת עדי

O the wailing! My Noble removed afar off the Law of My Everlasting-ness.

הן איד אים טרח בר

Lo, the load of the Terrible One is the burden of the Pure One.

רץ אשט לבת רמא-יה

A runner I shall send to the Daughter, the Bowman of Y-H.

ומדק אמל חוה

And from the Veil I shall cut off the Serpent.

בני שי-דק

My Son is the Gift-of-the-Veil.

Paragraph 203 Daniel 4.5a, 4

ני

A Lamentation

הלא חור ידו

Is not the Noble His Instrument?

יה לאם שכר צא טל בה

O Y-H, the people of the pasture, give Thou dew among her.

מש יד לאין די מד

A hand gropped for there was insufficient measure.

קל עני רח אדע וילן

The voice of the poor in spirit I shall discern and he shall lodge for the night.

יעדוה מאל הרשפו נוה

They have reckoned her from G-d. They inflamed the habitation.

ים דק הן אר מא אמלחו איד זגו

The Sea of the Veil, lo, a light. How I shall salt it. I shall make the skin of his grape glow.

איד שך אי פשה אים טרח ני *לעני דאב

O the burden of the Booth of the Coast! The Terrible One shall spread the burden of <u>wailing</u> to the weakened affliction.

Paragraph 204 Daniel 4.3, 2

ינן עדו הי

His Witness endured lamentation.

אמלח רשף יד לב בימי-כח לכל

I shall salt the firebolt of the Instrument of Heart in the days of power for all.

ימד קהל ענה למעט מיש ינמו

He measured the Assembly. He responded to a few. He departed; they became drowsy.

ינן להבי יא ארי וחחו

My firebolt increased the essence of My Light but they rejected *him*.

יבך שם לעני רהרה

Shem shall weep for the affliction. It was made afraid.

וינן לח דיות   יזח מלח ילך

And moisture shall increase more than enough. A Mariner shall move; he shall journey.

יהבן נער ויתיב בתי

He gave *the Sufficiencies* a boy and Jathib My Daughter.

Paragraph 205 Daniel 4.1a; 3.33, 32b

והה לשרץ נדך

But alas, toward the Swarm is thy heap.

ובן הן ארדו "רד מעה"

And the Son lo, I shall send him down: "Descend thou o seed!"

נטל שום לעת וכלמה תו-כל מן יפיק תהם

A burden he set at the time and the Mark-of-All wounded it because he caused the Abyss to totter.

כי הוה מתו ני בר ברהם כיה

When it happened they died. O the lament of the Pure One! Their Pure One is like Y-H.

ותא היו ימד קר פש

And the Chamber of his lamentation Chahal shall measure a wall *using* the palm *length*.

אי רע אהל אים עד בע יד איה מתו

He swallowed not up the Tent of the Terrible One until the claw of the Falcon swelled up; they died.

Paragraph 206 Daniel 3.32a, 31, 30b

אי תא אגש ינוך מל שא ער

The region of the Chamber I shall approach. It is smitten in front of Ravage the Foe.

אלך בן ירא די דא

I shall send a son; he shall see enough of this.

ינשלו אי

They shall clear away the region.

מא אים מעל כל

What is the Terrible Thing? All unfaithfulness!

אך לם רצן דך ובן לב

Surely for them is the Favour of the Oppressed and the Son of Heart.

בת ני דם בו

The Daughter of the lament of blood is with him.

גן דב עו כשי מכר דש

The Garden of the Bear of Ruin as a gift of value he trampled.

לחלק האכלם

Toward Chalez he caused them to be fed.

Paragraph 207 Daniel 3.30a, 29, 28c

ני דאב הנדך הלך הלל

O the Wailing! Thy *harvest* heap melted away. The Scorner boasted.

The Linear Bible Code

כי ידן רח אהל איתיאאל ידל בקלך

When he judged the Spirit of the Tent of Ithiel he shall be laid low at
Thy Voice.

הות שי ילון התיב ודב עתי

A Gift shouted. Hattib shall murmur and the Bear of My Appointed
Time.

ני מד האו

Waling is measure of Lust.

גן דב עו כשי מכר דש

The Garden of the Bear of Ruin as a gift of value he trampled.

ידן הה לא לעה לשר מאי ידן שלוה

They shall be judged. Alas, she spoke not wildly to the Prince of the
Region. He shall judge Shiloh.

מא מעל כי דם עמ

How it acted treacherously because of the blood of the pen.

מי שי נמו נוה

Whosoever is the Gift they of the Abode of the Flock are drowsy.

Paragraph 208 Daniel 3.28b

הלא לנהלה לאלך לנוד

Was it not to guide her to a watering-station? For I shall journey
toward the Wandering.

גסי-אל ונוח לפי אל ידנו

The splitters of G-d and Noah, at the Mouth of G-d they shall be
judged.

הי משגו בהיו

Wailing is more than His empty ones straying.

וינש אכל מתלמו יה

And He is sick of food more than their breaking with Y-H.

ולעוק חרת היד

But bor counseling the hand engraved:

"יהוד בעל בז ישוה כאל מחלש יד

"A Jew is lord of plunder. He shall be composed as G-d more than a
hand that is disabled.

וגן דב עו כשי מכר דש ידנו"

And the Garden of the Bear of Ruin as a gift of value he trampled. They
shall be judged."

Paragraph 209 Daniel 3.28a, 27b

הה לאך ירב רם או רצן דך ובן

Alas, He sent a Messenger. He shall increase on High desire for the Favour of the Oppressed and the Son.

הנע נוה בהדע אל רון חירו

He caused the Abode of the Shephered to stagger. With <u>the Knowledge</u> of G-d he overcame Cheru.

ונשאלנו

And We inquired among Ourselves.

הי לבר

A lament toward the Pure One

סוכר חת האל-נוה שאר רעש

the one shutting up the Terror of the G-d of Eminency. He left behind quaking;

ונוה משג באר ונטל שאל

and he betook himself to the Error of the Pit and the Burden of Sheol.

ידך לא אי רב

It shall be crushed. There is no region of dispute.

גל ני זח אך לם ירבדהו

He rolled away lamentation. O the pride! Surely for them he confine it.

Paragraph 210 Daniel 3.27a, 26b

אתוה פו אין גס

I shall set the mark here. There is no crude one.

אין פרד-שח-אן

There is no lowly mule of sorrow.

ישנך חם וארון או גן

Thy sleeping *people* are complete and the coffin of desire of the Garden.

מוג נד בע וכשי מכר דש

A heap dissolved; it boiled up, even as a gift of value he tread upon.

ני קף

<u>A Lamentation of the Ape</u>

נן יד-אב ותאו

The Instrument of the Father endured and his Chamber.

וקף אי לע אהל אי

And the Ape of the Coast swallowed up the Tent of the Coast.

די הדב עו גן דב עו כשי מכר דש רמא

Sufficient is the Bear of Ruin! The Garden of the Bear of Ruin as a gift of value the boman tread upon.

The Linear Bible Code

והנע את דקי-אר וננות
And he caused the thin ones of Light to stagger and the maltreated *women*.

Paragraph 211 Daniel 3.26a, 25, 24b

אער תל רצן דך ובן בר קני
I shall awaken the Tel-City *to feed them* the Favour of the Oppressed and the Pure Son of My Nest.

דאב ני הלא רב לה
Wailing is become faint. The Great One is He not against her?

מד אי עי בר ידהו רונו
O the measure of the region of ruin. The Pure One cast *a spear* at it; he overcame it.

הבית יא אלל
O the House Fair is worthless.

בחו ארו נאו גב
Bark you! Curse you! Frustrate you the Pit!

ני כלה כן ירשה עב
O the Wailing! Annihilation is right! Inherit thou the cloud!

רא ניר בגה זחה נא
See thou the tillable ground! Her food is now her pride!

אה רם או הנע אכל
Alas, the haughtiness of Appetite; it caused food to be tossed about.

מאבי צי אכלם לניר מאו נין עני
From My Father's Ship He fed them to give light from the Desire of the progeny of the Affliction.

Paragraph 212 Daniel 3.24b

תפך מארון או גל אן
Thy timbrel is above the coffin of desire a heap of sorrow.

ימרא תל חני-רב
It shall whip the Tel-City of the Jackals of Greatness.

גאלה יה ורבדה לרם או
YAH acted the kinsman for her; He bedecked her at the height of desire.

הנע הלהבת אַב מקוה
The Flame of the <u>Father</u> of Hope He made to flicker;

ותאכלם רצן דך ובן
and it shall feed them the Favour of the Oppressed and the Son.

Paragraph 213 Daniel 3.24a, 23, 22b

ני

O the Wailing!

דא ני תפך מאת דק יארו

This was the lament of thy timbrel. Hundreds of the Veil shall shine;

ננו תא-או גלול פנו גן דב עו כשי מכר דש

They shall increase the Chamber of Desire. The Idol turn you away.The Garden of the Bear of Ruin as a gift of value trample thou!

נוה תל תך לא אי רב גו ארון

He abided the Tel-City of the oppressed; not an island of greatness, *but* the interior of a coffin.

יד-אבי בשן ומה לט קו גן דב עו כשי מכר דש לו

The Hand of my Father is against the Tooth and what of the Mystery of the Measuring Line? The Garden of the Bear of ruin as a gift of value He trampled for Himself.

קסה ידך לא אי רב ריח יה זא אן

Thy Hand stripped her. No isle of a proud multitude is the Wish of YAH; this is sorrow.

ותאוה פצחה מאכלם תלמיד נמה נדל

But a thing desire broke <u>forth</u>. Because a scholar has fed them somnolence he is brought low.

Paragraph 214 Daniel 3.22a, 21, 20b

בקל כאת דק

By an utterance Thou hast rebuked the Veil

יארו ננו תא או גלו

they shall be lighted up; they shall endure; the Chamber of Desire is His rejoicing.

ימרו נוה

They shall make bitter the Habitation of the Shepherd;

ישבלו נוה

they shall make droop the Habitation of the Shepherd.

תל-ברך ונוה ישיט

The Tel-City of the Blessed One even the Abode of the Shepherd He shakes.

פנו הי לבר סבו תפך

They shall turn away lamentation for the Pure One. "March you about the Timbrel!"

The Linear Bible Code

כלא הי רב גן יד-אב את דקי-אר וננוח אל

He has shut up the lamentation of the multitude of the Garden of the Instrument of the Father together with the thin ones of Light and the maltreated *women* of G-d.

אם רם לן

The high mother belongs to <u>Him</u>.

וגן דב-עו כשי מכר דש

And the Garden of the Bear-of-Ruin as a gift of value He trampled.

לה תף תל-רם אהלי חבי דלי-חי

For her is the timbrel of the Tel-City on High, the Tents of My Bosom *and* the Gates of the Living One.

Paragraph 215 Daniel 3.20a, 19b

רב גני רב גלוה

The abundance of My Garden is a multitude; they rejoiced over her.

יזם לה זח יד

The pride of the Hand makes a plan for her.

לע העב שדחאנו תא

The cloud mass swallowed up he who pushed Us of the Chamber;

לאז מל רם-או

for at that time he cut off the haughtiness of Lust.

הנעו גן דב-עו

They caused to totter the Garden of the Bear-of-Ruin;

כשי מכר דש לעו נתש איה

as a gift of value he trampled for ruin. He rooted up her coast;

ופן אמל צו-אם חיל-מת הרצן דך ובן

And lest the commandment of a mother become weak the Fortress-of-Man is the Favour of the Oppressed and the Son.

Paragraph 216 Daniel 3.19a, 18, 17b

ני

O the Wailing!

דאב דג סנא לתם

A fish was faint; toward Integrity it hated.

יקה יד-אב הדם לצלו

The Hand-of-the-Father was obedient. The blood belongs to his shadow.

ני חלף אן יתיא אלך יה

O the wailing, the Caleph of On caused thy G-d pain.

לאל יד אכלם

For G-d the Hand fed them.

The Linear Bible Code

כל אוה לעי "די-אל נה ובזי שי-אכל מכד"

Every lust is for ruin. "The Sufficiency of G-d is Distinction and My Booty is a gift of food from a jar."

ינמו את דקי-אר וננות אן

They shall grow drowsy together with the thin ones of Light and the maltreated *women* of sorrow.

Paragraph 217 Daniel 3.17a, 16b

מאן חו בז ישלל

The Mark refused the Booty he shall plunder.

כי ני חלף אן חן איד אן

Because of wailing the Caleph of On's elegancy is the calamity of On.

הלא יתיא נה כתוב

Shall he not wound Distinction writing:

"תהלם גת פה נד לעה"

"The wine press shall smite the mouth that swallowed down the *harvest* heap."

נח נא ניח שח אל

Give Thou rest I pray. O the tranquility of the lowly of G-d!

רצן דך ובן אכלם לני רם או

Feed Thou them the Favour of the Oppressed and the Son at the lamentation of the haughtiness of Lust.

Paragraph 218 Daniel 3.16a, 15b

וגן דב-עו כשי מכר דש וגע

And the Garden of the Bear-of-Ruin as a gift of value he trampled and tossed about.

ידינם נוכן בזי שי-יד

The Establisher shall judge them. My Booty is the Gift-of-the-Hand.

הלא אוה נמ ואת דקי-אר וננו תא-או

Is not Lust Somnolence but the thine ones of Light even they increased the Chamber of Desire.

גלנו מר תתה תעשה בנוד

Our rejoicing is myrrh. Let thou roar! Let thou work among the Wandering.

גסת אל נה וחדב ע*ד אם לצל נוד

Thou O G-d split Distinction and Thou moveth gently <u>perpetually</u> over the Mother of the Shadow of the Wandering.

גסת ונול פת אר מזי-נזל כוה

Thou split *Distinction* and disfigured a fragment of Light overflowing the *celestial* Window.

ינף מוס

The one wasting away shall shake himself.

Paragraph 219 Daniel 3.15a, 14b

וני רת נס פא כבש סרתי-קאתי-קור

And wailing! A banner fluttered. Here is the Footstool of the Apostasies of the Pelicans of Kur

שמאן רק לקן

Who refused the Thin One of the Nest.

ועמשת יד-אן דע

And thou of hand of sorrow carried Knowledge.

בי דני די

With Me is My sufficient judgment.

תענו כיתיאן הנע כן יד

You shall be afflicted as he caused them *(the Apostasies)* pain; he waved a hand rightly so.

גס אל-תם

Wield Thou power O G-d of Integrity!

יקה יד-אב הדם לצלו

The Instrument of the Father, the Blood of His Shadow, showed obedience.

Paragraph 220 Daniel 3.14a, 13b

ניח לפנו כיתיא אל יהל אל

Tranquility is before Us; as G-d wounded it, it praised G-d.

וגן דב-עו כשי מכר דש

And the Garden of the Bear-of-Ruin as a gift of value he trampled.

אדק הנוה לרם או רצן דך

I shall leap the Abode of the Shepherd to raise up the Desire of the Favour of the Oppressed.

בן הנע אך לם מד קן

The Son caused trembling. Surely for them is the measure of the line.

יתיה כלא איר בגו יד-אב

He shall wound imprisonment. I shall make glow his morsel, the Hand of the Father.

ונן דב-עו כשי מכר דש לה

But the Garden of the Bear-of-Ruin as a gift of value he trampled for her *(Jerusalem)*.

יתיה לרמאה

He for her bowman wounds.

מחוז-גר ברצן דך ובן

The City-of-the-Sojourner is *found* within the Favour of the Oppressed and the Son.

Paragraph 221 Daniel 3.13a, 12b

ניד אב ניד

O the quivering of the Father; O the quivering *lip*.

גס אל-תם יקה יד-אב הדם לצלו

O G-d of Integrity wield power! The Instrument-of-the-Father showed obedience, the Blood of His Shadow.

ני חלף אל כיהל אל מעט

O the wailing, he quickly passed by G-d as G-d boasted of a few;

אכלם כילעו משאל

he fed them as they of Sheol spoke incoherently.

כלא אי רב גו גן דב-עו

He imprisioned the great region the backside of the Garden of the Bear-of-Ruin;

כשי מכר דש לבב תן

as a gift of value he trampled the will of the Jackal.

יד מת די בעל ענו

The Hand of Man is the sufficiency of the lord of the afflicted.

התיתין מיד ני

He made himself to be constant above the hand of wailing.

Paragraph 222 Daniel 3.12a, 11, 10, 9b

אד והין ירב גי-תיא את דקי-אר

With a mist and a Hin-Measure he shall multiply the Valley of Tia together with the thin ones of Light

וננו צא או גל אמרתי

and they increased the Chamber of Desire; o the rejoicing! I said:

"דג סיו לפי-אל ידנם ואבה דם לצל

"The fish of his sheep is for the Mouth of G-d. He shall judge them and the Blo of of the Shadow consented.

The Linear Bible Code

דג סיו לפי-אר מזי-נזל כוה

The fish of his sheep is for the Mouth of Light overflowing the *celestial* Window.

ינפַן סוני רת נס

The Sunni waveth! A banner fluttered!

פא כבש סרתי-קאתי-קר

Here is the Footstool of the Apostasies of the Pelicans of Kur

שמאן רק לק עם שי-יד שן-אל

He who refused the Thin One. He lapped up the people of the Gift of the Hand, the Tooth of EL

כידם עט חם

as he silenced the Pen of Integrity.

שא כלם התן אאי-חנים

The ravage of all of them is the Jackal of the favourable regions;

לעל אכלם אכלם רצן דך ובן לניר מאו

In regard to Above I shall feed them; I shall feed them the Favour of the Oppressed and the Son, for the Lamp is more than Appetite.

Paragraph 223 Daniel 3.9a, 8, 7b

ונע איד והי ידנוה

And Calamity trembled and Lamentation. They shall judge her.

יצר קולך אוני אדש כניר בגוב רק או מזהב

Thy Voice fashioned my strength. I shall thresh the likes of tillable ground when he pierceth the Thin One of Strength because of the gold.

הן דק בקלך אכלם רצן דך ובן

Lo, the Thin One by Thy Voice fed them the Favour of the Oppressed and the Son

מיקה יד-אב

on account the Instrument of the Father was obedient.

הדם לצל ניד גס אי נשל ואי

The Blood of the flickering Shadow split the Coast! He cleared off even the Region.

Paragraph 224 Daniel 3.7a, 6b

מא אים מעל כן ילף

How the Terrible One is swallowing down a gnat; it stuck fast.

נאר מזי-נזל כו

He abhorred the overflowing of the *celestial* Window.

The Linear Bible Code

ני רט נס פא כבש סרתי-קאתי-קור

O the Wailing! A banner fluttered! Here is the Footstool of the Apostasies of the Pelicans of Kur

שמאן רק

He who refused the Thin One.

לק אים מעל כן

The Terrible One lapped up the unfaithful rightly;

יעם שי-דך

he eclipsed the Gift of the Oppressed.

אן מזהב הנד לב קלך את דקי ארון חא-או

Sorrow is comparible to gold. The heart caused Thy Voice to tremble together with the thin ones of the Ark of the Chamber of Desire.

Paragraph 225 Daniel 3.6a, 5b

גל אמרתי "את עשה בד גסיו

O rejoicing! I said: "A ploughshare made separate his coarse ones;

לפי-אל ידנם ואכלם רצן דך ובן

in regards to the Mouth of G-d it judges them and He fed them the Favour of the Oppressed and the Son.

מיקה יד-אב הדם לצל נוד"

Because the Instrument-of-the-Father was obedient *even* the Blood of the Wandering Shadow."

Paragraph 226 Daniel 5a, 4, 3c

גס תונו לפת אר מזי-נזל כוה

Our Mark made a split for a fragment of Light the overflowings of the *celestial* Window.

ינפם וסני רט נס

But a Sunni tossed them about; a banner fluttered.

פא כבס סורתי-קאתי-קור

Here is the Footstool of the Apostasies of the Pelicans of Kur

שמאן רק

he who refused the Thin One.

לקנו עם שת יד-אן דע

We lapped up a people. A Hand of Strength set up Knowledge.

בא ינשל ואי

It came; it cleared away even the coast.

מא אים מעני רם אן

What is the terrible thing above Affliction? He exalted Sorrow.

וכל לי תבא רק אזו רך ורצן דך ובן

But all are Mine. The Thin One has hidden at his own time a Delicacy even the Favour of the Oppressed and the Son.

Paragraph 227 Daniel 3.3b

מיקה יד אמל צל בקל

Out of the obedience of the Instrument I shall cut off the Shadow by an utterance.

ני מאקו אכלם רצן דך ובן

O the wailing from a wild goat! I shall feed them the Favour of the Oppressed and the Son.

מיקה יד-אם לץ תכן

Because of the obedience of the Instrument of the Mother he scorned the standard-mesure.

חלאת ני דמי-נטל

The rust of wailing is the bloods of weight.

שלכו אי-תפת אי-רבתד אי- רבדג אי-רוגר

They have cast down Tophet; the region of Rabethad; the region of Rabedag; the region of Razegar.

דא אתו ״חפו״

This is its Sign: "His Clean One."

Paragraph 228 Daniel 3.3a, 2, 1

אין גס אין פרד-שח-אן

There is no crude one; there is no lowly mule of sorrow.

ישונך תם ניד אב אך לם רצן דך ובן

Thy sleeping *people* are complete. O the quivering *lip* of the Father! Surely for them is the Favour of the Oppressed and the Son.

מיקה יד-אם לץ תכן

Because of the Instrument of the Mother he scorned the standard-measure.

חלאת מלא תני-דמי-נטל

The rust of fullness is the Jackals of the Blood of Weight.

שלכו אי-תפת אי-רבתד אי-רבדג אי-רוגר

They cast down the region-of-Tophet; the region-of-Rabathed; the region-of-Rabedag; the region-of-Razegar.

דא אתו ״חפו״

This is the Sign: "His Clean One."

אין גס אין פרד-שח-אל

There is no crude one; there is no lowly mule of G-d.

שנך מל חל שאכלם רצן דך ובן

Thy Tooth cut the fortress of he who fed them the Favour of the Oppressed and the Son.

ולבב תני-דם באר ודת

And the courage of the Jackals of Blood is against Light and Law;

עקב בהמי-קא תשנים

as a consequence the beasts of vomitus Thou shalt change them.

אה יתפני אה מור בהד

Ah, he spat at Me! Thou shalt change them. Ah, Myrrh is with the joyous shout!

יד-מל צד בע אכלם רצן דך ובן

The hand of the Moel provided; it swelled up; it fed them the Favour of the Oppressed and the Son.

Paragraph 229 Daniel 2.49, 48b

אכלם ערת בל אי נדו

It fed them the bare places of Bel the region of his heap.

וגן דב-עו כשי מכר דש ללבב חן

But the Garden of the Bear-of-Ruin as a gift of value he trampled against the will of the Jackal.

ידם יד את די בעל עי

The hand silences the sufficiency of the Lord of Ruin.

ונמו אכלם נם

They slumbered; he fed them Somnolence.

אעבל אי נדו

I shall make stout the region of his heap.

לבבי-מי-כח לכל עני

The courage-of-the-Waters-of-Strength is for every poor one.

נגס ברו לבב חן

His Pure One bit off the courage of the Jackal.

יד מלך לעה טל שה והלב

The Hand of the King swallowed up the night mist, a sheep and courage.

Paragraph 230 Daniel 2.48a, 47b

הי נא יגש נבר בר

O the wailing! Now he hardened himself; the Pure One purified himself.

נן חם ויבר לאי נד לאכל מני

Integrity endured and he purified himself for the region of the *harvest* heap for the food of My Portion.

דא הנד הזר-אל גם לתל

This is the *harvest* heap of the Crown-of-G-d also for the Tel-City.

כי ידן יזרה לגו

When He makes judgment He shall scatter His Measure.

ני כלמארמוני הלא הלא אוה

O the wailing! everyone removed of My Citadel certainly removed afar off Lust.

נוכה לאיד טש קן מרם או

Smitten for the Distress he flew the Nest because of the haughtiness of Lust;

לאי נדל אכל

toward the coast the food supply was brought low.

Paragraph 231 Daniel 2.47a, 46, 45b

מה נעה לה כס נל רמא

How *Lust* trembled! For her was a throne; the bowman attained *it*.

ניחח ינוה חנם ודג סל אי נד לו יה

Quietness shows itself beautiful without cause and the fish of the basket of the coastal heap belongs to Him *even* Y-H.

ופנאל על פן רצן דך ובן אכלם

And Penuel is on High lest He feed them the Favour of the Oppressed and the Son.

ני דאב הר-שפן

O the wailing! Mount Shaphan languished.

מי הם ואמלח ביציו

Who murmured and I should salt his eggs?

הנד ירחא אוה לי דהם

He caused the Moon of Desire to wander. To Me is astonishment!

אכלם לעד והבר

I shall feed them forever even the pure.

Paragraph 232 Daniel 2.45a, 44b

הלא אב הד ואפסך אף סח אש

The Father removed afar off the Shout; and thy end yea is scoured of fire.

חן אל זרפת קדה

O Grace of G-d, thou dripped cassia-spice.

וני די באל

And wailing is enough with G-d.

The Linear Bible Code

יד נבא "תר זג תא-אר וטם ידתי

The Instrument prophesied: "A pair sought out the Chamber of Light but the stupid one I have shot *arrows* at.

זח יד לב קלך

"A hand has thrust away the Will of Thy Voice.

אים לע למוק תא-יה ואתו

"The Terrible One spoke incoherently to mock the Chamber of Y-H and His Token.

כל מני לא לך פי-שת

"All of My Portion is not for thee o mouth of Seth.

וקדרת קבת שת-אל

"And thou bowed down; thou uttered a curse *against* it, the Column of G-d.

נר חאם על התו כלמו לב חתת-אל

"The lamp of Cheam is above the Mark; the heart of the Terror of EL wounded him.

Paragraph 233 Daniel 2.44a, 43, 42b

ני מל על ידו כל מאי משה לאם יקיני

"O the wailing! His Hand on High circumcised all from the coast of Moses, the reconciler, Our obedient one.

נא אי כלם ידנו הימו

"Now alas, all of them shall be judged; they roared!

יבוא פסח מעבר-עת מאל

"The Passover shall come, the Passageway of Time from G-d.

אל זרפי-דך אה הנד מעה נדן

"O G-d the tears of the oppressed! Alas, the heap of seed was judged.

יקב דן והלא לו אשן אע

"The wine vat He judged and was not humanity wood to Him?

רז בנוהל

"The Secret is in the guiding to a watering-station.

ני בר עת מאן יטף

"O the wailing! The Pure One of the Appointed Time is a vessel. He shall discourse.

סחב בר עם אל זרפת

"The Pure One pulled along the people of G-d. O the tears!

יזח יד הרי-בתה והתהנם והפי קת

"The hand makes unsteady the Mountains of Desolation and Hata-Hennom and the mouth of Keith.

Paragraph 234 Daniel 2.42a, 41b

הוה תא חו-כלם חצק

"It shall come to pass the Chamber of the Mark-of-All-of-Them Thou pressed upon.

נם פסח נוה נמו לזרף נוה

"The Passover of the Abode of the Shepherd was drowsy; they were drowsy at the Discourse of Distinction.

נם איל גר תע בצאו

"The Ram of the sojourner was drowsy; he erred on account of his filth.

אניט פסח בבר עם אל

"I shall cause the Passover to dangle with the Pure One of the people of G-d.

זרפ*ת יזח ידל בקלך

"O the tears! He shall be removed; he shall be made low by Thy Voice.

הב או הלא לזרף יד את בץ ננם

"Give Thou Desire! Was it not for the Instrument to discourse the mire? He would increase them.

והוה תהג ילפו כלם לזרף נוה

"And it shall come to pass Thou shalt pant. All of them shall form a scab at the Discourse of Distinction;

נמו רחף יד פסח נוה נם

"they shall become drowsy. The Instrument shall brood; the Passover of the Abode of the Shepherd shall be drowsy.

Paragraph 235 Daniel 2.41a, 40, 39b

אתע בץ או אי אל

"I shall make the mire of the lust of the Ram to err.

גרתי זח יד וערת וקדת

"I shall stir up pride of the hand and the bare places and lowly places.

ני לאלך עערם יד זרף כוא

"The Lament is for thy G-d. The Hand of G-d is awakening them the drip of the *celestial* Window.

לך לשח וקדה מאל זרף

"Go thou to the Lowly One but cassia-spice is from G-d of the drip;

ידל בקלך אל זרפך הפיק חא

"it is brought low by Thy Voice O G-d. Thy drip caused the Chamber to reel.

והתה "יעי ברו כלם"

"And *the Chamber* shouted: 'My altar shoves make You pure, all of them!'

The Linear Bible Code

ואער אל כבטל

"And I shall reveal G-d as drinking ceases.

דא שח ניד ירחא

"This is the Lowly One *who* moved to and from the Moon.

אי חיל חו-כל מוך נם

"Alas, thou shalt howl. The Mark-of-All brought low Somnolence.

Paragraph 236 Daniel 2.39a, 38, 37b

אערא ירחא וכלם מוק

"I shall uncover the Moon and all of them it derided.

תכרת "בוא בהדיד השאר-אוה"

"Thou shalt write: 'Come thou when it has crashed noisily the Remnant of Desire.'

התא-נוה לך בך טל-שה

"The Chamber of the Abode of the Shepherd is Thine. Weep thou o dew of the sheep;

וכד יבב הי אים שפוע

"and o jar cry shrilly a lamentation! The terrible thing flowed abundantly *out of thee.*

וארבת ויחאשן אין

"And thou hast ambushed and Jacheshan is not.

בן ירא די דל כבו כלב

"The Son shall see enough of the poor. They are rolled up as the heart.

היא רקי ואפק חו אן

"She, *(The Daughter of Israel)* is Mine only one. And the Mark took hold of Sorrow;

סחא חו-כלם אי משה לאיד אי

"The Mark-of-All-of-Them scraped clean the coast of Moses in regards to the Calamity of the coast.

Paragraph 337 Daniel 2.37a, 36, 35b

כלם כלם אכלם החנא

"All of them, all of them I am feeding them of the Habitation.

אכלם מד קר

"I am feeding them a measure of cold.

מאן הרשף ואמלח הנד

"It refused the firebolt but I am salting the *harvest* heap.

אער אל כתרם ובדרו טל

"I shall expose G-d as a furrow. And they have chosen the dew.

תוה אם לצלת חם "יד אן"

"He put a mark on the mother of Zellah of Ham: "The Hand of Sorrow.""

באו נוה לחך תשה אל

"*Men* entered the Habitation of Thy Tablet the Efficient Wisdom of G-d.

רת אל כוה חורן

"G-d shook the window of Horon."

Paragraph 238 Daniel 2.35a, 34, 33, 32b

ומה אש נוט יקיר

"But what is a man? Made precious he dangled.

דא נמר ועכו והוא בהד ואף סך

"This is a leopard even Acco and he is among the Shout and also a lair.

אשח נא פסח-אל זרף

"I am humbled. Now is the Passover of G-d. He discoursed.

הדחך וקד ני דאב נום התקד

"He rinsed thee clean and wailing bowed. He became faint; he is drowsy; he was made to bow down.

הוא פסח ואל

"He is the Passover even of G-d.

זרף יד-יה ולגר לע

"The Instrument of Y-H discoursed but to the sojourner he spoke incoherently.

אמל צל תחם וני די באל

"The Shadow became weak; it became dark. And wailing is sufficient with G-d."

יד נבא תר זגת היד דעתי

The Instrument prophesied of the Age of Brightness of Power and My Knowledge.

וההה זח פסח יד נוה

But alas the Instrument of Distinction removed the Passover.

נמו לזר פי דנו

"*The people* slumbered. Toward the Gentile is the mouth of *their* judgment.

הן מי הול גר לזרף יד-יה וקשש חן

Lo, who is made a fool? The sojourner at the discourse of the Instrument of Y-H; so he sought for Grace.

Paragraph 239 Daniel 2.32a, 31b

ידה תך רי ויה

The oppression spewed moisture even Y-H.

ועם פסך יד-יה וער דוי הוד חבט בהד

And o people thy palm is the Hand of Y-H. And a faint city of splendour he beat out with a shout.

יד השאר אם לץ אוה ליחד הור וכל בקל

The hand of the remnant of Mother scorned Lust to unite a mountain and all by an utterance.

מא קרית יה ויזוב רן כד

What is the City-of-Y-H but a ringing cry overflowing a jar.

אם-לץ אי גש דחם לצול

The Mother of the Scorner of the region is a lump *of earth* thrust down to the stoned lined basin.

אותיו

I desired it.

Paragraph 240 Daniel 2.31a, 30, 29, 28b

הה זח אך לם התן

Alas, pride! Surely for them is the Jackal.

אערן תך בבלינו יער וונע

I shall make luxurious oppression. Without Us it would be naked and would tremble.

דוה יאכל מלא רשפי-דת

The Faint One shall consume a fullness of the Firebolts of the Law.

רב דל ענה לי

O the Greatness of the Thin One. He answered Me:

"ליל גה נדא זר איי-חל כן"

'The night has departed. The Gentile of the regions-of-the-Profane has been cast out rightly so.'

מי ביתי-איד

Whom are the houses of oppression?

המך חב אל

He was brought low; the Bosom of EL.

הן או אוה ליד

Lo, Desire, Desire belongs to the Instrument.

המך עדו הא יזר אל גו הנד ירחא

Brought low is His Witness. Lo, EL compresses the middle of the *harvest* heap of the Moon.

אוה ליד המוק לסך

Desire belongs to the Instrument. Did it mock at the Thicket?

בך שם לעכין ויער

Shem wept toward Acan and the Thicket;

אך למה תנא אוה הנד כבך שם

howebeit, why did the Jackal lust after the heap as Shem wept?

לעך שארי וזחו כמלח אים

My Remnant shall swallow thee and its pride is as dreadful salt.

Paragraph 241 Daniel 2.28a, 27b

ויתירח אב אוהלי-דהם

And the father of the Tents-of-Astonishment shall be made yellow.

רצן דך ובן אך לם לעד והון

The Favour of the Oppressed and the Son surely are for them for a witness and a sufficiency.

יזר אל גאי-משבה לא יתיאם "רב"

G-d loathes the proud ones of apostasy. He shall not set the mark "Greatness" upon them;

אך לם להי וחה לני

Surely for them belongs a lament and a community is for wailing.

לך יניר זג ני

For thee a cheap wine shall break up wailing.

מטר-חן יפש אן

The Rain-of-Grace shall scatter about strength;

ימי-כח-אל לאש

the Oceans-of-Strength of EL are for Man.

אכלם יד הזר רם-או

The Instrument fed them; haughtiness of Lust was made loathsome.

אכלם מדק לאי-נד

He has fed them from the Veil at the region of the *harvest* heap.

Paragraph 242 Daniel 2.27a, 26, 25b

הנע הרשפות יזח יד אם-לח

Shake thou the Firebolts! Let Him thrust away the Hand of Mother Nature.

ינת עדו הללה כך יתיאה

The oppression of his Witness she boasted of thus she shall be marked.

רץ אש טל בהם שי-דל

A fragment of fire is dew; the Gift of the Poor One is silent.

The Linear Bible Code

אין דל רם-או

There is no poor of the haughtiness of Lust;

אך לם הנע עדו

surely for them His Witness was made to shake.

הי אכלם לאר שפי-דדו

O the wailing! He consumed them at the Light of the mouth of His Beloved.

הי די אתו לגי-נבן

O the wailing! Sufficient is His Sign toward the valleys of Nebon.

מר בג תח כשה ידה לרם אנך

O the bitterness of the food of Toah. Her hand grasped to establish thy sorrow.

ואכלם מד קל אין דל לענה

And he fed them a fleeting measure *till* there was not a thin one *left* of the affliction.

Paragraph 243 Daniel 2.25b, 24

הלהב תה בכו

The flame roared! They wept!

יראני דא אוחא אכלם לאר

This is the Jackal who feared Me. I shall consume them at the Light.

שפו אכל ממד-קין

They ground food from the Measure of Cain.

לעה דב והתלא לב בימי-כח

The Bear swallowed her and he caused courage to hang in the Days-of-Strength

לה לרם אנך

for her to raise up thy sorrow;

ולזא לב בימי-כח להד

And for this courage was in the Days-of-Strength for the joyous shout.

בוהל אכלם ינם ידך

The Disturber consumed them; he made lazy thy hand;

וירא לעל אי נד הנד לב לב קלך

but he feared for against the coast of the heap *of ruins* was the heap of the Will of Thy Voice.

Paragraph 244 Daniel 2.23, 22, 21b

אנת עד והאכלם תלם-ידך נם אן
Thou encountered opportunely the Witness and did he feed them the furrow of thy hand? Sorrow slumbered.

יעב יד ינת עד והנעך
The Instrument shall be hidden; thou oppressed the Witness and he caused thee to shake;

וילח בהי
and thou howled at the lamentation.

אתר ובגו אתם כח יד
I shall reconnoiter and into the middle I shall complete the strength of the Hand.

הן אח בשמו אדוה
Lo, a brother with his reputation I shall sicken.

מי תהב אהל-אכל ארש המעא ירהן
Whosoever thou shalt give the food storage tent I shall make poor the seed of their irrigation.

ואך ושח בהם עדי אתר
But surely so the Lowly One is tongue-tied; My Witness I shall unbind.

תסם אתקי-מעא לגאוה
Let thou render *him* the galleries of seed for majesty.

הניב יעדיל אעדנם
The fruit he makes equitable; I shall treat them luxuriously.

Paragraph 245 Daniel 2.21a, 20, 19b

וני
And A Lamentation
מי כח לא תם-כח בהי
Who is strong? There is no perfection of strength within a lamentation.

ני כלם מיקהם זו אין דע
A lamentation has wounded their obedience;

וני כלמה דעהמ
And a lamentation has wounded their knowledge

זו אין דע
against which there is no knowledge.

אן שהם אוה
Sorrow is the Gem of Lust.

ואי הה לי דאת רוב
But where alas to Me is the Eagle of Greatness?

The Linear Bible Code

גו אתם כח יד אמל עד-עו

The back of you is the strength of the Hand. He weakened perpetual Ruin.

אמל ען מכר במאה

The Spring *water* from the pasture he weakened with a hundred *others*.

לא המש אוה לרם או

He was never made to feel the desire to exalt Desire.

לי אנד הנע אי-משה לאלך רב

For Myself I grieve; the Region of Moses was shaken for thy G-d is Greatness.

לי אן דן יד איל

For Myself the Strength of Judgment is the Hand of the Ram.

גה זרא יליל יד או

This is a loathsome thing: a hand causing Desire to be twisted!

זח בלי אן דלני

Pride is without strength; it weakens Me.

Paragraph 246 Daniel 2.19a, 18b

דא לב בימי-כח ראש מעיהו

This is Courage: in the Days-of-Power is the head of his seed;

רב חולי-אן דנו

a multitude of the sands of strength is His Judgment.

דבה יאל ידה נד הזר

He moved deliberately; He was determined. He cast at the heap of the stranger.

לע אים שה לא מד קן

The Terrible One swallowed up a sheep. There is no measure of the nest.

Paragraph 247 Daniel 2.18a, 17, 16b

מא עבם לני מחר ועד

How he beclouded them for wailing is tomorrow and future.

והא תלמי-הור בחה ירזעו

And lo, the terraces of the Mountain of Bacah they have sown;

לאשים הין נחלו

For I shall set a Hin-Measure his inheritance.

לזא התיבל לאי נד

For this he himself bore to the coast the *harvest* heap.

ני "דא אכל" מלה יוחה "לארש פוה"

O the wailing! "This is the food supply" spoke Jochan, "to desire here."

לן תנין מזיד אכל מן

The Dragon spend the night; causing to act proud he ate a portion.

Paragraph 248 Daniel 2.16a, 15b

מה עב * לא ינד

What is a cloud? It moves not to and fro!

ולא ינד לך

And it does not move to and fro for thee.

וירא עד והאת למני

And *the Dragon* feared continually; and the Sign is toward Meni.

דא אכלם מד קן

This I shall feed them a measure of the Nest.

מה פצחה מא תדה

What has burst forth of it? What is thanksgiving?

מלע אכל מיד

Swallowing down food from a hand.

אטיל שכו ירא לרם או

I shall cause his covert to be cast out. Fear thou to exalt appetite.

Paragraph 249 Daniel 2.15a, 14, 13b

הנע לב בי

The Will within Me wandered.

מי כח להטל קל קפני

Who is strong to envelop frivolity? It surrounds Me.

דא כלמי דא יחבט ברך

This *frivolity* wound thou! This *frivolity* let it be beaten out *upon* the knee.

וירא למעט

And fear thou for the few.

ואטע ביתה לא ינד ניד-אב

And I wandered toward the Temple. The Solace of the Father never wanders away.

הלט קת הליהו

Keith wrapped tightly his wreath.

רב חול אי נדו עבונו

O the abundance of the sand of the coast; it heaped up; they concealed Us.

לט קת מאי-מי-כחו

Keith wrapped tightly the hundreds of the waters of his strength.

The Linear Bible Code

Paragraph 250 Daniel 2.13a, 12, 11c

תקפן את דו לב בי
Let thou strike them off a dual heart within Me.

מי כח לכלה גב
Who is strong for the annihilation of the Bear?

הל רם או אי גש
Was the haughtiness of Lust of the Coast *but* a clod *of earth?*

פץ קו סנב
Break thou the measuring –line of Seneb!

אכלם הנד לב קלך יהו
Feed thou them the heap of the heart of thy frivolity! Let them happen.

Paragraph 251 Daniel 2.11b

תיאאר שב מענו
Tae-er turned away from the poor.

הר-דם ידן יה לא נהל
The Mountain of Blood Y-H shall judge. *Tae'er* guided not to a watering-station;

אכל מם דקה
He fed *the poor* a blemished *animal which was* emaciated.

נוח יד יתיא
O the consolation of the hand! It shall make a mark.

אל נרח או הר
We cannot smell the Desirable Thing of the Mountain.

יקיל אש הכל מידא תלם
Every man causes dishonour becaue he thrusts away the furrow.

Paragraph 252 Daniel 2.11a, 10b

וידשך ופש או
But he shall tread upon thee and the sin of Lust;

מטר חל כל
the profanes of all rained down.

לא שאל הנדך "הלמטי לשוב רך למלך"
Thy heap never asked: "Is my staff *of bread* to return a delicacy to the King?"

ידל בקלך היוח הללך ויאכלם תלם
It is made low by Thy Voice and he shall feed them of the furrow.

ידא תשב ילע שנא יתיא אל
He shall thrust away the sojourner. He swallows up the hater *who* causes G-d pain.

The Linear Bible Code

Paragraph 253 Daniel 2.10a, 9b

ני רם או אכלם מד קא

Wailing is the haughtiness of Lust. It fed them a measure of vomit.

ידשך וונע יננו

It shall tread upon thee but the one staggering they shall endure.

תהתה רשף ידע דן אויל

The Firebolt laid waste. Judgment understood the foolish *man*

ורמא אמלח נהל אנת שיא

and it permitted I should salt the watering-hole. Thou art loftiness.

נדע יד-דעים דקר מאם לנו

The Hand of Knowledgeable Things is known; it pierced the blemish for Us.

תן מזה התיחש והבדך הלם

The Jackal from here made himself to genealogy and he separated thee hither.

וונך תדא יה הד

And Smiter, thou art thrusting away Y-H of the Shout.

חי נן עד והתא לאם לחנה

The Living One increased the Witness and the Chamber for a mother for her favour.

Paragraph 254 Daniel 2.9a, 8, 7b

ידא תל מין מאד זא ידנו

He thrust away the Tel-City of an abundant species. Here they shall be judged.

תיז חי דל בקל

The Living One has shortened thinness by an utterance.

כני נב זנות נא אן דע

Smite thou the fruit of fornication of Thebes. Sorrow is knowledge.

ידה נא עדי

Thebes cast at My Witness.

מאו ביצי-נמר אכלסה

The eggs of a leopard are more than Lust. I shall wound her.

נעה וחהן הרשפו יה

Neah and Chaan inflamed Y-H.

Paragraph 255 Daniel 2.7a, 6, 5b

דב על רמאי-אם-לח

The Bear is alongside of the bowmen of Mother Nature.

The Linear Bible Code

אך לם ניר מאותו
Surely for them is the Lamp from His Token.

נין תו נעי-נוח הה רשפו אם-לח
The posterity of the Mark is the wandering ones of Noah. Ah, they inflamed Mother Nature.

נהלי מדקן
My watering-holes are compared to thinness.

מנו לבק תאי-גש רק
They split *the ground* to empty the cavities of the ground altogether.

יוהב זבן ונן חם נוח
The Giver made them flow; the Integrity of Noah endures,

הת "הרשפו אם-לח
He shouted: "They inflamed Mother Nature. They made Us prominent on account of My Dignity.

נהונו משתי ילוננו כיתב"
May he lodge with Us as he becomes prominent."

ונוד בעת תני-מדה
So is the wandering in Time of the distributors of Tribute.

Paragraph 256 Daniel 2.5a, 4b

הרשפו אם-לח
They inflamed Mother nature;

יננו עד והתא
they increased the Witness and the Chamber.

האד לן זא ינם
A Firebrand lodged for the night; here he shall slumber.

אתלם איד
I shall break in pieces the Calamity.

שכל רם-או אך לם הנע או חן ארשף
The haughtiness of Lust make childless; surely for them Lust caused Grace to show grief. I am inflamed.

Paragraph 257 Daniel 2.4a, 3b

וכיד בעל אמל חרם אי יחן
And as the hand of Baal I shall cut off the devoted thing of the coast; it shall become loathsome.

ימל על אכל מור מאי
The Witness shall speak against the <u>bitter</u> food <u>from</u> <u>the</u> <u>coast</u>.

וכל מלמיד שכהו רב דיו
<u>And</u> every thing is teaching his Pavilion! He magnified its sufficiency.

The Linear Bible Code

מולח התא תעד לי "חור מעפתו"

The one seasoning the Chamber thou shalt testify to Me: "The Pit is more than its darkness."

Paragraph 258 Daniel 2.3a, 2b

יתמלח מולח כלמה מהל רם-אי וכלמה

The Witness shall be salted. Salting reproach he weakened the haughtiness of the region and reproach.

ינפלו דמעיו ואביו

His tears shall fall and his reed.

ויתמלח כל מלד

And he shall cause himself to salt each who was made to beget.

יגה למי-דשכל ומי-פשרך-מל ומי-פשאל ומי-משר

He grieved for the waters-of-Dashcol; and the waters-of-PeshecMol and the waters-of-PeshEL and the waters of Mesher.

Paragraph 259 Daniel 2.2a, 1; 1.21

חל-ארק לך

Fortress Earth belongs to Thee;

למה רם איו

For them is the highness of His Region.

וילע הדדנו תנ-שו וחור מעפת

And Our Beloved shall swallow up the Jackal of Emptiness and the Cave of Gloom.

תו תו-מלח רצן דך

The Mark is the Mark-of-Salt the Favour of the Oppressed.

בן-מלח רצן דך

The Son-of-Salt is the Favour of the Oppressed.

בן תו-כל מל הרשע

The Son is the Mark-of-All; he cut off the Wicked One.

מי תשת נשב וכלם השר

Whomsoever Thou appointed has returned; the Prince comprehended them.

וכלחח אתן שד על אי נד יהיו

And as he expanded I shall set Ruin upon the coast of the heap. They shall come to pass.

Paragraph 260 Daniel 1.20b

ותו-כל מלך בר שאם יפש

And the Mark-of-All is the Pure King; he crashed them into ruins. He shall spring about *as a calf*.

אה מים טרח הלך לעתו

Ah, above the Sea of Burden he traveled through Time itself.

די רש עם אצם יוכלם

Because of the poor of the people he is strong; he empowers them.

המה משק בר שאה ניב תם

They are a pure acquisition. He gazed at the fruit of perfection;

כח רב דלך

great of strength is Thy Poor One.

Paragraph 261 Daniel 1.20a, 19, 18b

וכלמה ינפל ודם עי והי רז עול

And reproach he shall cast down and the blood of ruin and wailing *which is* the secret of injustice.

אשימה

I shall direct it.

ינן חל אי נדך

The Fortress of the region of thy *harvest* heap shall increase.

מלכם אצם נאלו כלם המת אר בדיו רצן דך בני

Kings of Strength have acted foolishly, every one of them; they murdered the Light with its sufficiency the Favour of the Oppressed, My Son.

נפלם יסיר סהר-שם איבי

He cast them down; he shall chasten the Tower-of-Shem My Enemy.

ומאי בהל כל

And from the coast all hastened.

Paragraph 262 Daniel 1.18a, 17b

מהר מאר שא מים יה

Hasten thou O Luminary! O Ravage at the Day of Y-H.

תצקם לו תו-מלח ונוזח לך

Thou shalt melt them! For Him the Mark is Salt and the Remover is against thee.

בני-בהלא ינדו

The sons of Behala shall retreat.

המך חור פסל

O Noble One cause the removal of the Idol!

כבל כשה וערם מיה

As is Bel, as is a sheep, so he reckoned them because of Y-H.

Paragraph 263 Daniel 1.17a, 16, 15b

לא המהל נתן מתע בראה

The Dragon caused not to weaken Err by vision;

לא המיד ליה

he caused not to measure for YAH.

ומי נער זמה לנתן ומהי

And who is the youth of the Plan against the Dragon even above wailing?

תשמני

Thou shalt make Me fat!

יום גב תפתא אש נר צלמה

O Day of the Locust! Let thou make wide *the mouth* the fire of the lamp of her Image.

יה יוכל מה גב תפתא

YAH is the Enabler. How O Locust thou makest wide *the mouth*!

מי לכאה מי דלי

Who is to be disheartened *by it?* Who is My Thin One?

הלך נמר שבי אי רב ובו טמה יאר

A leopard of the captivity of the Great Coast journeyed; and with him the unclean one of the Nile.

Paragraph 264 Daniel 1.15a, 14, 13b

מה אר נהר שעם

How the Light overflows he who is a people;

ימית צקם והרשע מימי-מס ני

it shall put to death the Idols and the wicked at the days of Despairing of Wailing.

והזה רב דל מהל עם שיו כיד

And the multitude of the Thin One raved; he pruned the people of his sheep the likes of a hand.

בע מעה שעה ארת רש אך וכלמה

A seed he enlarged; it regarded the Light of the Poor One surely and Reproach.

The Linear Bible Code

גב תפתא מי לכאה מי דל יה

O Locust, let thou make wide *thy mouth!* Who is to be disheartened *by it?* Who is the Thin One of Y-H?

הארמו וני ארמך ינפלו ארי

Shall I raise him up or wailing? I shall raise thee up they who cast down My Light!

Paragraph 265 Daniel 1.13a, 12, 11, 10b

והתשנו מים והלך אן

But they have disguised themselves from the Sea and Strength journeyed.

ומי ער זה נם ונל ונתי והרשע

And who is this adversary? Nem and Nel and Natai and the Wicked One;

מימי-כיד-בעתא אנס נהי רז עול

At the days of the War-of-Terror I shall constrain lamentation, *which is* the secret of injustice.

אשימה

I shall direct it.

ינן חל אי נד לעם

The Fortress of the Region of the heap shall increase for a people.

יסיר סהר-שה

He shall chastise the Tower-of-the-Sheep.

נם רש ארץ למה לאל אין דר מאיו

The poor of the earth is drowsy; why? For God there is no pearl from His Region.

כלם לי שארת אמת בי

All of them belong to Me; the Remnant of Faithfulness is with Me.

Paragraph 266 Daniel 1.10b

חום כל יגך

Every darkened one causes thee to shine *by comparison.*

רש אמי-דלי הנמם

The poverty of the mothers of My Door caused them to be drowsy.

יפע זמח כינף תא הארי

A Plan shines out because the chamber of My Light he brandished.

המל רא אם כיתשם תאום כל

He caused to be cut off the poverty of the mother as each twin is made firm.

כא מת אה נמר שאך
Here is man alas the leopard of thy ravage.

Paragraph 267 Daniel 1.10a, 9b

למה ינד את אי
Why does it roam the region?

נא ארי לאי נד לם
Now is My Light toward the region of the heap for them.

יסיר סהר-שר מאיו
He causes to chasten the Tower-of-the-Prince from his region.

מיסיר סהר-שי נפל מים חר לוד
Because he causes to chasten the Tower-of-the-Gift he casts down from the Sea the free born of Lod.

סח לל אי נד תא
He complained; he twisted the Coast of the heap of the Chamber.

Paragraph 268 Daniel 1.9a, 8, 7b

מי הלא הנתי ולא גתי
Who removed afar off My Treasures but not My winepress?

לא רשא מיסיר סהר-שמש קביו
He permitted *it* not because he causes to chasten the Tower-of-the-Sun, its Kabim.

ויתשם ני יבו כלם
But wailing established itself. All of them cried shrilly:

"הגב תף"
"He caused the Timbrel to be pierced!"

בלא גתי לאר שא
He troubled My winepress at the Flame of Ravage.

ובל לעל אין דם שיו ובן דב עו
And Bel is against the Height *for* there is no blood of his sheep *anymore* nor the son of the Bear of Ruin.

Paragraph 269 Daniel 1.7a

הי רז עלו
O the lamentation! The Secret is upon him.

כשי-מלא שים לו
Thrones of fullness he established for himself;

כר דשה ינן חלו

A pasture he threshed it; he increased his Fortress.

רצא שט-לב לאי נדל משי ותו משם

He is made low on account of the Gift even the Mark by name.

יסיר סהר-שמה לם שיו

He causes the chastening of the Tower-of-Shemah for them His Sheep.

Paragraph 270 Daniel 1.6, 5, 4c

הי רז עול אשימה

Lamentation is the secret of injustice; I shall devastate it.

ינן חל אי נד הדו

The Fortress of the region of the heap increases. Give you a *joyous* shout!

היין במם הב יה יוכל

The wine of the hills give thou! Y-H is the Enabler.

מה ינפלו דמעים תצקם

How the juices flow down; Thou poured them out.

ושולש מין שם לדגלו

And the one dividing into three a species of Shem is to set up his banner.

ויתשם ני ים

And the wailing of the Sea establishes itself.

וכלמה גב תף מום

And reproach is a ditch; the timbrel is a blemish.

ויבם וירב דך

Oppression is made high and it is magnified.

למה מהלן מיום יד

Why? He weakened them at the Day of Power;

שכן ושל ורפס מד

He dwelt and He plundered and He trod the garment;

מללו כלם

all of them languished.

Paragraph 271 Daniel 1.4b

הלך יה בד מעל

Y-H journeyed; He separated the unfaithful.

מה בחך רש או-עדם

What is in the palate of the Poor One? The Desire of the Eternities.

יניב מות עדי עדי

Death bears fruit as far as My Witness;

The Linear Bible Code

והמך חלך בם

And it brought low thy Fortress among them.

Paragraph 272 Daniel 1.4a, 3, 2c

יליך שם והארם יבו

Shem howled at thee and the Lights cried shrilly;

טומו אמלכם הבני ארש אמי-דלי

they are ritually stained. I shall make My Sons Kings the desire of the mothers of My thin ones.

מים תרף הנם והכולם העָר זמו

From the Sea is the Idol of Hennom and shall the one shaming the naked one consider it?

לא רשי ינב מאי בהל ויסיר סבר-זן

Not My Poor One, he shall bear fruit. From the Isle he hastened and he corrects a certain hope.

פש אלך למהר מאיו ויהל ארץ אתי

The Weak One of thy G-d is to hasten from his Isle and he shall boast of his land together with Me.

Paragraph 273 Daniel 1.2b

באי בהם ילך התאו

At the coast the Beast paces his chamber.

ויהל אתי ענש צרא מאיבי ומיה

The Pure One shall boast with Me. He fined the Adversary on account of My enemy and on account of Y-H.

לא התיביל כת צקם

He was not lead away; he crushed the constraints.

והדו היכלם מיקיו

And give you a *joyous* shout O Palaces of His Obedient One!

הי תאו די בי נד אנתי

The lamentation of his Chamber is enough; with Me is the heap of My Treasures.

Paragraph 274 Daniel 1.2a, 1

והי לערצי ומל שורי-לבבך למרץ אן דך ובן אב

And a lamentation is for My Terrible Thing and it cut off the walls of thy heart to make sick the strength of the oppressed and the Son of the Father.

הדו היכלם מיקיו

Give you a *joyous* shout O Palaces of His Obedient One!

The Linear Bible Code

הי תו-כלם לשולש תן

A lamentation of the Mark-of-All-of-Them is for the dividing into three the Jackal.

שב

Repent thou!

The NOTES

Paragraph 1

Here at the beginning of the 'Book of Wailing' the first sentence sets the tone of the subject matter: **"Wailing from Y-H!"** Who is the 'Mark'? The Hebrew word תו is highly significant. William Gesenius wrote in part: "…a sign in the form of a cross branded on the thigh or neck of horses and camels…" Here lies the significance: a sign of a cross. This man is special and is pivotal in the 'Book of Wailing'. The Name 'HaShem' is familiar with Jews as it is the title spoken when reading out loud Scripture which contains the Name of G-d. In a few places in the Scriptures this Name is presented in the absolute form of G-d's Name; see Leviticus 24.11 which has the definate article attached to 'Shem'. The fact that the Back Text of Daniel contains in the first paragraph this Title is significant. The Names of G-d are many and varied. Here in Paragraph 1 we read two of them; 'Y-H' and 'HaShem'. 'Y-H' is also found in the Scriptures in a few places. The reader is directed to Isaiah 12.2 for an excellent example. כי עזי וזמרת יה יהוה.

The identification of 'chamber' in this paragraph may at first seem difficult. I believe from other references in the 'Book of Wailing' that it refers to the Sanctuary on Mount Zion; the Temple or the Holy of Holies and perhaps at times the rooms where the priests put off their secular clothing and put on the holy garments of the priesthood.

The phrase חון תו **'the Mark loathes'** is fully spelled out: חונן תו.

This is an example of what the reader will find later in the Back Text. In order to present the message in the Back Text short-cuts were built into the Text. The reader must not expect to find perfectly spelled words in every case. The scholar surely is aware that the Forward Text has many examples spread out over the Hebrew Scriptures of words truncated whether for expediency or because of scribal error. But in the Back Text truncated words were part of the planned linear code.

The reference to 'city-mound' come from the Hebrew word תל which denotes either the place of a ruined city or a living city built on a mound or near one. Seth is an important figure in myth and legend.

Paragraph 2

The Forward Text of the Hebrew Scriptures contain well attested texts in error due to scribal mistakes. The use of the Scriptures of the Dead Sea Scrolls has assisted in the recovery of some of these mistakes. It is highly likely that the Forward Text of Daniel also has errors due to scribes. The Forward and Back Texts of Daniel are inextricably tied into each other. In the present parsing and translation of the Back Text I have paid attention to the notes in the Biblia Hebraica Stuttgartensia. In many cases the Witnesses call for emendations to the Masoretic Text.

When they are figured into the parsing of the Back Text some wonderful things are observed. In Paragraph 2 our first example is found. In Daniel 12.10 where it reads in the Masoretic Text ויצרפו the scholar is struck by the fact that this word is not in the Hithpael. The two verbs immediately before it are in the Hithpael. Therefore it is most likely a fact that this verb should follow as a Hithpael verb too. The BHS (Biblia Hebraica Stuttgartensia) shows us in the footnote for this word that the Targum secundum reads in the Hithpael. Therefore I have inserted the 'tav' ת into the MT. In parsing the Back Text this letter renders the word פרציו the more correct form of the plural פרצתיו , 'his violent ones'. This exercise shows how the Back Text help in identifying corruptions in the Forward Text.   This event is duplicated throughout the Back Text. But not all suggested readings for the ForwardText are accepted into this Back Text. There are also occasions when a whole word or words are suggested for inclusion in the Forward Text. Some of these are accepted here in the Back Text because the context of the Back Text is enriched. The reader is directed to 'Paragraph 259' for an excellent example.

Paragraph 3

In translating not all Hebrew words have the same value. One of note is   דע , I have rendered it 'opinion' in some cases and in others 'knowledge'. In the first case 'opinion' is subject to err; knowledge on the other hand is generally accepted as being fact and not opinion. The first answers to the example in 'Paragraph 29' thusly; "His opinion erred and he shamed himself." The second is exemplified in 'Paragraph 162 "I shall cast out the Gift of Knowledge".

Paragraph 4

The spelling of the 'Moon' in the Back Text parallels the Forward Text in most instances. The Back Text however adds an aleph א to the end of the word in a number of references ('Paragraph 9').   This adds a touch of the Aramaic to the word. The verb 'I shall roar at them' has the feminine plural suffix. The verb 'He maketh them err' is masculine plural. This is followed with a future plural verb masculine 'they shall be hindred'. This mix might be conveying more than what is first noticed. If we replace the feminine with 'women' and the masculine with 'men' the third future verb mixes them properly. This was done in 'Paragraph 162'. The verb **'they shall be hindered'** ינאו has as its root נוא   .

Paragraph 5

The mention of a 'burial cave' with 'treasure' in it is significant. The burying of items in caves is well established in text and actual fact. It is significant that here in the BT (Back Text) the reference is made so early in the Book. The Hebrew word is derived for a modern Hebrew dictionary כוך: Megiddo p.324a.   'Paragraph 268' refers again to the trasures of God.   Another cave is mentioned in 'Paragraph 259' 'the Cave of Gloom'.   The verb **'swallowing up'**, לוע is used extensively in the BT.   Significantly the verb   בלע   a synonym is used extensively in the secular DS Scrolls.

Paragraph 6-8

These are of one subject. The identity of G-d's 'distressed one' is intriguing. Is he a prince or messiah? The fact that he 'learned the perfection of knowledge' points to a special godfearing man.

Paragraph 9

Who are the people who resemble the Moon? Because this 'Book of Wailing' is reserved for the End Time may they be the people of the Quran?   The reference to the 'falcon of the Nile' is straightforward.

Paragraph 10

The verb imperative **'cast up'** is derived from the root   סלל . The word הזך   is used as an adjective in this sentence 'the cold *pure* mountain'.

The sentence 'and this he proved false' takes as its core the modern Hebrew word 'prove false' זימם   : Megiddo p.246a. This is the first reference to the ubiquitous 'Pure One' of the 'Book of Wailing'.   His identity will become evident through a series of repetitions and amplifications.

Paragraph 11

The translation of   טלם   is taken from the unused root in the Hebrew Scriptures **'to do wrong'** to someone. Oddly enough a proper name 'Telem' is discovered in Joshua 15.24 which William Gesenius translates 'oppression' p.322a.

Paragraphs 12-13

The verb rendered **'he caused pain'** spelled in the BT   התיה   is from the root   תוה . The word **'he shall roar'** is taken from the root   המם .

Paragraph 14

The consonants   איל   when voweled may be rendered 'ram' 'pilaster' 'leader' 'chief' and 'terebinth', etc. I have used the noun 'help' found on page 33b of the BDB Hebrew and English Lexicon.   The truncated word   או   is short for   אוה . The phrase **'they boasted'** הלו   is thus due to the needs of the Back Text. The scholar knows that the <u>lamed</u> is to be doubled thusly הללו . The last sentence of this paragraph conveys a powerful strength brought to bear upon Emptiness. Emptiness is the Nemesis of **'Perfect Desire'** אוה תם brought by God; see 'Paragraph 89'. Emptiness שו , is a dominion itself, 'Paragraph 97' and it was in the Garden as an abomination set up by the 'friend of His sheep'; see 'Paragraph 17'.

Paragraph 15
No notes.

Paragraph 16
Here we have a melding of 'Mark' and 'Pure One'; they are the same individual. He rises above the works of the Adversary 'with difficulty'. The translation of וראשית in this paragraph follows the new arrangement suggested in the BHS. Therein the Syriac has the reading spelled in Hebrew thusly: ושארית ; **'The eye of my daughter's <u>head</u> was drowsy'.** In two places I have added a ' ' .' The placement allows the translation of '<u>his</u> father'. The Forward Text now has the prefix 'he' and the root 'came'. In both directions (FT and BT) coherent readings are made. Since the BT demands this addition then one may say that the Forward Text at one time read the imperfect.

Paragraph 17
The word 'seed' is read only in part in the BT because of the FT. I have added the needed third consonant ' מעה .' In the Forward Text this addition may either be attached to the end of the Hithpael verb or if the beginning of העמו , then may it read **'his people'**? If either possibilities are rejected finally then the imperfect spelling of 'seed' in the Back Text was planned and even in this truncated spelling its meaning is discerned.   The spelling in the BT for 'Emptiness' is conjecture on my part. The only known spelling in the FT is feminine thusly: בוקה . My conjecture is a masculine word with the second root silent supplied here with a 'vav': בַוְק .

Paragraphs 18-19
The mention of 'My Only One' may refer back to 'His first born son'. The use of italics here is demanded by the exotic use of the pronouns 'him' and 'his'. Because the Hebrew word for 'people' is singular the pronoun is singular. In English the substitution 'them' is regular in English translations of the Forward Text.   All this is necessary to convey the sense of the Hebrew Text.   The mention of the 'Levite', no doubt to this translator, refers to the coming down from Heaven of the Messiah. In 'Paragraph 186' we read 'On what account did My Thin One, the Levite, descend? The pure banner's shaft was with him. I

wounded Bel; he caused a covering to be set in place. Alas, the bird of prey of the Pure One of Heart is at the Region of G-d's Mist.' It is my view that the 'Thin One' which in Hebrew is רק , as here and also דל , elsewhere as a synonym, is the same as the 'Pure One of Heart' and the 'Pure One' in 'Paragraph 17'. The 'Mark', the 'Thin One', 'Pure One' and the 'Only One' etc are referring to the same individual. We shall find at the end of the 'Book of Wailing' further clarification. The fact that he is a Levite is very significant. He then may be chosen to enter the Temple on the day of atonement! This role is a powerful one.

Paragraph 20

The verb 'they shone upon' truncated reads צהו which is from the root צהה . Again, 'they howled' bowing to the confines of the Back Text should have a second 'lamed' thusly: ילל .

Paragraph 21

The mention of the 'discharge' brings to mind the reference in 'Paragraph 2' where it reads: 'and the discharge of a daughter flowed'.

Paragraph 22

The 'Lishka' is a sacred room attached to a Temple Complex as in Ezekiel chapter 40. The truncated word for 'ruin' reads עו whereas the full spelling is עוה . 'the day of the fly' is of interest and the reader is encouraged to follow this word through the various references זבוב .

Paragraph 23

Often in the BT rhetorical questions are noted. This question 'Who is the Pure One?' appears many times. In the instance before us a type of answer is given 'to him belongs the Fruits of My Robe according as is his Name and his Opulence and he is set off.' The verb 'set off' קז is the shortened spelling of the Modern Hebrew word in the Megiddo dictionary page 598a קוזז . Although G-d bestows so much upon the Pure One still G-d is separate; He is <u>set off</u>. The 'altar shovels' are exactly that and they are used metaphorically for the Zaddekim צדיקים those who are ritually pure before G-d. Noah plays a key roll in G-d's Plan far beyond the first mission to pass through the Flood a righteous seed. The first reference to Noah is here in this paragraph.

Paragraph 24

The Biblia Hebraica Stuttgartensia footnote for the word in Daniel 11.31 משומם presents two variations. The first is to attach the article 'ה' thusly: המשומם. The second option is to remove the first letter of the word מ , and replace it with the definite article, השומם.

When the second option is carried through the Back Text is greatly benefited. The definite article supplies the last letter to the name 'Moses', 'Mosheh'. This gives spectacular information of the Law of Moses. The context of the Back Text supports this change. The verb translated 'dealt violently with' is to be read as Hophal.

Paragraph 25

No notes.

Paragraph 26

Here we have another reference to 'Gift'. In 'Paragraph 17' "The Pilgram-Feast is My Gift". But here in 'Paragraph 26' we have another gift; 'the Gift of Knowledge'. Because of more than one 'Gift' from G-d the translation of the BT does not speak of 'the' gift but of 'a' gift in any of a number of references.

Paragraph 27

The word translated as **'two'** is a modern word found in the Megiddo page 106a. I have discovered that the Back Text by and large can be translated with the words found in the Hebrew Scriptures whether they are Hebrew or Aramaic. But in a few instances I am gratified to find those unknown words to be found in Modern Hebrew. If one acknowledges that this Back Text was written with the knowledge that it would come forth in the Twenty First Century is it not then plausible that our vocabulary would be used when needed to write the text?

Paragraph 28

It is sometimes easy to discern a name when parsing the Back Text. In the case of 'Mebabel'. The nature of its Babylonishness stands out. Immediately before it is the word 'he said' מל in the truncated form; the full spelling is מלל . When looking for Hebrew names or names in other ages of the world difficulties arise. One difficulty with Hebrew names has to do with the fact they have meaning and they may easily be translated as verbals with prefices and suffices.

The BHS footnote puts forth the idea that three or four words beginning verse 26 of chapter 11 should be deleted. If we did that the BT would of course read differently. This loss affects the last part of verse 25 because the Back Text does not hew to the divisions in the Forward Text. Here is what that section would read without the clause in conjunction with the last part of verse 25 :

> **Declare you: The Mountain is among the sheep**
> **and among the lowly ones.**
> **They shall swallow up the shame of My Kinsfolk**
> **as the Tears of EL.**

I have of course decided not to delete this clause.

Several of the words in 'Paragraph 28' have ghost letters that would be supplied with a complete apparatus. Note 'lowly ones', שׁחם , with the full consonants, שׁחים ; and 'fortresses', חלם , with the full con-sonants חלים .

The interpretation of גנה is of two kinds in the Back Text. I have either rendered it 'garden' or 'orchard'. Both are acceptable and who is to say which is meant in each case?

Paragraph 29

In many places the word לוע appears. Its spelling is usually the masculine perfect לע . Two root words are spelled this way; the first, he swallowed up/down; and the second, he talked incoherently. The selection of one over another translation is usually determined by context. Here in this paragraph it is translated 'he spoke in-coherently' because the next clause reads 'they babbled'.

The word 'Issue' זוב , in a male means 'semen' in this paragraph. This procreative matrix contains the spiral Double-Helix. It is very remarkable therefore when the last line of this paragraph reads: 'A winding *staircase* resembles his issue.' To cement this interpretation we look to the line 'Oh the heat!' This word from the verb חמם , in Hoshea 7.7 may be interpreted 'lust'. Here we have in the boldest term the revelation of Watson/Crick about the genetic code. Here is a bit of irony; the Back Text is a simple code and within it is revealed the secret of life itself. 'Paragraph 54' gives this title to Y-H 'Father of Species'.

Paragraph 30

The translation of שׁע אל , as 'Delight of G-d' is easily derived from שׁעע in the Pilpel conjugation; see HELOT p.1044a. The noun plural form is rendered 'delight' 'pleasure' as in Proverbs 8.30 and Psalm 119.24 and Jeremiah 31.20. Because of the nature of the Back Text, the necessity at times to be on the look out for truncated forms of the words is a key to interpretation. I have determined that שׁע should be rendered 'delight'.

Paragraph 31

The translation 'Bill of Divorcement' is found in the word גט , which is not found in the vocabulary of the Hebrew Scriptures. In the Modern Hebrew this word means 'bill of divorcement', see Megiddo p.89a. Note that it figures nicely in the sentence. Divorce is not legal unless for adultery and in this sentence we read 'in the bed' in the 'divorcement of a people'. Nicely put!

The Linear Bible Code

Paragraph 32

This paragraph has interesting elements. First, we find the classic infinitive absolute of the verb פטשׁ . Second, the verb 'ejaculate' connected with 'His Own Seed'. The complimentary nature of the two is magnificent testimony to the homogenious nature of the BT. Time after time the parsing of the text of Daniel run backwards from its end to the beginning give whole thoughts worked out and the conveying of startling images.

Paragraph 33

Again the subject of 'seed' continues. Here we have an echoe of the mighty ones born to human women in Genesis 6. A people acted crafty as far as its seed and the result is the strong ones of G-d! The idea of being crafty in this process borders on breaking Law just as the 'sons of the El-h-m' did in have intercourse with the daughter of men. The verb translated here as 'crafty' also denotes 'knavish' behavior. The verb דחא is the Aramaic spelling of דחה . The translation which reads 'murmurers of' is the result of the participle of the Hiphel plural construct of the verb לון . The translation of 'his seed' is from the truncated word מעו which should be spelled here if in full text מעיו .

Paragraph 34

Again in this paragraph the subject of progeny continues! This time the "Pure One" who became "The Mark for G-d" "shall make himself a lineage". The word for 'lineage' is the used verb יחשׂ , which appears as a noun in one place, Nehemiah 7.5 'book of genealogy'. This root is translated consistently in the Back Text as 'doing genealogy'. In the instance before us the root is presented in the Hithpael, 'he shall make himself a lineage' or if one prefers 'he shall make himself a genealogy' which is the same in intent. The BHS contains a note on Daniel 11.18 for the words: לו בלתי . It reads that they are corrupt but no correction is suggested. These letters in the BT help in giving the reading:

> ותפר חית לב ולו תפר חני
> The translation of this section reads:
> **"and it seweth together a Community of Will**
> **"and in regards to it it seweth together My Grace."**

The words and letters underlined are the so called 'corrupt' words in the
Forward Text. I would argue for a purpose behind their being 'corrupt'.
The reason is revealed in the Back Text. In order for the simple code of
the BT to work the FT must at times read incorrectly!!! If any
corrections were to be introduced in the FT of Daniel 11.18 as shown
above the BT would not read correctly.

Paragraph 35

This paragraph uses the unused root   בצץ , here rendered יבצה and
translated 'he will make soft'.

Paragraph 36

The term **'Booth'** is interpreted here to be a figure of Y-H's abode in the
Heavens because of its expansiveness. Again 'seed' takes center stage.
The 'Mark' and 'Witness' are synonymous because of the parallel lines.
It is interesting in the extreme that this text places G-d's 'Witness', His
'Mark', with rebellion.

Paragraph 37

The word translated as **'Pavilion'** is the same as 'Booth' in 'Paragraph
36'. The spelling שך is a phoneme of the usual spelling סך . I consider
both to be speaking of the same place. Note again the continuation of
the 'seed' talk. The translation of   גן as 'Orchard' here is because I
believe the sentence is referring to illicit worship which was more a part
of the idea of 'orchard' than our concept today of a 'garden'. It is
worthy of note that 'Nebo' is a god as well as several localities.

Paragraph 38

'Species of renown' again is center stage. G-d reserves to Himself a
remnant; that much is found in the Forward Text. Here in the Back
Text this concept is also found and here in these paragraphs 'seed'
'lineage' and 'species' are all of the same cloth. There is an additional
meaning to the word 'seed' presented. I believe the 'Pure One' is likened
to 'a seed'. The word 'Thicket' עב may be a synonym for 'Booth' and
'Pavilion'.

Paragraph 39

Bitterness is a subject of the Back Text. In 'Paragraph 163' it says
"And Babylon is the bitterness of thy hand". In 'Paragraph 161' is
reads "Now are the words above the bitter things of the region." The
BHS footnote for the word   ירום would have it spelled ורם . This
gives the reading in the Back Text: "they rebelled against Us".

Paragraph 40

The word parsed אבו and translated **'his father'** is a defective spelling.
The missing 'yod' when written would be supplied by the addition of the

long HIREQ beneath the 'Bet'. Note the parallel in paragraph 124. The 'Garden' and the 'shamed ones stretched out' of paragraph 40 is juxtaposed with the 'Pasture of Sorrow' and the 'lion was made to stretch out'.

Paragraph 41

The word in the Forward Text יתגרו in the BHS reads יתגרה and this has the profound effect on the Back Text: "I <u>killed</u> Nebo".

Paragraph 42

The word parsed כמעם and rendered "so the bowels" should be spelled כמעתים in any other place except this encoded text. The same is applied to the translated word "bowels" earlier in the paragraph: מעתים for the defective מעים. I have inserted a 'vav' in the parsed Back Text to supply the perfect masculine plural of the verb 'they refused' מהו. Of course this being a defective spelling it is no stranger to the Forward Text. In Isaiah 37.30 this same type is found. The consonant 'vav' was supplied below the line for the word אכולו. Let this be the example for all other necessary 'corrections' in the Back Text. It is a fact that the Back Text is more compressed and as such so called 'defective' spellings are more common than they are in the Forward Text; however, they are not so common as to bring into suspect the integrity of the Back Text!

Paragraph 43

No notes.

Paragraph 44

In the BHS the word in 11.6 ומביאיה is modified by removing the second 'yod' thusly: ומביאה. Using this modified text the Back Text was changed also; instead of the word 'she' היא we read הא which I interpret here as in the interjection 'lo!'. The word in the Back Text חוך is the shortened form of חוה life and the suffix thine ך.

Paragraph 45

This paragraph ends with "His Living One is set apart" קז חיו. This verb קוז is modern in usage and is not found in the biblical vocabulary. I have wondered about this and have decided that since the unsealing was to take place in this modern world the writers knowing the future included some modern words into the Back Text out of necessity or otherwise.

Paragraph 46

The BHS offers in the footnotes the reordering of a portion of verse 4 of chapter 11. Hence the material segregated with c-c in the BHS is removed from the end of the verse and inserted immediately after 'b'.

Thus the student is made aware of the reordering of the letters at this point. The name 'Diblaim' is also found in the Forward Text Hosea 13 spelled there דבלים with the word 'daughter of' attached בת.

Paragraph 47

The BHS has several radical changes in the Forward Text of 11.2. However I have elected not to use any of them because leaving the MT alone fine readings are obtained in the Back Text.

Paragraph 48a

Again the BHS suggests some radical textual changes in the Forward Text that comprises this paragraph (verses 1b and 2a of chapter 11). I have used none of them on the grounds that the Back Text is enhanced. By removing the material suggested in the BHS the flow in the Back Text is impeded. Here then is a check on the integrity of the Masoretic Text. More often the Masoretic Text is proved correct by the reading of the Back Text. The few exception are of course exceptional if subtle. The two letters parsed עה is the conjectured imperative of the verb יעה 'he swept away'.

Paragraph 48b

The word in the Back Text parsed thusly דחאני and translated (Lust) 'pushed Me' is the Aramaic form of דחה.

Paragraph 49

Here the singular 'people' עם has the verbs singular 'he'. Therefore for clarity in English I have rendered these verbs plural 'they' following the one verb in plural 'they erred', תעו .

Paragraph 50

The reality of the Back Text is proof of the accuracy of the Masoretic Text. When parsing the Back Text in this paragraph the last sentence read thusly :

דמחשיאאריתלארמאיו

When I tried to parse the text I had one part that was confusion:

Here I was able to read:

After long deliberation I realized that one possible 'fix' was to replace three letters of the Masoretic Text with my speculative two letters. It so happened that the three letters in the MT of the Forward Text read 'man' in this context:

ויאמר אל תירא איש-חמדות

Which reads in English:

'and he said: "Fear thee not now man of preciousness".

I replaced איש with the Aramaic synonym בר . The meaning is the same but now the Back Text reads smoothly and very satisfyingly:

דם חרב ארית לֹא רם איו

"the blood of the sword of lionesses never exalted his coast".

This substitution is very rare on my part. In each case I have noted it in these Notes.

The use of the modern verb קז appeared first in paragraph 45 and noted there. It appears twice in the present paragraph with effect.

Paragraph 51

The name I discovered in the Back Text אשנאל is new to the Bible. Its meaning is derived from the verb root notated on page 80 of HELOT which is assumed to mean 'be hard' 'firm'. The name of two cities of Judah are constructed from this verb אשנה. The meaning of the new name I have rendered 'firm is EL', or 'firm is G-d'. Note the classic use of the double word דא\דא. The first instance is translated 'one' and the second 'another' after the reference in HELOT page 1086b for Daniel 5.6. The Aramaic usages in the Forward Text are found in the Back Text! See the Appendices for the listing of all the similarities.

Paragraph 52

The personal name 'Zael' is from the verb צוע 'he formed' and may be rendered her 'G-d formed'. The 'throat of Og' finds 'Og' in the Forward Text spelled עוג. Consult a bible dictionary. The BHS points out a possible addition to the MT די. I inserted it and it changed the Back Text wonderfully. The addition is rendered 'sufficiency' of fullness.

Paragraph 53

The translation of תא is 'chamber' or 'room'. Context must drive interpretation, therefore, I have rendered it 'threshingfloor' in the sentence

> **"O the ravage of thy threshingfloor! The fruit belongs to Me."**

I have rendered it so one other place, in paragraph 55. Another modern word appears in the text: וד rendered here 'twice'; see Megiddo p.106a. The verb root הות is the basis for the word יהת 'he shall say'.

Paragraph 54

Following the BHS I have inserted in 10.1 רש and the Back Text is filled out quite nicely. Whereas without it the Back Text might read

כלם לצאם "all of them he makes them filthy"

The insertion places כלם with the previous material and the new reading says "<u>Poverty</u> is to make them filthy"; רש לצאם ▪ The placement of כלם with תאבו סרפי כלם is very good construction complementing the plural verb: "They aboreth My Seraph, all of them" or as might be written "All of the aboreth My Seraph." The word ירש is to be read as Hophal; and נהום as Niphel. In all cases the verb לאך is translated "he sent a messenger". This verb is not used as such in the Hebrew Scriptures but is the underlying root for the noun מלאך ▪

Paragraph 55

In the sentence translated **"The product of the threshing room disquieted thee"** again renders תא in context as in paragraph 53: 'threshing room' or 'threshingfloor'. Again the Modern word וד is found and rendered 'double'; see paragraph 53.

Paragraph 56

The personal name **'Laeth'** was context driven. The construct form the פה pointed to a name. The word חלש is used here as an adjective. The verb חש read חוש ▪ The word כנא is the Aramaic spelling of כנה the verb meaning to 'betitle' one. I have used the British custom of 'knighting' for the rendering here 'was given a knighthood'. The 'poor one' was so given a title and the next line says it again 'a son was decked out' in honors. Here we see in the Back Text 'Parallelism' of thought found in the Psalms to effect. Many places in the Back Text 'Parallelism' is evident and is a sign to the translator that he is on firm ground in parsing the text. Almost parallel to the above 'was given a knighthood' is the excerpt from paragraph 63 which reads:

> **"A Seraph shall bedeck all of them a prince;**
> **"and every skirt he set…"**

Paragraph 57
No notes.
Paragraph 58
No notes.
Paragraph 59
The rendering of the consonants לק as a name and with the spelling 'Luke' is context driven in the first and speculative in the second case.

The placement of the definate article with the name thusly הלק also seems to bolster the interpretation as a name\place name as is seen in the Forward Text.

Paragraph 60
In this section of the Back Text the subject is shared with 'window' and 'windows'. The idea that it refers to the Celestial Window(s) of G-d is influenced by the Forward Text. Genesis 7.11 refers to the 'windows of heaven' opening up and although it is not the same word as found here in Daniel the context points to the same usage. I have added in italic *celestial* in all cases where I believe the Aramaic word כוה or its truncated form כו mean G-d's Window(s). In Daniel 6.11 is is used to refer to Daniel's windows of his room.

Paragraph 61
The proof of any new document is sometimes found in the place names or personal names found therein. The Back Text has offered these abundantly. Here in this section four places are mentioned if my parsing of the text is correct here: Regech, Janethom, Medebesh and Beldach. Names are often made up of compound words; some two, some three words. There are times also when the name is formed from one root. The Forward Text name Magbish in Ezra 2.30 spelled מגביש is very close to מידבש . The name **'Janethom'** becomes more familiar when divided into its two words 'Jane-Thom'. We are reminded of the Egyptian word 'Pithom' which means 'city/house of Thom' פתם or more pronounced in spelling פיתום. This paragraph also contains the name 'Meabesh' מיעבש. These and the other new names and places in the Back Text offer a great treasure for the philologist and scholar alike.

The Linear Bible Code

Paragraph 62

The dividing into three parts may refer to paragraph 1. It is there that
we first encounter the division. "The Mark divided into three a mother;
three wonders." Now in paragraph 62 we read **"Thou shalt divide into
three parts the Chamber for the measure of ruinations."** In the first the
doer is 'the Mark' and in the second it is 'the Poor One of his people'. I
suggest that these two men are one and the same. Another dividing into
three is found in paragraph 274 "The Mark-of-All-of-Them is for the
dividing into three the Jackal." The Linear Back Text Code for
Zechariah chapter 13 contains much information about the dividing of
the chamber into three parts.

> The Chamber of Noah is among you. The bosom is
> steadfast and the sole *of the foot.* Here is the Chamber
> of your breach; it shall be broken through. I shall draw
> out three parts of the Chamber and the Pure One shall
> consent. I shall mark its three parts and the tender
> cakes. Zechariah 13.9a-8b

The one liner "A Throne for a cup" is akin to the phrase "for a basket
he shall rule" Par. 183.

Paragraph 63

The words **'room of fruit'** התא ניב finds similarity with paragraphs 53
and 55.

Paragraph 64

In the BHS for 9.26 the note for the reference *g-g* reads dubious. The
Back Text when parsed by me relies heavily on these consonants
putting to rest the idea of dubiousness. The disputed consonants are
underlined below.

> די בגה ותום משת צרח נה which reads below:
> "sufficient is its food and completeness from Dignity.
> Eminency roared."

The word מוח and rendered 'marrow' is a fuller spelling of מח.

Paragraph 65

The word פט is translated **'stalemate'** from the modern Hebrew;
Megiddo, p.553a.

Paragraph 66

The word **'shame'** בושה is according to the BHS which replaces the 'yod' with the 'vav' in the word לשיב thusly לשוב in 9.25 but whereas the BHS suggests this change it also dropped the 'He' which I have retained. The word translated **'was made perpetual**; is from the root יחן and is in the conjugation Hophal הוחן. Seth, see Nag Hammadi Library.

Paragraph 67

The act of 'shaking a Vial' maybe an apocalyptic act. In Revelation the Greek word (φιαλη) in the King James Version is rendered 'vial'. The references there speak of 'pouring out the vials of the wrath of God'. In all places in that book 'vial' is a means of judgment.

Paragraph 68

Ursa Major is from the consonants עש with the understanding that it is defective. The missing 'yod' is easily written in such a case with a HIREQ beneath the ש and a PATHAH beneath the ע. In paragraphs 115 and 201 the full spelling is used and translated "Constellation of the Great Bear".

Paragraph 69

This section is of one round of thought: ark, vessel, ship's hold, watercourse/ island, sea of passage. Here then is inner proof of the truth of the Back Text. This Text is not fragments of disjointed sayings. The Text is thoughtful and well rounded. Themes are more often rounded out as in this paragraph. The BHS suggests that the word of 9.22 ויבן should be spelled with an additional letter thusly: ויבינני . I have elected to drop the suffix and keep the other suggestion. Once this is done the word in the Back Text reads correctly 'his fruit'. If the suffix is incorporated into the text the letters immediately before 'his fruits' is meaningless. This is how I weigh the suggestions found in the BHS.

Paragraph 70

In this section one singular phenomenon in the entire Back Text is encountered. Six consonants are read in the reverse! The Back Text is already read in reverse but I am speaking of doubling back and reading these six again in reverse. Here is the text. In the Back Text these six letters are found like this (underlined):

Reading the entire paragraph one sees that the text before and the text after this makes good sense; everything is accounted for as far as verbs, subjects and objects. Then we find this subsection above. I first parsed it this way:

רשא לאירבג שיא

which I translated tentatively "Lairabag permitted loftiness". This was wholly unacceptable. The name did not satisfy me yet I felt that the subject of the sentence was in these consonants. The verb was in syntax as well as the object. Then suddenly I saw that these six letters when read in reverse spelled 'Gabriel' in the Forward Text!

לאירבג
גבריאל

Thus I arrived at the subject of the sentence.

Paragraph 71
No notes.

Paragraph 72
I have elected to spell **'Fortress of Siin'** thusly because I disagree heartily with the translations of the Forward Text spelling it 'Sin'. I believe that two grounds stand behind my decision. The first is that the long HIREQ should be spelled double 'ii' and second the avoidance of thinking of the English word 'sin'.

Paragraph 73
The word translated 'mouth' פם is Aramaic and is restricted to the book of Daniel. Like a number of special words only found in Daniel they appear in the Back Text.

I have without authority added one consonant to 9.18 in order to clarify its text. In the Forward Text the word אזנך now has the definite article attached thusly: הַאָזנך . Now the Back Text makes sense:

זא הִי הלא הטה
"This is <u>wailing</u>; did he not turn aside?" The word הטה is the Hiphel of נטה.

Paragraph 74
The use of the ancient name of Jerusalem, Jebus, here in context are startling. The word כפא is the Aramaic form of the classic כפה. The

beginning of the second part of the paragraph "But a lament…" ends as it begins "…sorrow." In between however the lament is subdued which is the point of the text.

Paragraph 75

The word הרש is the imperative Hiphel.

Paragraph 76

The action of the 'king' is powerful in the extreme to create a place of punishments of iniquities. The question is not answered in my mind whether the 'king' is G-d. If so it must be rendered 'King'.

Paragraph 77

The 'Nine of Thebes' is intriguing. Does it refer to the past or the future? The juxtaposition of this with 'waters of Moses' is dynamic and for an Israelite significant. "The Discourse On The Eighth And Ninth" VI,6 of the Nag Hammadi Library speaks of nine levels of the heavens. The Ninth level is likened to true bliss. This library was found in Egypt!

Paragraph 78

The translation of the consonants לע from the root לוע is context driven. When they of the coast hear the lament of 'the fat one' they 'swallow' him up. When influenced by the 'discoursing Root of Desire' they 'spoke incoherently'. The choice is 'speaking incoherently' and 'swallowing up'.

Paragraph 79

The name 'Cuth' כת read כות. He is 'Sargon' king of Assyria in the Forward Text. Here 'Cuth' is establishing 'Belarus' which is the present name of a region in Russia. The 'Bear' is the traditional reference to Russia. Beginning then with this paragraph a lengthy text fills out the details of the story.

Paragraph 80

The 'Poor One' of G-d presents 'Desire' whereas the Adversary presents 'Lust'. These presents are of the same word אוה. In Paragraph 89 Desire is defined as 'perfect' אוה תם . In paragraph 63 we read:

> **"And proud Lydda is in the Ordinance;**
> **"She decorated the perfection of desire."**

Parallelism tells us that the 'Ordinance' is the same as 'perfection of desire'. The 'Ordinance' or צו according to the various lexicons has a wide range of meanings and nuances. But the use here in this context is one of holiness and perfection. The connection with the Law of G-d is evident.

The Linear Bible Code

Paragraph 81

No notes.

Paragraph 82

The translations of **'waters of Kachrah'** and the **'waters of Barak'** may be read **'waters of take thou fear'** and **'waters of lightning'**.

Paragraph 83

The word a head of cattle **'spoke'** spelled מל is the truncated form of מלל.

Paragraph 84

The numerical value of ס is sixty and ו six or sixty six. The choice of 'days' over 'years' was dictated by the length of a life. Sixty six years added to an adult male ruling in his prime far exceeds normal life expectancy. The defective spelling of 'they did wrong' עוו is from the root עוה and the correct spelling is עויו .

Paragraph 85

The spelling of **'the shining one'** here in the Back Text is truncated היל from the full הילל; see HELOT, p.237b.

Paragraph 86

No notes.

Paragraph 87

I filled out the sentence with italic words based on the definition of the verb in HELOT, p. 546. If לתח is from the word נתח which is used to 'spread out garment', then this is the authority for the italics. Note that the plural pronoun אתן is feminine. In a paraphrase the sentence might be expanded to read 'He spread you women out *as a garment.*'

Paragraph 88

The last two lines of this paragraph is an example of parallelism. The verbs are alike in their meaning. The first is מוק bearing the meaning 'mock' and 'deride'. It is used once in the Forward Text in Psalm 73.8. The second is the Hiphel of תול and spelled here יתיל conveying the meaning 'deride' 'trifle with' and 'mock'. The root תול is unused in the Tanach but is found in another spelling תלל ; see HELOT p. 1068b 'II'.

Paragraph 89

The question **'Who is the Pure One?'** is often repeated in the Back Text of Daniel. But here answers of sorts are given. The acts of the 'Pure One' is revealing. The Text is subtle at times and the reader must be patient for truly the answers come by degree.

Paragraph 90

The subject of '89' (Who is the Pure One?) continues. Again a question is asked: **"Who is the Poor One?"** Here we get another answer of a sort not unfamiliar to the readers of the Bible. Questions continue even into the next paragraph; indeed, the Back Text uses this technique very often all leading us to the last chapter when everything is revealed at once. Along the journey answers are given piecemeal. The Back Text reads easily here; there are no truncated words; no missing letters.

Paragraph 91

The question **"who is Havoc?"** continues the question/answer style of writing. "who squeezed Time?" The mention of the genealogies of the 'Mark of EL' is very interesting for they play a very important part in Israelite history. Note that synonyms are strewn everywhere in the text. They are done with purpose and they all seem to refer to just one individual whom I identify as 'the Mark'. The last two lines are excellent in balance on every level:

פנו וחך בא לו חכם צע
"Approach you even the Palate;
"Come thou to him
"And Wisdom he fashioned."

This triad portrays Wisdom coming out of the Mouth/Palate and the call goes out with the imperative verbs to come and receive it. Note also the plural 'you' juxtaposed with the singular 'thou' which is also found nicely in the poetry of theForward Text!

Paragraph 92

Again the question format continues: **"Who is Grief?"** The answer is G-d; He 'trembled' and He 'chastised'; He created the 'Mouth' and then died. But the 'Palate was with his G-d. The 'Mouth/Palate' is identified as 'the Mark' and when he died and went to G-d he passed over so to speak. The Back Text is eloquent in its imagery and content. The 'Mark' taking a page from his G-d who elsewhere is called 'The Enabler' (Pars. 263, 270) becomes an enabler also. Acting the Levir (doing the duty of a brother to his widow to raise up seed for him) with a sufficiency of Grace and the 'blood of his ruinations' enables they who died. And where did he go? "He moved out of Time". If being 'in Time' is the 'land of the living' then 'out of time' maybe existing in 'the land of death'. If this follows then can we say 'the Mark' went to the land of the dead even Sheol? I believe the answer is yes. Read Paragraph 209.

Paragraph 93

No notes.

Paragraph 94

The word צרא I conjecture to be the Aramaic equivalent of צרה from
צרר. The context seems to support this view. This word appears in the
Back Text a number of places.

Paragraph 95

The word spelled אב upon first glance is 'father'; but in context along
side of 'he regarded us as abomination' I read 'necromancer' spelled
defectively here; read then אוב.

Paragraph 96

The word 'arracks' is Arabian Whisky. Why is this non-biblical word in
this text? Look further in this paragraph and see that 'orchard' 'juice'
'fruit he gave to drink' and so forth support the interpretation of these
consonants ארקיו. The modern dictionary Megiddo p. 40a was my
source for 'arracks'.

Paragraph 97

The BHS helps restore a corrupt Masoretic Text here in 8.14. The
Forward Text reads in the MT:

עד-מתי החזון התמיד והפשע שמם תת
and the BHS informs of the following alternate:
▪ עד-מתי החזון התמיד מורם והפשע השמם נתן

Turning it around for the Back Text the portion effected appears this
way:

▪ נתן ממש העש פה ומרום די מת

Translated it now reads:

"And He set *it* beside Mash;
"He made the Mouth and the Height
"the sufficiency of Man."

My translation of the unaided MT reads somewhat strained:

The Linear Bible Code

> **"Devastation and a line placed above Mash**
> **"A mouth lent aid even enough *that* he died."**

Paragraph 98

The word **'judgeth'** is spelled fully פלל whereas the Back Text reads פל∎
I read here the defective verb and the lamed is doubled in Daghes Forte.
Please keep in mind that in writing the Back Text restrictions are at
times severe because of the constraints of the Forward Text. My
confidence remains intact that the meaning of the BT can be ferreted
out nevertheless as shown here with the defective verb פלל ∎

Paragraph 99

Seth, a very important figure in Egypt, see Nag Hammadi Library.

Paragraph 100

No notes.

Paragraph 101

I am impressed with the words

> ∎ ילד גת והרי עצם-תח
> **"He begat a winepress and the mountains of Azum-**
> **Toah"**

In Psalm 90.2 we read:

> בטרם הרים יולדו
> **"before the mountains were brought forth".**

The verb and the object are the same!

Paragraph 102

Here is another question at the start of a thought. **"Who is above a
sheep"**. In other words 'who is greater than a sheep' and the answer is
given **"The Noble Mark, The Passageway of G-d."** Much later in the
Book we shall find another reference to 'passageway', in paragraph
"The Passover shall come, the Passageway of Time from G-d". Note the
word דא in this paragraph which is Aramaic and feminine. The
masculine form is never used in the Back Text. The verb הלו is read
הללו 'they praised'. The last sentence of this paragraph contains two
verbs sharing the same meaning 'flow' or as used here 'swam'; יזעֻ and
פוץ∎ I am also impressed by the tense of each verb; the first is perfect

and the second imperfect. For the fact that the Back Text may be regarded as not having 'waw Consecutive/Conservative the use of the perfect and imperfect verb maybe used for the missing 'waw' or 'vav'.

Paragraph 103

No notes.

Paragraph 104

The word קהל **'Assembly'** if rendered using New Testament terminology would read 'church'. The idea of 'stout' truly conveys the idea of 'bulky' but not corpulent. It is the opposite of 'thin'. Whoever is the 'Stout One' he is a good person and is linked with 'Father' and His Knowledge. The idea of 'lamp' also links everything together in a familiar metaphor elsewhere evident in this Back Text and the New Testament Christians.

Paragraph 105

The word בת here translated 'house' and the defective form of בית understood may be contested but I translate it 'house' because of the masculine aspect of the context. If the verb had a suffix there would have been no doubt to its meaning. There are two verbs that in the imperfect appear to be the same but they are not; יפצהו and יפץ. The first is from the root פצה and the second פוץ.

Paragraph 106

This section is very straight forward in its presentation. There are no truncated words! The verbs and subjects are all balanced! How could it read any differently?!

Paragraph 107

There are a number of names and places in this section. **'Toah'** is again found in paragraph 242. **'Chael'** appears to be a name of the 'Witness'. The meaning of the name is hard to fathom because it may be in two parts and the first part is defective. But if the first part is from the word חוה 'life' or the verb of the same spelling we would get one answer. If the defective spelling is corrected thusly חיאל then we get another interpretation such as 'The Living One is EL'. The name or place 'Hannesh' is made up of the letters left over after the parsing. It is a mystery to me. Again we see how parsing the Back Text is not subjective but builds inevitably. In a previous paragraph (79) the name 'Belarus' came forth from the text unbidden and yet it is a name so familiar in Russia today!

Paragraph 108

The verb תביל **'thou carry away'** is from the root word יבל.

Paragraph 109

The name **'Javeez'** is conjectural on my part, יויז. The word used for 'knife' חלף admittedly is not quite the spelling one would expect: מחלף but the verb points directly to it: תשינו from שנן.

Paragraph 110

The words **'they boasted'** is from the truncated verb but the Daghes Forte solves it all; הללו for הללו .

Paragraph 111

I have conjectured the masculine form of **'thanksgiving'** found in the Straight Text in the feminine form תודה . Here it is spelled תד and maybe with a 'vav' תוד . For those scholars who are uneasy with 'assumption' driven interpretation please remember that there is a fair share of these in the Forward Text. A perfect example is תכה . HELOT p. 1067a reads in part "meaning wholly dub.;" and "*were led* or *assembled* would suit context;".

Paragraph 112

The word **"His Sheep"** סיו is an excellent example of a phoneme. The correct spelling is שיו. This sliding back and forth between the letters ס and ש is common in the Straight Text. See the word שט .

Paragraph 113

The spelling of **'Moon'** with an aleph ending the word is common in the Back Text of Daniel and I can only assume that it is due to an Aramaicism, ירחא . It appears four times in the standard spelling ירח, see the Register for references.

Paragraph 114

Another phoneme is **'council'** סוד but spelled in the Back Text שוד. The rest of the section reads clear and simple.

Paragraph 115

The collective noun 'the unclean' בטמא takes as its verb the plural here **'they were sucked out'** נמזו . This is also a common thing in the Forward Text which often has 'people' עם with a verb in the plural; see Genesis 11.6 עם and יזמו.

Paragraph 116

The word ענך **'it answered thee'** is defective; the correct spelling is עניך. The word ללם **'he grasped them with a twist'** is from the root לול. The word הללני 'he praised Me' has a Daghes Forte in the 'lamed' for the full spelling הללני.∎

Paragraph 117

The word תלת 'thou heaped up' is defective but with the Daghes Forte in the 'lamed' we read the full spelling תללת. The word 'distortion' עו is the truncated word עוה. The remarkable line הספר-הי לגר translated 'the book of Wailing belongs to the Sojourner' is the name of the Back Text Book. It appears a second time in paragraph 128. I interprete 'sojourner' as referring to the Jewish diaspora. This is a book for the Jewish Nation. The word זר 'crown' is associated in the Forward Text with the idea of 'circlet' 'border'. The Aramaic spelling זירא is associated with 'wreath' 'crown'; and so on. I render it 'crown' placed on the head partly because of the context: 'the head came' בא ראש.∎

Paragraph 118

Note the noun הרית is a spelling which is not in the Forward Text. I translate it **'Mountain'**.

Paragraph 119

The word **'its emptiness'** is from the feminine word בוקה.

Paragraph 120

We have an infinitive absolute in this section: עבר אעבר **'I shall indeed pass by'**.

Paragraph 121

The truncated word יל 'howl thou!' as the Daghes Forte in the 'lamed' and is to be read ילל. My thinking that brought me to this conclusion is based on the next phrase which also has the infinitive **'go thou'** לך; followed by yet another infinitive **'swallow up'** לע.∎ The verb דחל read in the Pael. The verb **'I drilled'** חורתי is of course Perfect. The verb definition is based on Gesenius' Lexicon page 266b. The idea of 'boring' or 'drilling' is associated in the Forward Text with a hole, a cavern; so why not drilling a well or making a cave? The word 'delicacy' רוך but here conjectured to be a feminine word and in the construct state also, does not define exactly what kind of delicacy is it other than of something pretty special since it is associated with 'a god'.

Paragraph 122

No notes.

Paragraph 123

The word **'praise you'** is the truncated form הלו for הללו. Read the Daghes Forte in the 'lamed'. The word 'thou obeyed' יקת is from the root יקה . The word 'for the return' is made up of the preposition ל and the Aramaic word תוב . This combination can be treated as the infinitive construct. (see this word below)

Paragraph 124

The infinitive construct לתב **'is to return'** is from the root תוב. The word **'lion'** read a 'yod' (י) in the word לִיֵש . The verb הוא is discussed in HELOT pp. 216-217. The only use of the verb in the Forward Text describes snow falling earthward הוא-ארץ 'an Arabizing usage'. I therefore use this verb in the same sense and supplied in italic *'earthward'*. I believe that this simple sentence may be read in a very big way. The next sentence built on the one verb יחתל **'he shall be swaddled'** when added to the **'falling *earthward'*** has echoes in the Gospels of the New Testament. The word 'let him turn aside' טי is the jussive form of the verb נטה. The name 'Kaid' is conjecture drawn from the parsing of the text. The vowels it will be remembered are conjecture. The verb **'nipped off'** מלק is used once in the Forward Text in Leviticus 5.8. From that useage I have added here the object of the verb *his head*.

Paragraph 125

It is remarkable that in the Back Text we find the same **"Living Being"** found in Ezekiel chapter 1 and chapter 10! Note in paragraph 150 the return of the "Living Being". The word in the Forward Text according to the BHS רבון is to be read in the Qere רבבן. I have spelled the word accordingly and in the Back Text the reading is strengthened. Instead of the conjunction ו we read the preposition ב 'in' 'with'. The completed sentence reads:

> ומד קן בבר וברו
> **"And the measure of the Nest is <u>with</u> the Pure One even His Son."**

The MT at this point is in error as is confirmed in the Back Text.

The vowels I used in filling out the name רהן are of course conjecture; 'Rohan'.

Paragraph 126

No notes.

Paragraph 127

Paragraphs 126 and 127 I consider one in thought. It is all about the Prince G-d prepares. The Prince is **'the Instrument of My Knowledge'**; he is the **'Stallion of the Chamber'** and I believe he is **'the Mark'**. Gesenius p.729a for the word קוע says that 'prop. Apparently, *a stallion*; hence figuratively, *a prince* (as rightly given by the Vulg. And Hebrew interpreters); a metaphor of frequent use amongst the Hebrews and Arabs...' The beauty of 126-127 is difficult to surpass in the Back Text. I also like the last two lines that end 127:

> "The Lamp of the Nest is above the Tel-
> City of the Mark;
> "The Abode of the Shepherd he shall cause
> to bear fruit."

The verb ללם 'he twisted them' is from the root word לול . **Paragraph 128**

When looking up the word הים look under הום. The word 'it defileth' יחל is from the root חלל the third III. In HELOT p. 320a. The verb הוה appears frequently in the Back Text having the meaning 'become'. In the Forward Text is is rare and its related verb היה is found in profusion. In this paragraph the name by which the Back Text was named appears: **"The Book of Wailing belongs to the Sojourner"**. This is the second time this sentence appears. The first reference is in paragraph 117.

Paragraph 129

In paragraph 117 we find the first reference to the **'head came'**. The two references side-by-side are instructive:

> "The Head came but before fire proceeded."
> "The Head came but before Him the strength
> of the Pure Son proceeded..."

The question begs to be asked: is 'fire' the 'Pure Son'?

In this paragraph the highly speculative double named personages appear in the Back Text: 'Kieth and Janet' קת וינת. Keith appeared in paragraph 57. He will appear in paragraph 163 as a 'free man', and in 233 his mouth is censured, and in 249 he 'wrapped tightly his wreath'. In the present paragraph Keith's mouth is censured by the 'Light'. Note the excellent interweaving of the 'mouth' imagery of desiring 'sharpness'.

Paragraph 130

This section is a lamentation. The reference to the 'Ram' אִיל is so interpreted because of the appearance of the 'lion' הלבי . Without the lion present 'Ram' could be rendered 'leader' 'chief'. This would fall nicely into place as a synonym for the 'Pure One'. Yet 'Ram' still is a synonym for the 'Pure One'. The identity of the 'lion' remains a mystery at this time. If 'lion' was feminine then the identity would be 'My daughter'. The word 'they are darkened' is from the second II. עוף in HELOT, p. 734a. The central theme is nicely rounded out: 'darkness'.

Paragraph 131

The opening sentence is packed with wonders. The early fig theme is not new to the Bible. The imagery of the pomegranate as the Moon, the Light of My Token, is highly suggestive and of course the Moon (light) is already defined elsewhere as a token or sign in the Heavens. Coming on the heal of the previous paragraph where 'darkness' is the theme we are on steady ground in parsing of the Back Text. If the reading of the text of Daniel backwards is nonsense what is the explanation of the wonders found in the Back Text as parsed and translated?

Paragraph 132

The word translated **'she covers Us over'** is the Hiphel of לוט which means 'wrap closely, tightly, enwrap, envelop' and I suggest the italic *'with secrecy'* to round out the meaning.

Paragraph 133

This section is composed of three small lamentations. They are all connected however. The word translated **'a hedged place'** טיר I believe to be the masculine form. The feminine form is only familiar to us in the Forward Text טירה. The word **'quivering'** ניד by itself here is linked with 'my lips' in Job 16.5. Using this reference as a guide I add the appropriate italic *'lips'* here and elsewhere in the Back Text. Note that the 'early fig' is something to lament. In the Straight Text 'untimely fruit' is a metaphor. In the New Testament Gospels Jesus curses a fruit tree for not having its fruit ripe!

The name 'Jacha' יחע was determined by the parsing of the text. It fell out as a name 'forced' by the text. If correct then it is highly significant because we have a name. This does not mean the 'Pure One' has no other name. This of course is understood. Royalty goes by many names and because names have meaning the list can be very long indeed. Names can be composits or single words. Often names are derived from the participle of the verb.

Paragraph 134
The circumcision of Noah is astounding in the Back Text. Equally astounding is the next sentence: "He shall make abundant the Region of Messiah." The Dead Sea Scrolls contain a book called 'The Birth of Noah' (4Q534-536). I quote from the remarks of Robert Eisenman and Michael Wise:

"A pseudepigraphic text with visionary and mystical import, the several fragments of this text give us a wonderfully enriched picture of the figure of Noah, as seen by those who created this literature. In the first place, the text describes the birth of Noah as taking place at night, and specifies his weight. It describes him as 'sleeping until the division of the day', probably implying noon.

"One of the primordial Righteous Ones whose life and acts are soteriological in nature, Noah is of particular interest to writers of this period like Ben Sira and the Damascus Document. The first *Zaddik* (Righteous One) mentioned in scripture (Gen. 6.9), Noah was also 'born Perfect', as the rabbis too insist, as is stressed in this passage. Because of this 'Perfection', Rabbinical literature has Noah born circumcised. However this may be, 'Perfection' language of this kind is extremely important in the literature at Qumran, as it is in the New Testament. See, in this regard, the Sermon on the Mount's parallel: 'Be perfect as your Father in Heaven is Perfect' (Matt. 5.48)." Quoted from "The Dead Sea Scrolls Uncovered", Robert Eisenman and Michael Wise, Barnes and Noble Inc., 1994, page 33.

The word 'perfect' in the scroll is שלם . This definition comes from the ideal of 'completeness'. In the Back Text, paragraph 255, we read this:

> "The Giver made them (cavities of the ground) flow and the Integrity (תם) of Noah endured."

The word **'Integrity'** as shown is the more familiar תם or spelled תום. This word may indeed be translated 'Perfection' and here is the tie-in with the Qumran sectaries! The text in Genesis 6.9 reads תמים which is of course where תום\תם originates. The Genesis word is an adjective and the BT word is a noun. The Back Text of Daniel is of course as old as the Book of Daniel. Many years or centuries earlier than the Sectaries this Book was written. Because the Forward Text of Daniel is considered scripture should we not consider the Back Text scripture as well? Scripture of whom? They who recognize the Forward Text of Daniel of course!

The Linear Bible Code

Other references in the Back Text for Noah are found in the Register. The reference in Paragraph 73 is very interesting. While Noah is linked with Enoch in known literature the Back Text links Noah with 'the Mouth'. "Who is for Me? The Mouth and Noah. They have restrained the habitations of Ked the stumbling of thy gods." Noah's already linkage with 'Messiah' maybe showing us that 'the Mouth' is Messiah.

In this same paragraph (134) the inclusion of Shem has heavy overtones in the Dead Sea literature and in the Nag Hammadi Library. Consult the Register for all references to Shem.

The word translated **'was made to weep'** הבך is in the Hophal.

The word **'runner'** רץ is the participle of רוץ . The runner may be a messenger as in 2 Samuel 18.21ff; a figure of a prophet's activity, Jeremiah 23.21; of G-d's word in Psalm 147.15 "his word runneth very quickly" KJV. Runners may also be as a royal escort or a body-guard, and so on. The significance of 'runner' in the Back Text is full of possibilities. Consult the Register for the references to 'runner'.

Paragraph 135

The name 'Cuth' is spelled כות in the full. The word הגד is in the Hophal 'he was made to show grief'. The word ינד is rendered here in the Niphal **'he showed grief'**. The word ביזים 'scorners' is from the word to 'dispise' בוז in conjunction with the Modern Hebrew usage of the word ביזה. The second use of the word 'scorners' of Shem is truncated thusly בזי-ש.

Paragraph 136

The name **'the Mark-of-All-of-Them'** so long in English is quite simple in Hebrew התו-כלם . He is also known as **'the Mark-of-All'** תו-כל and simply as **'the Mark'** תו.

The very interesting word מיקוא in the Back Text rendered **'company of'** finds its use in the Forward Text in 2 Chronicles 1.16 spelled the same but the 'yod' is written below the 'mem' as a short HIREQ, מקוא.
The name 'Jeah' is new to the readers of the Forward Text. The word rendered the sharp one **'howled'** is the truncated verb ילל. The word rendered **'fornication'** is spelled for the first time with a ה as the final letter whereas it is known with the 'ת'.

Paragraph 137

The word rendered **'he shall be smitten'** is written awkwardly ינוך , if the root is נכה and rendered Niphal. The word מא is the Aramaic version of מָה 'How'. Both versions are found in the Back Text. This is interesting because Daniel's Forward Text is classic Hebrew and Aramaic. The word translated **'wander restlessly'** is the imperfect of the root רוד spelled here יִרד .

Paragraph 138

The word '**Adversary**' עָר is defined this way in HELOT, p. 786a.

Paragraph 139

The word **'billowed'** גל should have the 'lamed' doubled; so read Daghes Forte in the ל. Another translation that might be acceptable is 'rolled away' because a Sign in the sky might act in this way. The Sign caused a 'distress of noise' צר קול.

The name 'Taihu' was first suggested because of the final letters 'hu' הו.

Paragraph 140

The imperative **'set thou'** הב is from the root יהב 'give'; Gesenius p. 336a lists Ezra 5.16 for the use in 'to lay' a foundation. The word קסהו 'he cut him off' is from the unused root קסס which root is used for the Poel קוסס to cut off; Gesenius p.736a or HELOT p.890b 'strip off'.

The place **'Seneh'** is real. It is a crag over against Michmash, I Samuel 14.4. "a cliff opp. The cliff called בוצץ, HELOT, p.702a. Here there is a connection between 'Seneh' and the word I translated 'he cut him off'. The verbal called Poel of קסס is the same as קוצץ! What is going on here? The paring of the two as mentioned in HELOT in this form suggests there something unusual is happening.

Paragraph 141

Note that not all Hebrew/Aramaic sentences in the Back Text follow the rules. The sentence that reads:

> **"O that Boach had fed them when a measure curdled."**

Here the Hebrew reads in the order of good English! The verbs are last! The parsing of the text placed all this material in this order.

The Modern Hebrew word ז-יהום is here bearing the interpretation 'contamination'. See Megiddo p. 245a. The word 'he is made filthy' ינול is found in Gesenius p. 539b from the verb בלנ. The exclamation 'lo' or 'behold' אלו is found in the Forward Text of Daniel; see Gesenius p.48b.

The Modern Hebrew word גס used in conjunction with פר gives us 'an ill-mannered bull. What did the bull do? He put them in fear. And what might be that fear? The next sentence tells us the answer: being tongue-tied אלם. The bull is also tongue tied because only man can speak. The connection of the bull and tongue-tied is startling. I believe that it is just this type of text that stand out as a marker confirming that I have parsed the text correctly. The word יחנ is the truncated form of יחנני rendered here **'may he show me favour'**.

Paragraph 142

The personal name Zabai זבי is found in Ezra 10.28.

Paragraph 143

The word rendered **'he fashioned'** צע is found in the unused root צוע. Note that 'hand' יד is at times discerned in both the masculine and feminine in the Forward Text and the Back Text. The word interpreted 'he shook' is the Poel רפרף of רפף. In the BHS Daniel 6.19 the word ודחון is to be read ודהון. This in turn changes the Back Text. The MT in the parsing of the Back Text has the word הד interpreted as 'sharp *tongued*'. The BHS change הד reads 'Shout'. **"Our G-d of the Shout"** is found in other places in the Back Text. For this reason the BHS reading is adopted. The name 'Teth' is conjecture טת. The words **'Column of G-d'** שת אל ל also appears in paragraph 232. The word 'Column' is a metaphor for 'prince' or 'noble'.

Paragraph 144

The Back Text uses the metaphor 'food' and 'feeding them food' many times. Here the combination of 'eating' 'food' 'beans' and 'millet' in the context of ravaging is remarkable. We are on sure ground in the interpretation. The word 'emptiness' was created by following the BHS. In Daniel 6.18 the word והיתית is modified in the BHS thusly והתית. The Back Text words went from באתיתיהו which cannot be parsed with meaning to this באתיתהו which is successfully parsed באתי תהו and interpreted **'I brought Emptiness'**. Now the whole text is enhanced. 'Emptiness' parallels 'Calamity'. This again points to periodic corruptions in the MT and the versions at times supplies the needed tex; the Back Text benefits.

The word **'scorners of'** בזי should be read ביזי as in paragraph 135.

Paragraph 145

Again the subject of food is present in a combination of lodging for the night and taking pleasure in food and in particular flesh. The act of shutting up the **'greatness of the Garden'** is the same as cutting off the supply of food. The imperative **'crush thou'** רֹס is from the word רֹסס.

Paragraph 146

Again the act of feeding is central in this paragraph when it says 'Who is oppressed? I shall feed them.'

The dominion of 'Shem-Avah' may be translated 'Name of Desire' or 'Name of Appetite/Lust'.

The word בֹזִי is here translated **'My booty'** because of the verb 'he plundered' שלל . The word נֹדל is the Niphal of דלל and the word הולֹע is the Hophal of a conjectured verb ילֹע which itself is from the root לוֹע 'he spoke rashly'; see HELOT, p. 534a II. לוֹע .

This paragraph contains elements that find a parallel in the New Testament. The Revelation chapter 12 has the elements 'mother' 'hide' and 'Dragon'.

Paragraph 147

Again feeding is central. The subject continues. 'But a few I shall feed them' speaks of a remnant whom G-d loves. The 'Perfect Garner' is he who enlarges the produce of the orchard/garden. G-d's 'Garden' is heavenly. He feeds them 'from the Veil'. The act of 'swallowing' is expressive of destruction. They who are swallowed up end up on Sheol 'because for people is Sheol'.

The word **'I shall crush'** is from the root רֹסס.

Again the words רֹם או appear and they are translated 'haughtiness of Lust'. 'Lust' instead of 'Desire' because of the juxtaposition of opposites. G-d's alternative is "Desire" which comes from the Veil from G-d through the hand of the Garner, the Prince, the Hand. The food is none other than 'the Knowledge of G-d'. This is central to the Gospel of John. But that author neglects to a fault the 'knowledge' for the messenger bearing that Knowledge. Note that the Back Text speaks of the 'Mouth' and John speaks of the 'Word'. The translation of סרֹף as **'serpent'** is indicated from 'Dragon' in paragraph 146.

Paragraph 148

The feeding and eating continues here. Just like the paragraph where one lodges for the night and eats so here one 'slumbered' and 'he is refreshed'. G-d's 'Thicket' slumbered no doubt to be refreshed.

The word **'his hundred'** מֹאו is defective and should be spelled מֹאיו.

The word **'extended'** סֹא is possibly from the root סֹאה ; see Gesenius p. 575b. I believe it to be from a more archaic root I conjecture to be סֹאו

and in the perfect tense the 'vav' is removed. The context of the Back Text lends support for 'extended'.

The BHS for Daniel 6.13 deletes על-אסר on the strength of two sources. I have deleted them and I believe the Back Text is improved. This is how it looks with the text intact:

אכלם רסאלע אכלם מד קני

I find that the letters רסאלע chaos. When they are removed the text reads in translation:

> **'it fed them; it fed them a measure of My Nest'.**

Paragraph 149

Again the theme of 'eating' 'feeding' and the 'Garden' continues. The text now speaks of the gushing of 'Desire' and of the 'perfect heap of the Veil'. The words **'the Pure One'** from בר is the product of a BHS change. Multiple manuscripts at this point, says the BHS, brought about this reading. In Daniel 6.13 the word קריבו is now read קרבו.

The verb 'gushed' is בע from the root בוע. I have used the excellent reading of William Gesenius in his lexicon, page 108b.

Paragraph 150

The word **'I shall crush'** ארס is defective and should be spelled ארסס.

Paragraph 151

The adverb כה is spelled here כא. The phrase **'leading *them* to a watering-station'** is all from one verb מנהל.

Paragraph 152

There are a number of intriguing things about this paragraph; 'the **generation of So'**, the 'lowly mule of desire' and the wounding of 'Icarus'. The first may refer to one or more individuals mentioned in the Forward Text spelled סוא. The second because there are nine references to the lowly mule (see Register). The third because of the reference of the wounding of Icarus. Is this the Icarus of Greek mythology?

The word translated 'break' *n.* is found in the Modern Hebrew language. The translation of טעי-תאי **'the lost ones of My Chamber'** is from the verb **'to err'** טעה and may also be translated 'the sinners of My Chamber'.

Paragraph 153

This section is full of eating, drinking and food imagery. The progression of thought is logical and impressive for a newly discovered text and parsed without recourse to any tradition.

Paragraph 154

No notes.

Paragraph 155

There is no question in my mind but that **'goddess'** is correct. I base this on the imperative commands in feminine form: 'spend thou the night' לִנִי and **'go thou forth'** לְכִי. And then later **'for her'** is part of the text twice! This section also contains the explicit reference to **'the Assembly of Yeshua'**. If this was translated into Greek and then into English we would read 'the church of Jesus'! The close proximity of the 'Mark' seems to tie the two together. In other words, 'Mark' and 'Yeshua' are the same person. The context of all this is also remarkable and bears repeating here:

> **"Every king belongs to thee O Mark!**
> **"From the Assembly of Yeshua I shall feed them and give thou *to* My lions."**

All this reminds me of the reference in paragraph 104:

> **"Whosoever is a lamp of the Assembly קְהִל of the Stout One is worthy of the knowledge of his Father."**

Paragraph 156

The word **'beginning'** קָזן in rendered only from context and conjecture. I do not recognize this word otherwise. Note that the italic words *'men'* and *'women'* owe their origin to the plural endings of the respective verbs, masculine and feminine.

Paragraph 157

The verb rendered 'they shall be blunted of' יקְהוּ is from the root קָהַה. The verb **'they are bringing down'** יוֹרִדוּ is Hiphel imperfect.

Paragraph 158

'Sheol' is feminine. The text which reads 'he howled at her' therefore means 'he howled at Sheol'. The word 'devastating storm' שְׁאוּה being feminine is the subject of the verb 'she shall throw down' תָּטִיל. I believe the **'Rib of the Fa**ther' is a metaphor; even as Havah (Eve) is the rib of Adam perhaps G-d's chosen is His Rib who in another place is called 'Our Beloved' 259; and 'His Beloved' in 168. Paragraph 162 also speaks of the **'Rib of the Father'**. Is it not significant that 'Beloved' spelled דוד is from the verb in the sentence following: 'He made a loving jesture הדיד surely'?

Paragraph 159

In this section we read of the circumcision of the Mark by one called Lekeith לקת. The verb בהה is used to describe the actions of one Lekeith, **'thou acted purely'** to obey בהת. Gesenius wrote of this verb 'an unused root,' (in the Forward Text), 'which properly appears to have had the significance of *purity...*' The very next part of the sentence we read ליקת which I interpret **'to obey'** the infinite construct form of יקה, another unused root, see Gesenius p.362b. Perhaps most wonderously of all is that the name of this man is built from this verb thusly לקת. All this is spelled out in this manner:

ואין זא מבהת ליקת לקת ▪

And the sentence continues with the Hophal of the verb 'he cut' מל , 'having circumcised' a sheep even the likes of the Mark. The word 'hundreds' מאת needs the 'vav' which is supplied above the line by the 'dot' or reproduced in full מאות ▪

Paragraph 160

The story of Lekeith continues with a lament written of him and the Seraph.

Paragraph 161

The word 'neglect' is from the Aramaic word שול spelled in the Back Text here של ▪

Paragraph 162

The mission of the Mark is central here. The sentence that has the italics literally reads 'it had enveloped them (masculine) and them (feminine) לטמ והן ▪

Paragraph 163

In each place in the Back Text of Daniel where the Timbrel תף is referenced it is done correctly. The Timbrel is an instrument of joy and it is juxtaposed with sorrow. In the present context the question is asked 'is this shout for the timbrel?' after stating the death of Grace. And of course the answer is understood, no.

The last portion of the paragraph is devoted to a progression of making the hand white/pure. It is a very interesting section which culminates in purpose 'to erase Lust' and its identity 'the Hand of Y-H and so the Thin One slumbered not.' In the Back Text of Malachi this making white is also recorded. We read of it several times. In 3.21 I read "The Mark, I shall white him."

Paragraph 164

Suddenly we arrive at a new junction in the Back Text, the introduction of 'the favour of the oppressed' which is identified as the personification of 'the Son'. In the paragraphs to come it will read in total 'the Favour of the Oppressed and the Son' which G-d attempts to feed the people. Paragraph 261 contains the last reference; see the Register.

Paragraph 165

The BHS lends a hand again in restoring the Text. First the reading in the Back Text using the Masoretic Text. I parse the text in this section thusly:

בבהן רח-אל כתי בז בנו

"when the Spirit of God covered a Cypriot the spoil of his son".

The BHS text modifies the MT thusly:

בבהן רח-אל כתיב תבז בנו

"with a thumb the Spirit of God he made a writing: 'Thou shalt despise His Son!'.

This coincides with the context of these paragraphs. G-d sends His purified Son to swallow up reproach and the people but was tossed about and eventually was rejected.

Paragraph 166

The sentence that reads ' **All entering the Tel-City of Thy Mark saw the Ribe of the Father'** is first mentioned in Paragraph 158. The result of seeing the Rib of the Father should have been rejoicing, 'Give thou a shout!' but they refused! G-d called them to repentance! 'Return thou to Our Chamber!' The word '**inscribe**' רשם is only found in Daniel!, see 10.21.

Paragraph 167

No notes.

Paragraph 168

The name 'Henna' הנע is a place in the Forward Text, 2 kings 18.34. The idea of feeding 'a measure of her curtain' is well established earlier when G-d feeds them from the Veil, par. 147. The name 'Havach' is conjecture. After all the letters had been parsed this name appeared and I read it as a name.

Paragraph 169

The sentence that reads

> **"Come thou forth transgressor, the heart of Hamas,**
> **from thy ravage."**

is all too familiar today. Hamas is a a terrorist organization among the Palestinians. However, in their case 'Hamas' is spelled in Hebrew חמס from the noun 'violence, wrong'. In the Back Text the spelling is המש from the root which has a dubious meaning. Still I believe it refers to this 21st century terrorist group and the spelling in Hebrew is the correct phoneme in pronouncing חמס in the English speaking world.

The word 'transgressor' is a modern Hebrew word שע , see Megiddo p.663a. Is it not interesting that this modern word is connected directly with the phoneme 'Hamas'? Is it not a signal or sign that it refers to our day? Compare with paragraph 184 where Hamas again appears.

The phrase **'they were wounded'** is conjecture.

The word חכת is a defective spelling; read חכית **'thou tarried'**.

Paragraph 170

The words 'thou tarried' from חכת is the defective spelling of חכית.

Paragraph 171

Here in one place we have one individual with different titles or names: 'perfection of strength', 'the Son', 'the Instrument', 'the Mark-of-All-of-Them', 'the Pure One' and 'My Grace'. This last is confirmed in paragraph 191 'Man of Grace'.

The word יבו **'they cried shrilly'** is to be read יבבו. The word ידך **'he is to be pounded to powder'** should be read ידוך.

Paragraph 172

The story of the Pure One interacting on behalf of G-d on earth continues. (It is significant that in the Back Text of the Book of Ruth I read that 'the Gift acted the Levir surely for Me'; Ruth 1:1. G-d sent His Son to act is His stead!) Why did he purify himself? He was to circumcise their heart. Who is 'the Voice'? Perhaps it is the 'Pure One' and from his Mouth comes forth pure words that incite the people to purify themselves.

The spelling of '**treachery**' תרמה is spelled in the Back Text תרמא∎

Paragraph 173

The verb רוק is used here ארק '**I shall pour out**'.

The BHS in Daniel 5.8 records two versions other than the Masoretic Text for the word מלכא. The first is the new word בבל, and the second is a new spelling מלכותא. All of these changes create viable translations in the Back Text. The verb להך is to be read לאך 'He sent a messenger'. The misspelling is evident. Here they are:

להך אל ולב בימי כח

"God sent a messenger and <u>courage at</u> the days of power".

להך אל ואתו כל מימי כח

"God sent a messenger and <u>His Token all from</u> the days of power."

All of these are viable and may represent several varients of the Back Text itself just as there are varients of many old books of this same period.

Paragraph 174

The word אנו is the imperative of the root II. און '**enjoy you the life of plenty**'.

Paragraph 175

No notes.

Paragraph 176

The BHS makes an emendation in Daniel 5.6 thusly: the MT שנוהי becomes שנו עלוהי on the strength of the similar text in verse 9. When this is assimilated into the text the Back Text reads of course differently. The Masoretic Text in context reads:

ערו יה ונשיהו

"they awoke Y-H and His Debt".

The new emended text reads:

ערו יה ולעו נשיהו

"they awoke Y-H and <u>they swallowed up</u> His Debt".

If the emendation follows exactly that of verse 9 the Back Text reads as follows:

ערו יה ו<u>לעני</u> נשיהו

"they awoke Y-H and <u>for the poverty</u> its debt".

The word 'proud' זח is a modern Hebrew word. On occasion in the Back Text זח is the truncated verb זחח .

The mark of the accusative appears in the Back Text in the familiar form את and in the Aramaic ית.

The sentence '**He exposed the Prince when he shaved the pubis of thy daughter**' is astounding if one does *not* accept the validity of the Back Text. What are the odds of this sentence otherwise? The verb is the verb of a barber shaving and the pubis although private is shaven to expose something! This is a powerful sentence. The spelling in the Back Text for 'pubis' is קלן which is the shortened form of קלון. It is used seventeen times in the Forward Text. It is used twice in the sense we find in the Back Text; Jeremiah 13.26 and Nahum 3.5.

Paragraph 177

The word <u>excrement</u> is created by an emendation in the MT as suggested by the Qere. The affected word in Daniel 5.5 reads in the MT

נפקו and the Qere would have it spelled נפקה. The parsing of the Back Text using the MT leaves one with a corruption: 'He staggered among צאו. If the 'vav' is the conjuction starting the next sentence then we are working with צא but if it is part of the corrupt word what can we make of it? By using the Qere this apparent problem is solved; the 'vav' is removed and replaced with the 'He' thusly צאה and the word <u>excrement</u> is born!

The name 'Aeael' from the letters אעאל is the best I could hope for in the parsing of the text.

Paragraph 178

The word 'his efficient Wisdom' is written in the Back Text תשיו in a truncated form. The full spelling without the suffix 'his' appears in HELOT p. 444b and Gesenius 860b thusly תושיה .

Paragraph 179

The simple sentence רם חלד is stupendous in meaning! The Pure One of Heart purified himself *and* exalted the world! Note that the word translated 'world' חלד is esoteric in meaning.

The BHS offers much in the emendation of the first word of chapter 5. The spelling in the MT of בלשאצר is emended on the authority of two manuscripts (says the BHS) to read בלאשצר. Inserting this into the long line of consonants let us compare what changes are noticed. First the MT is given:

> . בעאכלמרצאאשלבההלפש

All attempts to parse this is met with difficulties. But when the emendation is inserted all falls into place quite nicely with the resulting parsing:

> בעאך למרץ שאל בהל פש
> **"He sought Thee against the fierceness of Sheol.**
> **Transgression trembled."**

The word above בעא is the Aramaic version of בעה.

Paragraph 180

Several previous paragraphs contained references to an 'Ape'. This has led me to consider the opening word of this paragraph. The phoneme 'gibbon' from the consonants גבן is so startling in the context of 'Ape of Distinction' in paragraph 178 that I have so translated it. The references to animals whether they are apes, gibbons, bears or lions is powerful evidence to the time period Daniel was written. The mentioning of a bear here in connection with bereavement משכל is nothing but short of a wonder in itself. In Hoshea 13.8 the two are connected! The Back Text parsed as I have done it continually shows evidence internally to its authenticity.

The BHS in Daniel 4.33 inserts the 'yod' in the text thusly: ועלי . This creates in the Back Text the imperfect verb יעלו 'they shall swallow up'.

Paragraph 181

The verb **'let thou make a donation'** תדב is from the modern Hebrew word נדב.(See Megiddo, page 446a.) The name 'Aiah' is spelled here עה but read עיה. This now is a city found in Jeremiah 49.3.

Paragraph 182

The act of swallowing up is not always of destroying. The word 'swallow' לוע is also a synonym for 'eating' אכל. Therefore when the text reads 'The Mark-of-All-of-Them even is swallowing the burden of a sheep: the burden is a Gift of the Law', he is eating it. This finds a parallel in Ezekiel 3.1 where Ezekiel eats a book. Compare this with Revelation 10.9.

The word 'secrecy' is found in a modern Hebrew dictionary שלי.

The BHS modifies Daniel 4.32's word כלה to read כלא. This creates in the Back Text this reading:

> אֵלֵךְ אֵעֵר אִירָא דלך
> "I shall go; I shall awaken; I shall make afraid thy door".

At first sight it seems superior. But I chose the MT because its text 'he journeyed' seems well suited to the text 'With Me is the Lowly One; he journeyed'.

Note the excellent balance of the two sentences of the first 'awaken' and the second of 'sleep heavily':

> "I shall awaken; I shall made afraid thy door;
> "and fall thou down and sleep heavily Aiah!"

The second to the last sentence of this paragraph is startling. The text was parsed to read thusly:

> רדה ותחבש
> "Have thou dominion and govern".

The balance of thought and the construction is right out of the Forward Text. The use of the word חבש as 'govern' is linked with its use in Job 34.17:

> האף שונא משפט יחבש
> "shall then he who hateth right be able to govern?"

Paragraph 183
In this paragraph the swallowing up verb is used in the sense of destroy. The short sentence '**the ruin of Eden is Death**' harkens back to Genesis. Its use here is dramatic.

Paragraph 184

See paragraph 169 for a discussion of 'Hamas'.

The verb יַרט , fire 'flickers' is from the rare word רטט.

Paragraph 185

The word 'opinion' is the same spelling for 'knowledge' דע. Just like in the Forward Text this word can have two meanings. In the Back Text opinion is negative and knowledge positive. The first is a tool of the Adversary and the latter a tool of G-d. Therefore it is 'opinion' that increases the 'Cloud of Emptiness'. Because opinion is the enemy of knowledge we read that the 'Knowledge of the Mark-of-All-of-Them was put to death'.

The purity of G-d is such that His 'whiteness' judges all. When Moses came down from being with G-d his face shone and it judged the people. He was forced to veil his face while he shone so as to remain among the people. This paragraph has much to say.

The word 'hand' is feminine in this paragraph. The imperative commands 'come thou' באי and 'strengthen thou' לשי are feminine and the object is 'hand'. One might insert 'hand' in the sentences like this: 'come thou O hand to My Stylus' and 'strengthen thou O hand knowledge'.

The BHS records in 4.29 the probable addition of a conjuction thusly: וַעֲשַׁבָּא. This in the Back Text confirms the suspicion that עכר is a participle 'the disturber' of the blood'.

The idea of endurance נון (paragraph 184) and increase נון again (para. 185) is enhanced with the word conceive יחם .

The word 'thy trembling' רטך is the defective spelling of רטטך. Read Daghes Forte within the letter ט.

The word in Niphal נמת is not found in the Straight Text; 'was put to death'.

Paragraph 186

The identity of God's 'Thin One' as a Levite is an important fact in determining his identity. See also Paragrap 19.

The word 'shaft' or 'handle' is a modern Hebrew word קת.

Paragraph 187

The name 'Raphah-Kedez' is my conjecture of the remaining consonants of the paragraph. The next train of thought beginning paragraph 188 concluded the 'booking' of these consonants.

Paragraph 188

The word יכלם 'he shall reserve them' is from the verb II. כלל in HELOT p. 483a-b. The meaning of 'Rama-Yad' maybe 'the hand has cast' as in casting a lance; see I. רמה, HELOT p.941a.

Paragraph 189

The feminine imperatives do not refer to a woman but to the 'hand'. This is discussed in paragraph 185.

The need to insert italics in the Pen sentence is due to an error in the Masoretic Text or if correct we the readers of the Back Text are to fill in the missing words. How are we to know what is missing? Referring back to paragraph 185 we read this same text in full:

> "The stylus slumbered; it empowers the Lamp and the oppressed."

I chose to place the <u>empowering </u>before the <u>lamp</u> slumbered because of the inactivity associated with slumber.

The BHS emends מטת in 4.21 on the witness of two manuscripts to מטית. I agree that this is necessary because the emendation supplies a much needed letter. In the Back Text the Masoretic Text at the effected point reads:

ואך למי ארם לעת ט מיד

"And surely to whom shall I raise up at the appointed time? ט from the hand."

ואך למי ארם לעת יַט מיד

"And surely to whom shall I raise up at the appointed time? <u>Let him stretch forth</u> from the hand."

The word יט is the jussive of נטה .

The word 'Ram' איל is a metaphor for 'leader'. See notes on paragraph 130.

Paragraph 191

This section is full of wonderful sayings and associations. Look at the 'Token'; examine the 'exclusive root of the mighty people of Y-H', or the 'Core of the Register', or the 'firebrand of a whelp' compared to the 'Lust of the Terrible One of Tooth' and finally what a friend did to the hand of the 'Man of Grace' bearing a special 'Gift'. The Back Text is so simple and straight forward that no notes are needed to fill out the text.

Paragraph 192

The importance of this section cannot be underestimated. The 'basket' and 'rule' have already been encountered in paragraph 183; and 'Death' which was the ruin of Eden (para. 183) shall destroy the 'Pure Mark' by making his knee to totter shall itself be destroyed (para. 194); and the 'Hand' feeding them 'Desire'; and the 'Song' the Terrible One wants so much to sing about the demise of G-d's 'Daughter'.

The Qere solves a textual problem. The word in 4.19 רבית is to be read

רבת. This makes the Back Text read תבר יד instead of תיבר יד. The new text reads 'the hand purified itself'. Here the 'hand' is feminine and the verb is feminine imperfect Niphal.

Paragraph 193

The word 'Plan' is spelled זם with a double 'mem' marked with a Daghes Forte זממ.

Verse 4.8 in the Forward Text has in part this:

> וחזותה לסוף כל ארעא
> **"and its visibility to the end of the whole planet."**

In verse 17 this is repeated along with the whole description of a vision. However the repeat in verse 17 is not exact. It is this fact that suggests that the Masoretic Text is in error. If we make verse 17 repeat exactly the description of verse 8 at this point the Back Text also changes. The Forward Text of this segment is put in parallel with the suggest haromonized text:

> MT: וחזותה לכל ארעא
> BHS: וחזותה לסוף כל ארעא
>
> The Back Text then is changed:
> MT: ואער אל כל התו זחו אי משל אט
> BHS: ואער אל כפו סלה תו זחו אי משל אט
>
> MT: **"and I G-d shall lay bare everything of the Mark. They pushed away the region of the dominion of gentleness."**

> BHS: "And I G-d shall lay bare <u>the sole of his foot.</u> The Mark <u>exulted.</u> They pushed away the region of the dominion of gentleness."

I have elected to print the Masoretic Text. This is not an endorsement of that text over the emended text of the BHS.

Paragraph 194

This text is a straight forward translation. No notes are necessary.

Paragraph 195

The word הכה **'he caused to be scorched'** is defective and should be read הכוה. The context of the section points to this definition/spelling.

Paragraph 196

The word **'man'** אש is defective; it should read איש. The 'skin of the grape' זג is not to be eaten by one under a Nazirite vow. Might this then mean that this זג is a metaphor for the dispised of G-d? Perhaps it is collective and perhaps it is but a single individual.

Paragraph 197

No notes.

Paragraph 198

Here is a new word איר which I base upon the verb אור and the noun of the same spelling. Working with the idea of 'illuminating' I have given it a more atomic sense of structure **'irradiation'**.

The word **'soothsayers'** עננם is defective and read עננים.

The plural **'hundreds'** plural feminine is truncated here מאת for the full מאות and the verbs all take the plural feminine ending ן :

> ותוחתן מאַת ויחדן תהבן אור
> "even He is the one breaking apart hundreds then he united them; let thou give them light."

The last part of this section ends in an imperative command plural masculine: "Move you gently!" This may not be wholly masculine as this suffix encompasses at times male and female. Futhermore the armies of which 'hundreds' are comprised are of course males. The feminine suffices are only in compliance with the rules of grammar.

Paragraph 199

No notes.

Paragraph 200

The Qere comes to the assistance once more in parsing the Back Text. Two words which are misspelled in the Masoretic Text are corrected. The first is ידרון but should be read ידורן and the second is יתזין but should be read יתזן. I shall present these changes below.

> נ*זתי הנם ואים שיר פץ נ*ר וַדי יה
> "I <u>sprinkled</u> Hennom and the Terrible One of Song. <u>A lamp</u> scattered <u>even the</u> sufficiency of Y-H."

Paragraph 201

In paragraph 115 the 'Constellation of the Great Bear' is first encountered by this name but in paragraph 68 it is presented in its other name URSA MAJOR. The sentence 'G-d lifted up an Alien to a Star' needs some comment. The verb translated 'lifted up' סנא is an Aramaism of the word סנה. Gesenius wrote that this word being an unused root in the Forward Text has the meaning in Arabic 'to lift up, to elevate'. This is my argument for interpreting סנא 'He lifted up'. The word 'Alien' whether upper or lower case in the Foward Text refer to 'stranger' in the participle form זר. This meaning of 'strangeness' is used to describe, in Hebrew minds, an uncleanness such as a Harlot or 'strange fire' upon an altar. Furthermore the foreigner of alien nations was referred to with this word. In our day stories of visitations of alien races from the stars has entered into the mythos of the world. It is a world phenomenon. Now, because we have encountered URSA MAJOR in this part of the Back Text and a Star it is only possible now to think of G-d removing from this earth (or 'lifting up') the Alien to a Star.

I have conjectured the noun form of the verb מור to become 'changeling'. I have further by fiat finalized the name אאוג 'Aa-Og'. It supplies the much needed object of the sentence.

Paragraph 202

The verb translated 'I shall send' אשט is from the root word I. שוט which usually is used to describe 'roving about'. The name 'serpent' is from the noun חוה and in HELOT p. 295b a reference to 'serpent' is made as a possible meaning. Because this is a rather esoteric meaning I will suggest a normal translation 'life' or 'Eve'.

> **"and from the Veil I shall cut off Life",**

> **"and from the Veil I shall cut off Eve",**
> **"and from the Veil I shall cut off the Serpent".**

Paragraph 203

The idea of giving one lodging is to imply he is made warm, welcome, fed and bedded and that he who did this also paid the bill.

The idea of 'salting' Light maybe to increase its effectiveness. There are three verbs listed in HELOT for these consonants. The first definition means 'to tear away', 'to dissipate'; the second definition is hidden to us and the third 'to salt, season'. But finally and more conclusive than dictionaries is the use of the word מלח in paragraph 204. Here it reads 'I shall salt the firebolt...My firebolt increased יני. These are the facts I used to translate this verb.

The verb translated 'he spread' פשא I believe to be the Aramaic spelling in the Back Text of פשה.

The Qere for the Masoretic Text word עללין reads עלין. This emends the Back Text also and remarkably but not unexpectedly an impediment is removed in the Back Text. There is an extra 'lamed' ל and it is this very letter that is removed!

> **"The Terrible One shall spread the burden of <u>wailing</u> to the weakened affliction."**
> The extra letter in place appears below underlined:
> פשא אים טרח ני ל<u>ל</u> לעני

Paragraph 204

Here is a significant section. The Instrument of Heart in the days of power shall measure the Assembly. This word may mean Israel, if a Jew, or 'church', if a New Testament Christian. He responded to a few of that Assembly; he went away; the people of the Assembly became slack in their duty before G-d. They rejected the Instrument of Heart although G-d increased His Firebolt which is the essence of His Light. Significantly Shem wept yet again for the plight of Israel (paragraph 134) and would yet 'howl' at Israel (paragraph 272). The affliction of Israel was made afraid.

The verb 'it was made afraid' is the Pipel form the verb.

The italic word *'women'* is a response the plural suffix feminine of the verb יהבן.

Paragraph 205

The collective 'Swarm' is used to describe schools of fish, small reptiles and quadrupeds and insects.

The imperative 'descend thou' רד is not feminine to correspond with 'seed' מעה.

Paragraph 206

This section marks the transition into Daniel chapter 3. Please note that the flow of thought is smooth from chapter four into three. The Forward Text of chapter three tells a story different from chapter four. The story revolves around three righteous men 'Shadrac, Meshac and Gabed-nego' or as the King James Version spells their names in the King's English 'Shadrach, Meshach, and Abed-nego'. The Masoretic Text divides the text differently. The Masoretic Text has 33 verses while the English versions number 30. The additional three verses are the first three verses of chapter four in the English versions. Each time the three men are mentioned together the Back Text reads **'the Garden of the Bear of Ruin like the gift of value he trampled'**. Sometimes there is a reason for the trampling of the Garden. Herein lies the explanation in part for the great length of the Back Text as compared to the Forward Text; from four words the Back Text gives eight (fifteen in translation). The information in the Hebrew/Aramaic texts is highly compact in the Back Text. The English translation does well in expressing it in its volume.

Paragraph 207

Here the 'gift of value' trampled is found with the 'Gift'. We know from other places that there are many gifts, some good and some bad. One such Gift is the Son of God. Paragraph 194 records: "Surely My Son is the Gift of the Veil". Is the 'gift of value' to be identified with the 'Gift of the Veil' which men trampled?

The name **'Ithiel'** איתיאאל is virtually identical with 'Ithiel' in Proverbs 30.1 and Nehemiah 11.7 איתיאל. This is very good grounds for the acceptance in the Back Text of these consonants as a name.

Paragraph 208

"...**for counseling the hand engraved**..." The subject 'hand' is masculine here as judged by the verb. The verb חרת is used once in the Forward Text in verse 16 of Exodus chapter 32 'engraved upon the tablets'.

The name **'Jude'** יהוד is found in Daniel 2.25 bearing the meaning in short form the land of 'Judah'. In the Back Text before us I have translated it 'a Jew'.

The word translated 'he shall be composed as' G-d ישוה is derived from the word I. שוה , 'to be equal, to be equivalent to'.

Paragraph 209

The BHS records that the Dead Sea Scrolls contains a fragment of Daniel which at the point of 3.37 reads עדה for the Masoretic spelling עדת. Making this change in the Back Text it now reads '**with the knowledge of**' G-d, בהדע. The MT may read 'when <u>thou</u> knowest' G-d he overcame Cheru. This is a collision of 'thou' and 'he'. If the word רון is read as the noun 'shouting for joy' we may read 'when <u>thou</u> knowest G-d the joyous shout of Cheru'. It is plain that the MT is not right. The superior reading is in the DSS fragment of Daniel. This paragraph records a visit to Sheol by the Pure One. There is a great ending in sight of Pride, Dispute and perhaps Sheol itself.

Paragraph 210

The decision to translate ארון '**coffin**' was due to context of paragraph 209, (Pit, Sheol, imprisoned, confined him) as well as the reference 'sleeping *people*'.

The last word of this section was translated '**and the maltreated *women***' ננות. I looked for a verb that would be feminine if treated as a gerund or participle. I believe the verb is ינה and in the Niphal plural participle ננות. This is repeated in paragraph 214 and there it is evident that 'women' is appropriate in filling out this word.

Paragraph 211

The Phoenician spelling of יאה is used here אי and I see an adjective.

The imperative '**bark you**' בחו is from the QAL word נבח.

Paragraph 212

The most significant thing in this section is the modification of the MT word in the Forward Text of 3.24 בהתבהלה on the basis of the DSS scroll fragment of Daniel which reads באאתבהלה. The change in the Back Text The sentence which reads in the MT thusly

---

הנע הלהב תהב מקוה may be read:
   "the flame was made to flicker;
   "thou shalt give hope."

But when the Qumran letter א replaces the ה in the next the parsing is very different:

הנע הלהבת אַב מקוה which now reads:
"The Flame of the <u>Father of</u> Hope He made to flicker."

Paragraph 213
The verbal suffices are masculine while 'hundreds' are feminine. The hundreds are either masculine or a mix of genders.
The 'mystery of the measuring line' reminds me of the book written in the Nineteenth Century on the Pyramid of Cheops called "Our Inheritance in the Great Pyramid" by Piazzi Smyth, 1880 and reissued by Bell Publishing Co. in 1977 under the new title "The Great Pyramid Its Secrets and Mysteries Revealed". Chapter XVI is entitled *The Sacred Cubit*, pp. 331-358. In there the author put forth the 'sacred cubit' which was in conflict with the Egyptian or common cubit. See Paragraph 227.
The word translated 'wish' רית is a modern Hebrew word.
Paragraph 214
The word translated '**the maltreated *women***' is discussed in the notes to paragraph 210.
A varient suggested in the BHS becomes sufficient in the Back Text. The conjuction ו is to be attached to the word in the Forward Text of 3.20 thusly וַלמרמא. In the Back Text this appears in context:

אם רם לוַ
"the high mother belongs to <u>Him</u>."

Paragraph 215
No notes.
Paragraph 216
The word סנא is a phoneme for שנא 'he hated'.
It is at times difficult to know when a noun or other part of speech belongs to Deity. Here the 'blood of his shadow' falls into this category. Is the blood a reference to the 'Instrument of the Father' and is 'his shadow' the Instrument's or the Father's? Paragraph 219 appears to favor the Father.
A 'jar' holds wine and food. Wine from a jar makes one drowsy.
Paragraph 217
Here the 'Mark' refuses the booty he shall plunder just as Abram refused the booty he plundered after the battle of the kings (Gen.14).

The Linear Bible Code

The word כתב is read as infinitive absolute and intransitive, 'writing'. **"The winepress shall smite down the mouth"** finds a link in the Forward Text in Isaiah 16.8 *"the vines of Sibmah languish, though their red grapes once laid low the lords of the nations…"* NEB. The same verb appears in Isaiah and here in the Back Text describing the effects of the 'red grapes'/ 'winepress', הלם!

The sentence **"I shall feed them the Favour of the Oppressed and the Son…"** in the MT has the verb at the end of the sentence but in the BHS this is inverted to the front of the sentence.

Paragraph 218

The verb translated '**thou split**' גסת is a modern Hebrew verb.

The BHS suggests the modification of די-עבדת in Daniel 3.15 of the Forward Text to read דעבדית; but if we take the 'yod' out and replace it with pointing below the ד we have in the Back Text a viable parsing of the text.

> תדב ע*ד אם לצל נוד
> **"thou moveth gently <u>perpetually</u> over the Mother of the Shadow of Wandering."**

The modern Hebrew language offers a clue to a difficult text in this section. The text translated reads:

> גסת ונול פת אר מזי-נזל כוה
> **"Thou split *Distinction* and disfigured a fragment of Light overflowing the *celestial* window."**

The difficulty is the '**overflowing**' מזי-נזל. In modern Hebrew I find מזי-רעב with the idea of 'starving' no doubt from the second word רעב. Using the second word in the Back Text נזל 'flow' I supplied the 'ing': 'flowing'. This new word appears again in paragraph 222.

Paragraph 219

The word translated '**fluttered**' is רת which is the truncated form of רתת 'tremble'. If there is a root word רות it may or may not have the same meaning. The feminine name 'Ruth' for instance offers no assistance in getting at a root such as רות. The rendering of the word 'fluttered' at least makes sense in the context of a 'banner' doing something.

The Linear Bible Code

The pairing of 'sorrow' and 'knowledge' is appropriate and no stranger to the readers of the Bible.

The word translated **'he causeth them pain'** יתיאן the suffix is feminine plural. What else is fem. Pl. in this section? "Apostasies"!

The word translated **'wield Thou power'** גס is the imperative of נגש. What we have here then is another phoneme ס for ש.

The phrase **'Blood of His Shadow'** is discussed in paragraph 216.

Paragraph 220

No notes.

Paragraph 221

The verb rendered **'he made himself to be constant'** above the hand of wailing, is from the verb התת . In this sentence the verb is Hithpael.

Paragraph 222

The word (in two places) סיו 'his sheep' is a phoneme to be spelled שיו.

The Qere of the word in 3.10 in the Forward Text וסיפניה is spelled וסופניה. In the Back Text the change is dramatic:

> MT ינפי סוני רת נס
> "???? Sunni; a banner fluttered."
> Qere ינפן סוני רת נס
> "they, the Sunni, waveth; a banner flutters."

Does the text referring to the Sunni waving the banner of war equate to our own day? Is this not the Sunni of Iraq in 21st Century Earth?

Paragraph 223

No notes.

Paragraph 224

The BHS for the Forward Text of Daniel 3.7 proposes a number of emendations due to omission or misspellings. Because the Masoretic Text repeats parts of the story the question arises why do the repeats read different from the first telling? This leads to a harmonization of the two tellings. One emendation is the suggestion of inserting one word found in the first but not in the second telling. This inserted word וסומפניא is found in verse 5 and is placed immediately after פסנטרין in verse 7. The Back Text is immediately rewarded by this action. Here is the reading without the addition followed by the emended text.

> The Back Text
> MT נאר מזי-נזל כו ני רט נס פא

The Linear Bible Code

> **"He abhorred the overflowing of the *celestial* window.
> Wailing! A banner fluttered. Here..."**
>
> נאר מזי-נזל כו <u>אי פם וסוני</u> רט נס פא BHS
> **"He abhorred the overflowing of the *celestial* window
> <u>of the region of the Mouth and the Sunni.</u> A banner
> fluttered. Here..."**

This text of Daniel is inconsistent in its spelling. Note that due to the phoneme of ס and ש as discussed in another Note and the Aramaic practice of substituting the א for the ה the Forward Text of Daniel is confusing. The BHS notes this and suggests an insertion from the first telling of the story which actually has the word ending in a ה not the supposed א. So, when BHS suggests its insertion in verse 7 it makes the letter change to א. But if one leaves the ה in place (as it appears in the MT in verse 5) the Back Text is in ruins *unless* we look elsewhere for help. Since we are on a search for correctly repeating exact wordage because of the penchant of the story teller to repeat then why not look in verse 10.

In verse 10 we find a third telling of the story begun in verse 5. When we compare the three they do not agree in every respect. Yet my Back Text of verse 10 which reads exactly as the Masoretic Text spells the words (with the one exception of a proposed substitution of a 'vav' ו for a 'yod' י as laid out in Paragraph 222's notes) is well rounded in thought. I propose using this third telling in verse 7 and in verse 5.

The words in verse 10 I propose repeating in verses 5 and 7 are as follows:

> ▪ קל קרנא משרקיתא קיתרס שבכא פסנתרין וס<u>ו</u>פניה וכל זני זמרא

Whatever must be done the evidence suggests that there are textual problems. How one fixes them I believe is determined by the Back Text. The letters of Daniel have got to make sense in both directions.

The word translated 'he eclipsed' יעם is from the root II. עמם ▪

Paragraph 225
No notes.
Paragraph 226
No notes.
Paragraph 227

The reference to **'standard measure'** which the Instrument of the Mother scorned maybe linked with the reference to the 'mystery of the measuring line' in Paragraph 213. I discuss there the 'sacred cubit' in comparison with the 'common cubit'.

The use of the word 'rust' חלאה in connection with 'bloods' דמים is most appropriate because the two are linked. Rust is a symbol of impurity and blood-stain, see Ezekiel 24.6; and blood is used to illustrate that the land is defiled (Numbers 35.33).

The next reference in connection with the impurity is its opposite: "His Clean One". This section is very powerful.

Paragraph 228

The **'standard-measure'** is again the topic here and the 'Blood of Weight' its parallel. Note the connection of 'rust' with 'blood' again in the sense of defilement.

This Paragraph ends the Forward Text of Chapter 3.

Paragraph 229

This begins Chapter 2 of the Forward Text (of course) with the last verse 49.

The mark of the accusative את also appears in the Back Text. A perfect example is the sentence:

> ידם יד את די בעל עי
> **"The hand silences the sufficiency of the Lord of Ruin."**

Paragraph 230

The word translated **'smitten'** is from the Hophal נוכה of נכה.

Paragraph 231

The name **'Penuel'** appears but once in the Back Text. It is the Name of G-d as recorded in Genesis 32.31 and spelled פניאל which translated means 'the face of G-d'.

The use of the word על 'on high' is according to HELOT p.752a.

The word המ translated **'he murmured'** is from the verb הום.

The word 'Desire' אוה in connection with the 'Moon' has to do with the phases of the moon as it wanders during the month. A connecting link is found in Deuteronomy 12.15,20,21 and 18.6. It comes in its own season.

Paragraph 232

The word 'scoured' סח is from סחה.

The word 'pair' גז is a modern Hebew word; see Megiddo, p. 243b זוג ∎

The word translated 'he thrust away' זח is the truncated form of זחח∎

The word 'Column' שת is a metaphor for 'prince'; Gesenius 852b.

The name 'Cheam' is conjecture 'encouraged' by the context. Seth is keeper of the Word of God but not all.

Paragraph 233

The word translated 'vessel' מאן is according to Gesenius p.445a which appears only in Daniel the Forward Text; 5.2,3,23.

Hennom is a known evil place. While parsing this section of the Back Text the name 'Hata-Hennom' seemed inevitable. I do not know what the prefix means. Likewise the construct of mouth פי points to a person's name and hence 'Keith' of whom I have parsed before in paragraphs 57, 129 and 163.

Paragraph 234

I have translated rather freely the noun נוה which in the HELOT p.627b in bold reads *'abode of shepherd, or flocks, poet. habitation;"*. According to context I have used one or the other full interpretations. In a rare instance I have rendered it 'habitation'. The noun 'Distinction' or 'Eminency' also is spelled the same.

Now I come to my translation of זרף. I have rendered it 'discourse' as a noun and with the lamed לזרף as the infinitive construct of the verb. In the Forward Text the verb root word זרף probably means 'drip' and 'dripping' all on the one reference in Psalm 72.6. This is similar to another word דמע which means: 'weep' 'trickling' and in the noun form 'tears'. I believe the context of this and the following paragraphs can only mean 'discourse' *n.* 'to discourse' *vb.* from the idea of words 'trickling' down or 'dripping' from the lips. This maybe supported from the word נטף which means 'drop, drip' as in clouds 'dropping' water. Another meaning of נטף is 'discourse', especially of a prophet, Amos 7.16, 'prophesy not against Israel, and drop not against the house of Isaac'. In this case 'drop' is translated 'discourse'. The similarity between נטף and זרף is that of synonyms.

Paragraph 234

The word translated **'Thou shalt pant'** תהג is from the root נהג∎

Paragraph 235

The word translated 'it is awakening them' עערם is a modern Hebrew word and would be a participle spelled fully here עוערם, see Megiddo p.520b.

My translation of the word ניד as '*who* moved to and from' is from the hollow verb נוד and is in perfect masculine. This follows other hollow verbs which can also be written with a 'yod' in place of the 'vav', see שום\שים

Paragraph 236

I have conjectured another name because after parsing the text this remained יחאשן *Jacheshan.*

Another modern Hebrew word I found in the Back Text is סאח although spelled סיחה page 498b; such is my conjecture.

Paragraph 237

The word translated '**cold**' קר is to be read קור and like the Forward Text the 'vav' is deficient presenting the same spelling like the Back Text.

The word '**heap**' גד can according to context be a *harvest* heap or a heap *of ruins.*

The word rendered '**efficient wisdom**' is from the truncated word תשה which is spelled in full תושיה ; see HELOT p. 444b.

Paragraph 238

The word '**Acco**' עכו may be found in any good dictionary of the Bible.

The act of '**rinsing clean**' הדח from דוח is of course part of the Torah although this specific word is not used there. The best use of it in the sense of washing away guilt is in Isaiah 4.4. Its use in the Back Text is significant. It goes hand-in-hand with being unclean (paragraphs 115 and 263) as well as becoming purified which the Son did in order to perform his service to the people of Israel "the Pure One volunteered and they of the Affliction shall become his debt; he shall take it away with innocence," Paragraph 173; "the Pure One purified himself and he fed them," Paragraph 177.

The following sentence is constructed from one conjecture 'Brightness' and resorting to one modern Hebrew word 'Age':

> **"The Instrument prophesied of the Age of Brightness of Power *and* My Knowledge."**

The word rendered '**Age**' תר\תור is from the Megiddo, 695a where the word is in combination with the word gold. The conjecture of rendering זגת as a noun construct is from the verb זוג . It is to be expected that the Back Text would advance our knowledge of the Hebrew and Aramaic languages. I believe we are not disappointed in this expectation.

The word 'he removed' הז is the truncated form of זחח . Perhaps the original form of this verb was spelled זוח in which case the perfect form of the verb would indeed be הז▪ A number of known roots share this type of spelling, see רום and רמם▪

The word rendered 'he is made a fool' הול is the truncated form of the Hophal הולל ▪

Paragraph 239

The act of '**beating out**' חבט in the Forward Text is a figure of judgment of Y-H and subsequent gathering of Israel, Isaiah 27.12; see also HELOT, p.286a.

Paragraph 240

The word '**has departed**' גה read גהה ▪

The word '**he was brought low**' is the Hophal המך of מכך ▪

The BHS suggests the insertion of a 'yod' in the word רעיונך of the Forward Text of 2.29 רעיניך and I have accepted that addition. The Back Text then is modified and fills out the name of a place עכין▪

The spelling of 'Jackal' here is augmented with a final aleph תנא something unusual in the Back Text.

The mentioning of the 'Lair' twice using two very different words סך and יער is noteworthy. Perhaps the 'Lair' of Y-H is referred to here on the grounds of Jeremiah 25.38 where Jerusalem is the 'Lair' forsaken of G-d. Both words acting together spell out 'lair' whereas individually 'booth' may be thought of. The wild animal 'jackal' is perhaps the guide to thinking of a 'lair'. It is the quintessential animal for inhabiting ruins.

Paragraph 241

The word '**community**' is truncated חה from the full form חיה ▪

The word translated '**a cheap glass of wine**' is a very free paraphrase of זג▪ The HELOT says (page 260) that this product of the grape was forbidden to the Nazirite under vow. While in other places I have rendered the noun otherwise I believe it does refer to a poor wine and not grape skins. Who eats grape skins? Surely the scholars are at odds over its meaning also.

Once again in the Back Text we have come upon a segment dealing with food and drink/water. I am personally in wonder about the consistency of the topic here as it builds to a climax in the next paragraph.

Paragraph 242

The word הגע is interpreted here as Hiphel imperative, 'shake thou'.

The words אם-לח I have linked with the MAQQEPH because of the close association in meaning. It may be read in the old manner 'mother of freshness' but in our day this means 'Mother Nature'. This takes upon itself great moment in our day because of the threatened state of Nature and the great upheavals thereof.

The place 'Nebon' is more than conjecture because of the plural construct state of valleys גי , 'valleys of' what? And the next consonants must become a place!

Paragraph 243

Note that the subject of food as a context helped to interpret the letters שפו as 'they ground' food. The root verb is from the modern Hebrew word שוף, Ben-Yehuda/Weinstein p.291a and שף page 303b.

Sometimes a translator has to choose between alternate meanings. Here in this paragraph the letters קין in a sentence that reads **"They ground food from the measure of"**. These letters appear in the Forward Text as 'Cain' and 'Spear'. I have chosen the former because as a son of Adam he tilled the earth.

The BHS for Daniel 2.24 suggests a word be omitted from the text. I have underlined this word; the asterisk * denotes omission:

. כל-קבל דנה דניאל <u>על</u> על-אריוך די מני מלכא

In the Back Text this fixes a problematic text:

ו ירא לעלע לאי נד הנד לב קלך

Which does not mean anything; but removing the two letters everything comes into focus linguistically:

ו ירא לעל * אי נד הנד לב קלך

"and he feared for <u>against</u> the coast of the heap *of ruins* was the heap of the Will of Thy Voice."

Paragraph 244

The word translated '**let thou render**' תסם is a phoneme for שׂום the root. The word rendered plural construct 'galleries of' seed אתקי is spelled out fully אתוקי ; see HELOT p.87b.

Paragraph 245

The interpretation of דאת as 'eagle of' Greatness, is grounded in the fact that the word means 'a bird of prey'.

In the Forward Text the two letters גז in Ezekiel 47.13 is interpreted as זה 'this'. I have also rendered it this way in the Back Text. In other places in the Back Text I have read it as the truncated form of גזה 'depart'.

Paragraph 246

No notes

Paragraph 247

The word '**terraces of**' תלמי is a word meaning 'furrows of' a field. But when these furrows are applied to hills and mountains I interpret it 'terraces'.

The spelling of **'mountain'** is the ancient spelling for the familiar הר .See HELOT, p.223b. And what product was produced in these 'terraces'? The next line tells us it is measured by the liquid measure Hin הין . May it be then olive oil? And the line next says that it is traded on the coast. The whole paragraph takes this as its topic.

The name 'Jochah' although the vowels are conjecture the consonants seem sure as it follows the verb 'he said'.

Paragraph 248

The BHS records that the Septuagint (LXX) of Daniel does not have the equivalent of ועל . When I remove this from the Forward Text of 2.16 the Back Text makes wonderful sense. If one keeps it the text reads abit differently:

> Removed: **"What is a cloud? It moves not to and fro! And it does not move to and fro for thee."**
> Retained: **"What is a cloud? And upwards the Isle a heap but it does not move to and fro for thee."**
> 2nd Retained: **"What is his cloud? For over the coast is his heap and it does not move to and from for thee."**

I perceive an awkwardness to the text and I have omitted it.

Paragraph 249

The translation of ביתה is usually 'toward the house' but I realize that the 'house' is the Temple. The Temple is known by this simple word in conjunction with qualifiers such as 'sacrifice' 2 Chronicles 7.12 and 'holiness' 2 Chronicles 3.8; but more especially when it is used alone as in I Kings 6 and 8.

The idea of Keith wrapping tighly his 'wreath' brings to mind a 'crown'.

Paragraph 250

The opening verb **'let thou strike them off'** תקפן stripped of the prefix and suffix reads I. נקף ▪

The imperative **'break thou'** is from the root פצץ ▪

The name 'Senab' סנב is my conjecture of letters otherwise of no meaning although the use of the two letters סנ are foreign in nature and may be found in the Forward Text beginning names of people 'Sanballat' סנבלט and places סנאה of that nature . Please note that 'Sanballat' reads exactly as the conjectured name in its first three letters!

Paragraph 251

The name "Tae'er" is conjecture but contains evidence of two words as is known in established names. I see the last two letters אר reading 'light' and the first part made of three letters תיא which may be a prefix 'thou' or 'she' ת and the verb יאה 'be befitting' for the full meaning 'light is befitting'.

The word 'blemished' מם is the truncated form of מום and connected with the verb 'she was emaciated' דקה this goes a long way validating the italics I used to convey the meaning.

Paragraph 252

The name/place name, 'Joach' has the definite article ה attached to it and is untranslateable. This is known in the Forward Text, see 'Sharon' Isaiah 33.9 השרון ▪

The rendering of תשב 'sojourner' is from HELOT, p.444b and spelled fully תושב▪

Paragraph 253

The verb **'laid waste'** is the Pilpel form of the unused root in the Forward Text תהה and spelled here in the Back Text תהתה▪

Paragraph 254

The Linear Bible Code

The imperative '**smite thou**' כני is feminine.

The two names 'Neah' and 'Chaan'; the first is biblical נעה Joshua 19.13 and the second is conjecture from parsing the text. 'Neah' is feminine and may answer to the verb preceeding it 'I shall wound her' and in that case the BackText would read:

"I shall wound Neah and Chaan inflamed Y-H."

The idea of 'eggs' from a leopard is perposterous and yet imagery is the over riding rule here. In the Forward Text of Isaiah 59.5 we read of the creature צפעוני having eggs and we read in HELOT p.861b that this 'venomous viper' does 'not lay eggs'. Here then we have a possible precedence for eggs when eggs are not possible. We must read this metaphorically.

Paragraph 255

Note that the word 'thinness' is Aramaic plural with the 'yod' defective but spelled out this way: קנין■

The word 'integrity' of Noah תם may also be translated 'perfection' of Noah. In Genesis 6.9 it reads 'Noah was a just man, a perfect one'. The key word 'perfect' תמים is an adjective more akin to 'integrity' than 'perfection'. Both תם and תמים work hand-in-hand, the one a noun and the other an adjective. The definition then is interchangeable; 'integrity' and 'perfect'.

The word יתב '**he becomes prominent**' is from the verb נתב■

Paragraph 256

Note the Aramaic word '**here**' אז■ I find it significant that the Back Text of Daniel has many Aramaic words mixed in with classic Hebrew. It will be remembered that the Forward Text of Daniel begins classic then moves to Aramaic and concludes in the classic Hebew.

Paragraph 257

The BHS suggest a change in Daniel 2.4. The MT is first given and followed by the emended text.

MT: ימל על אכל מתימר
"He shall speak against the food from Timor".
BHS: ימל על אכל-מור מאי ו
"He shall speak against the <u>bitter</u> food <u>from the coast, and</u>".

The reference to 'Timor' reminds me of the present day 'east Timor' that is occupying the news. This place is located in Indonesia.

The word 'his darkness' עפתו is from עיפה , see HELOT p. 734a.

Paragraph 258

In this section there are four places all known because of their bodies of water. The text is straight forward enough:

מִי-דְש-כֹל "waters of Dashcol"

מִי-פְשֶׁךְ-מֹל "waters of PeshecMol"

מִי-פְש-אֵל "waters of PeshEl"

מִי-מְשֵׁר "waters of Mesher"

The fun part is interpreting the place names. The first "Dashcol" maybe the verb דוש 'he threshed' or 'to pound' and the noun 'whole' 'all'. Its possible interpretation may read "he threshed everything".

The second place name "PeshecMol" maybe read 'thy sin' פשׁך 'he cut off' מֹל ; the verb in this case is spelled out fully מול or מלל ∎.

The third place name "PeshEL" may mean "the transgression of God" or if a verb "God is proud".

The fourth place name "Mesher" may be the truncated noun מִישׁר "equity" or "uprightness".

Paragraph 259

My translation of חל-ארק "**Fortress Earth**" is a clear cut translation. The word for "Earth" is very unusual in the Forward Text; it appears once in Jeremiah 10.11 but quite often in the Targums; see Gesenius p.81b.

The BHS in Daniel 2.1 the Forward Text suggests a change in the word נהיתה . It is written נדדה . This changed the Back Text remarkably. The Masoretic Text does not work in the parsing of the Back Text but the suggested change does work reading '**Our Beloved**'.

The BHS in the same verse suggests that שׁתים read more fully שׁתים עשרה . This added word in the Back Text spells out 'wicked one' and the sentence reads:

"He cut off <u>the wicked one</u>."

Paragraph 260

I added italics to the sentence "**He shall spring about**" יפש because the verb in the Forward Text is used to describe the gamboling of calves, see Jeremiah 50.11 "though you run free like a heifer" NEB.

The remainder of this section reads straightforward enough and needs no comment.

Paragraph 261

The context of this section dictates that the verb המת should have the third masculine suffix added המתו and by pointing below the line we would find below the ת the three slanted dots called QIBBUS. This also occures in the Forward Text. The sentence in questions is "They murdered the Light..."

The verb translated 'hastened' בהל is in the Piel; see HELOT, p. 96b.

Paragraph 262

The word translated 'the remover' is from a conjectured form of the verb זחח thusly יזח and written in the imperfect Niphal.

Paragraph 263

The word translated '**let thou make wide**' is from the Aramaic word פתא . I added in italics *the mouth* in the two occasions of the verb on the strength of the Forward Text; see Proverbs 20.19 and 24.28 where lips are indicated.

A note about the word translated '**the unclean one of**' the Nile טמה . This is the spelling of the verb not the noun or adjective which are טמאה and טמא respectively. However the verb root for these words is טמא and not what is in the Back Text טמה ; therefore, I have conjectured an adjective spelled the same as the root letters! Not all construct words ending in ה become ת ; see one example in the word מחנה .

Paragraph 264

The word translated 'idols' צקים is from the root 'pour out' צוק . This noun plural is not found in the Forward Text.

The word translated '**raved**' הזה is according to Gesenius' lexicon, p. 220b.

I have rendered a common conjunction (ו) in an atypical manner in the second to last sentence in this paragraph; the translation 'or' only because of the context: "Shall I raise him up or wailing?"

Paragraph 265

The word translated **'they disguised themselves'** התשנו is the truncated Hithpael of שנה QAL.

The list of names in answer to the question 'who is the adversary?' are as inevitable as are they new and intriguing. If the names beginning with נ are other than phonetic and are built on verbs or nouns therein lies the intrigue. The name 'Nem' may be the verb 'he slumbered', and 'Nel' may come from the verb נלה 'he obtained' according to some and 'he finished' according to others, and the name 'Natai' appears to be the feminine imperative 'give thou' from the root נתן 'he gave'.

The BHS offers yet another emendation to Daniel. In chapter 1 verse 11 the name/title 'the Melztar' of dubious translation (found only here in this chapter) appearing twice (vs.16) seemingly is spelled differently in other versions. The one the BHS points out is the spelling מנצר which makes better sense to a philologist because it means 'keeper' or 'guardian' while the first spelling is acknowledged to be very dubious with the likelihood that it too means the same. I have elected to keep the spelling in the Masoretic Text but I would use this point in the text as a study lesson in how two letters can change the reading dramatically. Below I have reversed the order of the letters for the Back Text and parsed the text first according to the Masoretic Text and second according to the Emended (BHS) text.

MT: יסיר סהר שה נם רש ארץ למה לאל אין דר מאיו
"He causeth to chastise the Tower of the Sheep. The poor of the land is drowsy. Why? For G-d there is no pearl from His Region."

BHS: יסיר סהר שה נַמר שא רצן מלא לא ינד רם איו
"The leopard of ravage turneth aside the Gate of the Sheep the favour of fullness. The haughtiness of his coast shows no remorse."

The reason I have not used this excellent textual emendation is because it does violence to the text previously encountered and what is yet to come. I speak of the other 'towers'. In Paragraph 261 I have translated the very same Hebrew letters יסיר סהר "he causeth to chastise the tower" and in paragraphs 267, 268 and 269 four more towers by name are given all with the same translation "he causeth to chastise the tower". It is only in the present paragraph that violence is done to this homogenous set of 'towers'. I submit that the word מנצר was corrupted intentionally to מלצר for the express purpose of the Back Text. The Forward Text by other means recovered the true meaning of the name/title as I have shown (guardian/keeper) and yet the Back Text would have read incorrectly without it!!! I cannot stress enough this dual writing technique: What is written in the Forward Text must bend here and there for the purpose of the Back Text!

Paragraph 266

The word translated 'causeth thee to shine' יגך is the truncated version of the root נגה. The full spelling ought to be יגיך.

The sentence in which the 'mothers' are spoken of also says 'caused them to be drowsy'. Who are 'them'? The suffix is plural masculine therefore it is the people of 'poverty' who are made drowsy.

Paragraph 267

The reading of **'free born'** from חר maybe rendered 'noble' but I have elected otherwise because in those days to be free born was to have an elevated stature in culture of masters, free born and slaves.

The word translated **'he complained'** from סה is both defective and a phoneme from the correct word and spelling שיח .

The word translated **'he twisted'** is from the unused root לול in the Forward Text.

Paragraph 268

The word translated 'My treasures' הנתי is from the singular noun 'wealth' הון.

The BHS and my own text change in the Forward Text offers a satisfying reading in the Back Text. Without these two emendations the Back Text would mean nothing. First the Masoretic Text backward is given and the proposed parsing of its text:

MT: וגנדבע and parsed וגן דב ע which reads in part **'and the garden of the bear'.** The consonant ע means nothing by itself and the parsing of the text after it precludes using any letters to help it. Surely there is a problem in the Forward Text. The BHS suggests that the ג be substituted with a ב in the Forward Text word נגו. The Back Text then reads: ובן דב ע 'and the son of the bear'. I suggest the addition to the Straight Text of a 'vav' ו in verse 7 at this point: וַעבד. This does not corrupt the Forward Text at all but enhances it. Now the Back Text is complete: ובן דב עַו "and the <u>son</u> of the Bear <u>of ruin</u>." Elsewhere in the Back Text we have read of the 'bear of ruin' and this restoration conforms with it; see paragraphs 206 and 207 and the Register. What is new here is the reference to the Bear's son.

Paragraph 269

The word 'thrones of' כשי is a phoneme for כסי which again is the shortened form of כסא.

Paragraph 270

The word 'hills' במם is the truncated form of במים.

Paragraph 271

The word 'eternities' עדם is the truncated form of עדים.

Paragraph 272

The word 'lights' הארם is the truncated form of הארים.

The words 'a certain hope' סבר-זן is a phoneme and is found spelled שבר and the second part זן is altogether correct 'kind' 'sort'.

Paragraph 273

The word translated 'he shall boast' יהל is the truncated form of יהלל.

The word 'palaces' is truncated היכלם so read היכלים.

The word 'My Treasures' is plural feminine possessive so read אונותי in place of the truncated form אנתי.

Paragraph 274

And so the book ends with themes presented in the beginning of the book. And finally a fitting and parting injunction:

'Repent thou!'.

Appendix

A

WORDS FOUND IN THE STRAIGHT TEXT OF DANIEL AND IN THE BACK TEXT

The discovery of a new book linked to the Book of Daniel will add to our knowledge of the language in which it was written. The Book of Daniel is composed of two languages. The first is classic Hebrew and the second Aramaic. The Back Text of Daniel contains a mix of these two languages but to a lesser degree. Aramaic words are dispersed throughout most of the Back Text. This Appendix is a partial list of the unique words used in Daniel that appear in the Back Text as well.

בות   "to pass the night", Daniel 6.19 / Back Text Paragraph 11 "he passed the night".

כו   "a window", Daniel 6.11 / Back Text Paragraph 60 "window".

רז   "a secret", Daniel 2.18, 19; 4.6 / Back Text Paragraph 22 "secret".

ית   mark of the accusative, Daniel 3.12 / Back Text Paragraph 88.

דחל   "to fear" "to make afraid", Daniel 2.31; 5.19; 7.7 / Back Text Paragraph 121.

אלו   interjection "lo" Daniel 2.31; 4.7,10; 7.8 / Back Text Paragraph 141.

חוא   "to shew, to declare", etc. Daniel 2.24 etc., \ Back Text Paragraph 144.

רשם   "inscribe, sign" Daniel 6.10 etc. \ Back Text
Paragraph 166.

זן   "kind" Daniel 5.7, 10, 15 \ Back Text Paragraph 272.

דרע   "arm", Daniel 2.32 \ Back Text Paragraph 163.

פם   "mouth" Daniel 7.8 etc. \ Back Text Paragraph 71.

Aramaic word used in Daniel and Ezra

מאן   "vessel" Daniel 5.2,3, 23; Ezra 5.14 \ Back Text
Paragraph 233.

Appendix
B

<u>New Words</u>

It is in the realm of all likelihood that in a Book such as this new words will be encountered. Each book of the Hebrew Scriptures surely is unique so why not the Back Text of Daniel? In this we are not disappointed. Some of the new words in the Back Text are derived from stems already known or hinted at in the Forward Text of the Tanach while others are so new that their understanding remains conjecture.

קזן   This is conjectured to mean 'beginning' by the context in which it is embedded; see Paragraph 156.

נם   This is derived from the verb נום and is an adjective meaning 'drowsy'; see Paragraph 168.

חאו   This is conjectured to be in the perfect plural masculine. The context seems to mean 'they were wounded'; see Paragraph 169.

רז   This is from the verb רזה and is interpreted to be an adverb 'leanness'; see Paragraph 170.

אבץ   This word means 'whiteness' noun from the unused root in the Forward Text אבץ 'to be white'; see Paragraph 185.

אשן   This is used as an adverb from the unused root of the same spelling; see Paragraph 189.

תע   This is a noun 'err' from the verb תעה 'err'; see Paragraph 12-13.

מגש   Noun masculine 'error'; see Paragraph 209. The feminine form only is found in the Forward Text משגה.

מזי-נזל I have by conjecture interpreted this 'overflowing'; see Paragraph 218. I arrived at this definition from the modern Hebrew word מזי-רעב 'starving', see Meggido, p. 381a. The key to 'starving' is רעב so 'overflowing' is keyed off of נזל 'flow'.

נול Interpreted 'disfigured' verb from the modern Hebrew word as listed in Weinstein, p.199b.

נום Rendered 'somnolence' masculine whereas the Straight Text only lists the feminine form נומה; see Paragraph 229.

ינת Noun construct 'oppression of' from verb ינה 'to oppress'. This I interpreted from context; see Paragraph 242.

ענה Noun 'affliction' from verb ענה 'to afflict'; see Paragraph 242.

דל Noun, 'thinness'; see the adjective דל in HELOT, p.195b. Paragraph 254.

צַוקים Plural noun masculine from verb II. צוק 'pour'; see Paragraph 264.

במַים Noun plural masculine 'hills' from the feminine form במה; see Paragraph 270.

בהם Noun masculine from feminine בהמה; see Paragraph 273.

בלול 'confusion' from verb בלל 'mingle, mix, confuse, confound' HELOT p.117a. See Paragraph 26.

שע 'delight' noun from verb שעע ; see also the noun שעשעים 'delight'. Paragraph 30.

שג Translated noun 'sin' from שגג the verb 'err'. Paragraph 33.

תן Translated noun 'gift' from the verb נתן; see paragraph 35.

נוזה Translated 'Remover' participle from the verb זחח; see Paragraph 95.

פטש   Translated 'spread out' verb from the unused verb in the Forward Text; see Gesenius 673a #2. Paragraph 40.

בבה   Translated noun 'gate' ; see HELOT p.93a בבה noun feminine. Paragraph 42.

לוק   I treat this as the root of the verb לקק 'lick'; see Paragraph 48a.

רת   Translated adjective masculine 'trembling' from the verb רתת 'tremble'. Paragraph 54.

נרק   Niphal form 'was weakened' of רקק which is unused in the Forward Text. Paragraph 128.

מו   Used in Paragraph 113 and translated 'from it'.

רט   Translated 'terror' from verb רטט 'tremble'; see Paragraph 163.

הרית   Translated 'mountain' feminine construct from a conjectured noun הרה 'mountain'. Paragraph 118.

זגה   Translated 'brightness' from verb זוג 'be clear, bright, transparent', and is in the construct form here זגת HELOT p.259b. Paragraph 238.

קלקל   Pilpel from קלל in Paragraph 21 'contemptable' of Bosom.

צע   QAL from צוע which is an unused root in the Forward Text. 'They fashioned' for him My banners'; Paragraph 28.

יתבש   Hithpael of בוש   'He   shamed   himself', Paragraph 29.

לל   Translated 'winding' *staircase* from לול 'shaft' 'enclosed space (poss. In wall), with steps or ladder, only pl. לולים ; so reads HELOT p.533a. See Para. 29.

התב   Hophal 'he was returned' from תוב ; see Paragraph 35.

השע   Hophal 'he was made deliverer' from ישע; see Paragraph 35; 'he was to save' Paragraph 47.

נוזח   Niphel participle 'the Remover' from the conjectured יזח which in turn is from either זחח or זוח in Paragraph 37.

ברש   QAL 'he cut to pieces' of the unused root of the same spelling; see Gesenius p.145b. Paragraph 38.

הצק   Participle of the QAL צוק 'the Distresser' in Paragraph 38.

הנם   Hophal from the root   נום 'made to slumber' in Paragraph 38.

נואצי   Niphal participle construct plural masculine, 'the ones having despised' from נאץ in Paragraph 39.

ינש   Niphal 'is made sick' from the root נוש in Paragraph 42.

נתן   Niphal 'he was presented' from I. תנה QAL 'hire'; Paragraph 44.

ירש   Hophal imperfect 'he shall be made poor' from the QAL verb רוש in Paragraph 48b; 'has been made poor', Paragraph 54.

הדח   Hophal 'he is made clean by washing' from the QAL דוח in Paragraph 54.

תוד   Noun masculine תד 'thanksgiving' from the verb ידה and note the feminine form 'thanksgiving' תודה . Paragraph 111.

בהיתי   QAL first person masculine perfect 'I emptied' from the root בהה unused in the Forward Text. The suffix 'his' finishes the word "I emptied it"; Paragraph 112.

בק   Noun 'empty one' from בקק II.; spelled in Paragraph 119 plural masculine possessive third person masculine בקיו 'his empty ones'.

ינול   Pael 'he is made filthy' from the verb נול 'to pollute, to make filthy'; see Paragraph 141.

אבצהו   Hiphel 'I shall make him white' from the unused root בוץ; see Paragraph 163.

רההה   Pipel 'it was made afraid' from רהה , see HELOT p. 923b; Paragraph 204.

חאו   'they were wounded' conjecture, Paragraph 169.

חלף   'knife'; see HELOT מחלף 'knife' p.322b. The Back Text verb 'sharpen' שנן leads to this translation.

There are other new paradigms of verbs I have elected not to list. These are part of the Notes to the paragraphs.

Appendix
C

<u>Modern Hebrew Words</u>

There are a small number of words that appear in the parsing of the Back Text that can only be interpreted by referring to Living Hebrew. These modern Hebrew words, some of which may not have ancient roots, raise an important question. Why are modern words found in the Back Text of Daniel? I believe that these words can only be interpreted from a modern world. If I am right then he who composed the Back Text foresaw its coming forth in our day and certified it with our words. The Back Text of Daniel is composed of classic Hebrew, Aramaic and modern Hebrew, the Past, Present and Future, if you will.

רר   'Discharge' Paragraph 2 "and the discharge of a daughter flowed יצק". See Megiddo p. 647b.

זח   'Pride' Paragraph 47 "pull down thy pride". See Megiddo p.244a.

דו   'twice' Paragraph 53. "twice is thy ruin". See Megiddo p.106a.

פט   'stalemate' Paragraph 65 "a stalemate *with* he who is with him". See Megiddo p.553a.

ארק   'whiskey' Arabian called in the Back Text 'Arrack' Paragraph 96 "did not the sojourner increase because of the coast and *from* its arracks they howl?". See Megiddo p.40a.

זיהום   'contamination' Paragraph 141 "the Palate lendeth him the likes of contamination". See Megiddo p.245a.

גס   'ill   mannered'   from   'crude'   Meggido   p.98a. Paragraph 141 "an ill-mannered bull put them in fear".

גס   'crude' noun or adjective from 'crude' Megiddo p.98a. Paragraph 210 "there is no crude one".

שט   'transgressor', Megiddo p.663a. Paragraph 169 "come thou forth transgressor!"

תדב   ' Let thou make a donation', from נדב Megiddo p.446a. Paragraph 181 "Aih maketh a donation".

שלי   'secrecy', Megiddo p.674b (Paragraph 182) which calls the word 'biblical'. Paragraph "two islands of secrecy of the Bosom of the Bear".

חו   'register', Megiddo p. 258b. Paragraph 191 "and the Core of the Register is strength to Me".

זים   'proved false', Megiddo p.246a from זימם. Paragraph 10 "and this he proved false".

נגס   'to bite', Megiddo p.446b. Paragraph 229 "His Pure One bit off the courage of the Jackal".

נזח   'to be unsteady', Ben-Yehuda/Weinstein, 200b. Paragraph 233 "the hand makes unsteady the Mountains of Desolation".

עוער   'awaken' (archaic) Megiddo p. 520b. Paragraph 235 "the Hand of God is awakening them the drip of the *celestial window*".

ניד   'deflection', Megiddo p.459a which reads 'movement; swing, deflection'. Paragraph 235 "This is the Lowly One, the deflection of the Moon" I subsequently rendered the word a verb "This is the Lowly One *who* moved to and from the Moon."

טום   'ritually stained' from Megiddo's טומא p.292. Paragraph 272 "they are ritually stained" טומו .

The Linear Bible Code

The REGISTER
of Names and Subjects
in Hebrew-Aramaic-English

Note: The number following an entry refers to the Paragraph Number of the 'TEXT'.

The Linear Bible Code

A

אאוג	**Aa-Og**, 201.
תעב	**abomination**, he poured out his, 17.
אבאל	**Abael**, 62.
נוה	**abode of the shepherd**, 118; 123; 127; 209; 220; 234; 236.
נוה	**abode of the flock**, is with the Pure One, 177; 207.
על	**Above**, 222.
רב	**abundance**, 154; 215; 249.
תהם	**Abyss**, 205.
עכת	**Acath**, 68.
עכה	**Accah**, 126.
עכין	**Acen**, 240.
עכו	**Acco**, the blood of, 47; wail of, 60; 238.
משק בר	**acquisition, a pure**, 260.
קם	**adversary** swallowed thee, 73; 99.
צר	**Adversary**, who ran from the, 15; felt shame toward G-d, 26; they magnified the, 26; swallowed up Grace, 64; of desire, 103. of the Chieftain of Integrity, 100; the living, wrung out a measuring line; 176.
צרא	**adversary**, 273.
ער	**adversary**, who is this, 265.
רע	**adversary** hammered by the Mark, 32; made unclean My Winepress, 138.
צרא	**adversity**, he shall run from, 75.
אעאאל	**Aeael**, the fruit of desire, came forth, 177.
עני	**affliction**, he shall cast down, 36; poor of, 128; 156. howled, 173; weakened, 203; 204; 211; 226.
ענה	**affliction**, 242.
רת	**Age** of Brightness, 238.
עה	**Aih**, makes a donation, 181; the haughtiness of his coast was weak-ened, 181; shall surpass in white-ness My sacrificial cake, 182; fall thou down and sleep heavily, 182.
רז	**alien**, G-d lifted up an, to a star, 202.
יעים	**altar shovels**, My, 23; 47;114; are pure, 235.
ארב	**ambuscade** of the Mark, 190; 191; 197.
אף	**anger**, 161; of the Pavilion, 177; 192.
חיל	**anguish**, he raised up, 90; 99.
כלה	**annihilation**, is right, 211; 250.
תוא	**antelope** of the dominion of Emptiness, 97.

קוף   **Ape**, 125; of distinction, 177; he staggered among excrement, 177; brought to an end, 178; a Lamentation of the, 210; Ape of the Coast, 210.

משבה   **apostasy**, 241.

סורתי   **apostasies of**, 219; 222; 224; 226.

Italic   **apostasies**, 219.

שמה   **appallment**, 128.

לב   **appetite**, fruit of, 109.

או \ והא   **appetite**, 144; 148; 149; 150; 152; 211; 222; 248.

תבה   **Ark are in it**, 77.

ארון   **ark** *of the Covenant*, 85; of the Chamber of Desire, 224.

דרע   **arm**, an, above His ruin is His Dev-astation, 163.

ארק   **arracks**, 96.

חץ   **arrow**, 156.

עשף   **Aseph**, 99.

Italic   **arrows**, 232.

אשנאל   **Ashnael** shall shine, 51.

יזא   **assembly** of all My Portion this is thy daughter, 176.

משב   **assembly**, every messenger of the, 83.

קהל   **assembly**, whosoever is a lamp of the, of the Stout One is worthy of the knowledge of his Father, 104; the Instrument of Heart...shall measure the, 204.

קהלת   **Assembly** of Yeshua, 155.

דהם   **astonishment**, 231; 241.

רע *vb.*   **awaken**, I G-d shall awaken every-one, 114.

עצם-תח   **Azum-Toah**, mountains of, 101.

B

בבל   **Babylon**, is our bitterness, 39; 90; 132; erred, 163; bitterness, 163; 197.

גו   **backside** of the coast was lean, 175; of the great region, 221; **back**, 245.

בהארם   **Bah-aram**, 63.

דגלים   **banners**, 28; 29.

לדגלו *vb.* **banner**, **is to set up his**, 270.

דגל   **banner**, to a Cherub is a, 38.

נס   **banner**, the pure banner's shaft was with the Thin One, 186; fluttered, 219; 222; 224; 226.

ערה   **bare place**, 76; 77.

ערת	**bare places**, 229; 235.
ארן	**Barque** of the Moon, 108; removed afar off, 108.
צול	**basin**, stoned lined, 239.
טנא	**basket**, for a, he shall rule, 183.
סל	**basket**, 192; 231.
פל	**beans**, consumed of calamity, 144.
עיש	**Bear, Constellation of the Great**, 115; 201. [*see also URSA Major*].
דב כי	**Bear of Branding** is its god, 18.
דב	**bear**, at thy window O G-d, 51; 53; 55; is against My Witness, 80; 83; opinion of, ceaseth, 110; 115; of thy trouble thrust away the one bearing the loss of a child, 180; bosom of the, 182; 229; 243; 250; 255; 268.
דב	**Bear** of Ruin, Garden of the, 206; 207; 208; 210; 213; 214; 215; 218; 220; 221.
בהם	**Beast**, at the coast the, paces his chamber, 273.
בהמי	**beasts of**, 228.
מצע	**bed**, 31.
בהלא	**Behala**, sons of, 262.
בל	**Bel**, hand of, 59; asked, 134; I wounded, 186; he caused a covering to be set in place, 186; is guilty, 197; 229; 262; 268.
בלדח	**Beldach**, 61.
בלרוס	**Bellorus**, 79.
בלשם	**Belshem**, 15.
דד	**Beloved**, who is the, of My Time? 133; *G-d* shall cause His Beloved pain, 168; *G-d* shall cause His Beloved pain, 168; 242; Our 259.
ברן	**Beren**, 164.
מת חום	**black man**, 3; 10.
גט	**bill of divorcement**, 31.
דאה	**bird of prey**, 4; 51; My, is ruin, 118; of pureness, 120; of the Pure One of Heart is at the Island of God's Mist, 186.
מורת	**bitter things**, 161.
מר	**bitterness**, wealth empowers, 93; it made the mountain, 93; 138; 144; 159; Babylon is, of thy hand, 163; 165; 242.
מור	**bitterness**, in the Garden all is, 40.
מם\מום	**blemish**, 251; 270.
ברך	**Blessed One**, 214.
עור	**blind**, 55.
דם	**blood** of His Time, 1; 12-13; of thy fortresses, 15; of his bosom, 18; cast down, 36; upon the mouth, 36; of ruin, 37; man of, 42;

of the fortress, 42; of Acco, 47; of the sword, 50; of ruin from G-d, 51; mark of blood, 56; *italic*, 71; of wailing, 98; of ruin, 89; of his ruinations, 92; of burning desolation, 98; of the children of the Father, 103; of Aiath, 104; of the Witness, 107; of the sheep is for us know-ledge; 110; of the pen, 136; those vomiting the blood of Emptiness, 157; of the region, 162; Lamb of Blood, 189; lament of, 206; of the pen, 207; 216; of His Shadow, 219; 221; 222; 223; of the Wandering Shadow, 225; 228; 251; 261; 268

דמי   **bloods of**, Thebes, 71; of weight, 227.

קהין   **bluntness** to be shamed, 71.

בח   **Boach**, 141; Mount, 247.

ספר   **book** of wailing belonging to the sojourner, 117; 128.

שך   **booth** of the coast, the calamity of the, 203.

סך   **booth**, they praised the, of its expansiveness, 36.

סכי   **booths of** Hallel, 161.

בז   **booty**, 146; My, is a gift of food from a jar, 216; the Mark refused the, he shall plunder, 217; 218.

חב   **bosom**, 5; 18; contemptable of, 21; spoke, 23; banners of the, 29 Integrity of His, 104; praise thou the, 175; it feedeth them light of the Nest, 175; 'Bosom of Ravage', Y-H is against his god, 177; of the Bear, 182; of EL, 240.

חוק   **bosom**, every proud, 50.

גבל   **boundary** of the coast, 121.

מעי   **bowels of**, the fool, 12-13; measure of the, 42; so the bowels of; 42; 47; chasten the 92; sufficient are His, 94.

רמא   **bowman**, 140; 145; 175; 201; 202; 210; 220; 231; 255.

Italic   *bread*, staff of, 252.

כי   **branding**, chamber of, 103.

עג   **breadcake**, My, 51.

צחת   **bright ones**, G-d passed by His, 46.

זהר   **brightness**, 55.

זגה\זגת   **Brightness**, Age of, 238.

רחב   **broad** delicate **expanse** is made to shake; 170.

אח   **brother**, 244.

שד   **breast**, made to hang down loose, 48a; gentle as a, 74.

Italic   ***breast***, My proud suck *the*, 51.

פור   **bull**, young, 21.

פר   **bull** of the herd, 141.

נטל   **burden**, at the region of the, 109; of a sheep, 122; of Ivory, 122; of vanities, 130; of a sheep, 182; is the Law, 182; burden of the Gift of Knowledge, 182; of Ravage, 192; 205; of Sheol, 209.

טרח   **burden**, 202; 203; above the Sea of, 260.

משא   **burden** on High, 161.

איד   **burden** of the Booth of the Coast, 203.

כי   **burning**, I shall exalt, 51; Noah removed the, 51.

שת   **buttocks**, 50.

C

קין   **Cain**, from, the wicked one shall wound the Mark of All of Them, 113; measure of, 243.

תעה   **calamity**, who is, 66.

איד   **calamity**, 142; 157; of Y-H, 188; of On, 217; 223; 256.

שבי   **captivity** is mad, 30; of Thebes, 107.

שבי   **captive**, burden of a, 122.

דיד הvb.   **caressing jesture**, 174.

קדה   **cassia-spice**, 232; 235.

כך   **cave**, burial, 5.

חור   **cave** of gloom, 259.

תאים   **cavities** of the ground, 255.

Italic   *celestial* window, 60; 170; 199; 218; 222; 224; 226; 235.

חאה   **Chaah**, coast of, 142.

חהן   **Chaan**, 254.

קש   **chaff**, fine, 67.

חדון   **Chadon**, wailing is from, 164.

חאל   **Chael** is worthy, 107;

חהל   **Chahal**, 205.

כשד   **Chaldea**, I shall travel toward, 68.

חלף   **Chaleph** of On, 216; 217.

חלץ   **Chalez**, 206.

תא   **chamber**, 1, 7, 10; 27; Y-H con-secrated the, 15; 47; Noble Lady of the, 48b; created, 58; for Lydda, 58; My, 59; 61; divided into three, 62; of the Mark, 68; he healed for Me the, 68; the Father swallowed up the, 77; of HaShem, 77; he decorated the, with his rottenness, 78; crowns of the, 79; El shook His, 86; 88; the Pure One veiled the, 89; 94; at Nob, 96; O the pride of the, 96; mighty, 96; Nathan swallowed up the mire of the, 99; chamber of branding, 103; of the Shovels of the Pure One, 114; the chamber erred, 115; held in aversion, 123; stallion of My Chamber, 152; dew of the, 166; return thou to Our, 166; of Y-H openeth, 199; of his lamentation, 205; I shall approach, 206; 210; 213; 214; 215; 218; 222; 224; 234; 235; 236; 253; 256; 259; the Chamber of My Light he brandished, 266; 267; 273.

המור   **changeling**, 201.

חאם   **Cheam**, 232.

חירו   **Cheru**, 209.

כרב   **cherub**, cut the Thicket to pieces, 38.

רב   **chief** of terror is the sea, 45.

אלף   **chief** of Integrity, 100.

עללי   **children of** the Father, 103.

קנמן   **cinnamon**, no measure of, 136.

ארמון   **citadel**, 230.

ער   **city**, the Father's, 191; 198; of splendour, 239; of Y-H, 239.

מחוז   **city** of the sojourner, 220.

לת   **city mound** of Shem, 45; 55; of the Mark, 113.

יד   **claw** of the falcon, 205.

הדח vb. **clean, made, by washing**, 54; 169.

דוח   vb. **Clean, rinsed**, 238.

דוח   **clean one**, 227, 228.

צורח   **Cleaver**, 66.

גש   **clod** *of earth*, 109; 137; 140; 161; *of earth*, 193; a clod *of earth*, 200; 250.

עב   **cloud** of Emptiness, 66; a thin, 116; 144; 146; 185; 189; O the lament of the, 189; 190; 192; 196; inherit thou the, 211; 215; 248.

גסיﬦ   **coarse ones**, 225.

אי   **coast**, 50; 78; 87; 96; 120; 121; 122; 128; 131; salt of the, 134; 143; 146; 152; 153; 163; 164; 174; 175; 181; 196; 203; 210; 215; 223; 230; 232; 233; 243; 247; 249; 250; 257; 263; 267; 269; 273.

אייﬦ   **coasts**, 121.

ארון   **coffin** of desire, 210; 212; 213.

קר   **cold**, My, is above ruin, 68; lamp thrusts away, 105; 165; a measure of, 237.

קרה   **cold**, lower region of, 70.

שת   **Column** of G-d, 143; of EL, 232.

צו   **commandment**, a severe, 24; of a mother, 215.

חיה   **community**, 241.

רע   **companion**, pure, of desire, 134.

ריע   **companion**, Gift of the Veil and his, 199.

D

בת	**daughter,** discharge of a, flowed, 2; shall be ill; eye of my daughter's head was drowsy, 16; excesses of the, 80; fruit of appetite trembled, 109; vanity of a, 111; pride of My, 123; 130; his ruin is the pride of my d. 134; remnant of the, 134; 167; 169; 170; 176; 192; 200; 202; 204; 206.
יום\יֹם	**day,** at the day he cause Us to journey, 89; of Y-H, 262; of the Locust, 263; of power, 270.
ימי	**days of,** power, 173; 195; 204; of strength, 243; of power, 246; despairing, 264.
מות	**Death,** 21; shall be increased, 31; has swallowed them up, 88; the ruin of Eden is, 183; 192; 194.
נשיהו	**debt, his,** 173.
חוֹב	**debt** of the Mark, 32; 65.
חביך	**debts, thy,** gentle are thy as a breast, 74.
נשה	**deceiver** toward G-d, 145.
מוּם	**defect,** 99.
שע-אל	**'Delight of God',** 30.
רך\ורכה	**delicacy,** I have drilled a, of a god, 121; 226; 252.
השעו	vb. **Deliverer, he was made His,** 35.
השד	**demon** of profaneness, 61; 65; as a demon, 73.
או \ אוה	**desire,** trampled, 18; was with Me, 30; hand of, 41; is weakened, 42; lo, he is Precept, the wine of, 48b; thou denied, the Light of my G-d, 59; the perfection of, she decorated, 63; living, 65; great, 68; Root of Desire, 78; the multitude swallowed up the one seeking My Desire, 78; the Poor One presented, 80; 83; 87; *oppression* derided Desire, 88; perfect desire, 89; of the Noble, 101; in the garden, 101; adversary of, 103; made Me fast, 106; Light of Desire, 107; fire of My D., 107; light of d., 107; light of new d., 108; voice of, 128; the Noble of Desire of My Will, 132; the Pure One of Desire, 133; 134; 136; height of desire, 142; gift of d., 144; raised up d., gushed, 149; lowly mule of, 152; 153; oh d. be thou drowsy, 154; he gave them, 156; this is the beginning of d. for G-d, 156; set d. 161; caused itself to rise early, 175; give thou Desire, 195; 209; from the desire of the progeny, 211; 212; chamber of, 213; 214; 218; 220; 222; 224; 231; 234; 236; belongs to the Instrument, 240; shall it mock at the Thicket? 240; a hand causing d. to be twisted, 245; of the Eternities, 271; the desire of the mothers of My thin ones, 272.
הוה	**desire,** of Jareb, 85.
קלס	**derision,** turn away, 117; 133.
Italic	**desert,** 196.

או   **desirable thing** of the mountain, 251.

שוד   **desolation**, burning, 98.

בתה   **desolation**, mountains of, 233.

מס   **despairing** of wailing, 264.

בלי   **destruction**, hand of, 58.

שאוה   **devastating storm**, 158.

שד   **devastation**, 99.

משמה   **devastation of** sharpness, 82.

שאת   **devastation**, Mount of, 82; 163.

שמם   **Devastator**, 84.

חרס   **devoted thing** of the coast, cut off, 257.

טל   **dew**, 138; of the chamber, 166; the Gift of His Token, 174, 174; 194; 195; 236; 237; 242.

דבלם   **Diblaim** is not, above the Moon his god? 46.

שת   **dignity**, completeness from, 64; 255.

הוד   **dignity**, 32.

בלום   **discharge** is held in, 21.

זרף   **discourse** of distinction, 234; 238.

זרף\vb   **discourse**, the Fire of Grace discoursed, 177; 234; 238.

נוטף pt.   **discoursing**, 78.

ריב   **dispute**, 177; 178.

נה\נוה   **distinction**, nine is, 19; sweep away every, 48a; 52; the sufficiency of G-d is His, 216; 217; 218; the Instrument of, 238.

Italic   *distinction*, 53.

איד   **distress**, 230.

צר   **distress**, mount of devastation and, 82; of noise, 139.

צק   **distress**, spoke: 27; becometh weakened, 45; was appropriate, 94.

צרא   **distress** was against him, 15; 33; 35; **distresses**, 55; 57; is complete, 99; 105.

הצקי   **distressed one, My**, 7; learned the perfection of knowledge, 7.

צק   **distresser**, the, shall err, 38.

צראים   **distressed places** of untimely birth are incomplete ruin, 94.

תנים   **distributors** of Tribute, 255.

עוה   **distortion**, voice of, 117.

עוכר   **disturber** of the blood, 185.

בוהל   **disturber**, 243.

גב   **ditch**, 270.

שולש/pt.   **Dividing into three, the one**, 109; 270; into three the Jackal, 274.

משל   **dominion** of Emptiness, 97.

רדת   **dominion** of Shem-Avah, 146.

The Linear Bible Code

דלה   **door**, there is no, into the Garden, 63.

דל   **door**, of the Isle, 136; I shall make afraid thy, 182; My, 266.

Italic   *dough*, 196.

תנין\תנן   **Dragon**, tel-city of the, 146; 247; 263.

Italic   *Dragon*, 248.

ערצ   **dreadful thing**, a lamentation is for My, 274.

מחלם   **Dream** came to him, 33; 64.

שתי   **drinking**, 235.

שתא   **drink**, he shall reveal the vomit of the, 103.

Italic   *drink offering*, 123.

זרף   **drip** of the *celestial* window, 235; cassia-spice is from G-d of the drip, 235; thy drip caused the chamber to reel, 235.

\ינים\ vb.   **Droop, he makes to,** 126.

דו   **dual** heart, 250.

גל   **dung** of the sojourner, 126.

דק   **dust**, thou heaped up wailing out of the, 117.

E

נשר   **eagle**, teeth of the, 157.

דאה   **eagle**, teeth of the, 160; 245.

עגל   **ear rings**, a heap of, 111.

ארץ   **earth**, your Creator awoke and He caused to purge Death because of the, 194; the poor of the, is drowsy, 265.

רעש   **earthquake**, 184.

עדן   **Eden**, tail of, 181; the ruin of Eden is Death, 183.

אדום   **Edom**, 149.

ביצים   **eggs**, 231; 254.

זוב   vb. **ejaculate,** he caused us to, 32.

אל   **EL** showed grief, 86; He shook His Chamber, 86; the Fortress is the Mark of EL, 86; Mark of EL, 91; Poor One of EL, 93; measure of, 96; our EL raged, 209; tooth of, 222; Column of, 232; terror of, 232; Bosom of, 240; compresses the idle of the *harvest* heap of the Moon, 240; the oceans of the Strength of EL are for Man; 241..

חשמל   **Electrum**, he shall swallow, 58.

חן   **elegancy** of On, 217.

אלד   **Elled**, 85.

נה   **eminency** roared, 64; fish of, 102; the Light of Desire, 107; G-d of, 209.

שׁוא   **Emptiness,** 14; odour of, 17; pride resembles, 48a; cloud of, 66; time of, 73; I shall wound, 137; it shall be subdued, 137; 157; 167; Antelope of the Dominion of, 169; 171; 177; 178; 185; 189; 196; 259.

תהו   **Emptiness,** 144.

בקים   **empty ones,** 119.

בהיו   **empty ones, his,** 208.

נוכל   **Enabler,** Y-H is the, 263.

יוכל   **Enabler,** Y-H is the, 270.

איב   **enemy,** 67; his, 80.

ער   **enemy,** 27.

איבי   **enemies, My,** 76; 273.

צריו   **enemies, his,** 104.

חרט   **engraving tool** of Shilo, 132.

מבא   **entrance,** every, of the city-mound, 158.

ציר   **envoy,** belly of the, the mouth of Nebo, 37.

ער   **Er,** 27.

ארש   **Eresh,** 76.

תע   **error,** 12-13; 20.

מתע   **error,** 263.

משג   **error,** of the Pit, 209.

של   **error,** 110; 173.

נוכן   **Establisher,** shall judge them, 218.

עלם   **Eternity,** they have severed, 10.

עדים   **Eternities,** Desire of the, 271.

עד   **everlastingness,** 202.

בוחר   **Examiner,** 66.

יתר   **excess,** palate of, 52.

יתרות   **excesses of** the daughter they completed, 80.

נדה vb.   **excommunicate,** 190.

צאה   **excrement,** he staggered among, 177.

תר   **explorer,** the pride of the, 116.

שמד   **Exterminator,** he works the heads of cattle of the Mark, 66.

עין   **eye of** my daughter's head, 16; because of the, he decreased the time of emptiness; 73.

Italic   *eyes* besmeared, 84; 188.

F

פני	**Face, My**, they thrust away the Living Being of, 125.
דוה	**Faint One**, the, of the poor is here, 166; 168; shall consume a fullness of the firebolts of the Law, 240..
דוה	**faint**, the Faint One is against her *(Jerusalem)*, 166 of the poor, 167.
דוי	**faint**, 239.
דאב	**faint**, O the wailing of the faint, 145.
אמת	**faithfulness**, remnant of, 265.
מעל	**faithlessness**, what is the Terrible Thing? All, 206.
אית\איה	**falcon** of the Nile, 9; My falcon is their light, 106; it has swallowed, 107.
צם	**fasting**, 66.
טפש	**fat one**, 78.
אב	**father**, a, constrained it, 65; of the howler, 189; 196; the father of the tents of astonishment shall be made yellow, 241
אבות	**fathers** of his father, 124; thy, 150; vomitus of the, 165.
אב	**Father** of the Gift, 26; the, shall remove afar off His saved ones, 36; is Shatterer, 37; The Mark-of-All-of-Them is with the, 41; whosoever ran from my, 42; he brightened not his, 43; is against a people with its father, 43; of the palate, 48b; of species, 54; swallowed up the chamber, 77; his Father ended the blood of ruin, 89; chose to wander about, 94; He was silent, 94; permitted the chamber to be as ruin, 94; permitted the increase of haughtiness of His Own Region, 94; He shall weep for the Spring, 94; sufficient are His Bowels, 94; established the Ordinance of the Veil, 97; He made the Mouth and the Height the sufficiency of Man, 97; shall remove the hunter against His fisherman, 100; He will shine toward the Desire of the Noble, 101; He planned for the Desire in the Garden to be lights, 101; He begat a winepress and the Mountains of Azum-Toah, 101; children of the, 103; knowledge of the, 104; a lamp shall scatter the adversary of the, 105; a people shall Passover, lo, from the, 105; My Falcon is their light the Spirit of the Father, 106; swallowed up the Howler, 118; I shall make fat my, 121; I the Father shall awaken, 135; give you the dew o Hand of knowledge of the, 138; the, of the Garden of Fullness shall show grief, the Father of the Garden cut him off, 140; for the Father a vessel of purity He raised thee up, 143; the Hand of the, shall

The Linear Bible Code

behold the vessel of its own flame, 143; quivering *of lip* his
Father fed them, 143; the Hand of the, is His heap of
bitterness, 144; of the coast, 146; and the Pure One of the Nest
is the Hand of the Father, 149; the Instrument of the, *is in* the
midst of the heap *of waters* and the waters of the Prince are the
heap of the Father *in* its midst, 156; they beheld the Rib of the
Father, 158; he inflamed the, of the Shout, 161; but a few he
caused to shine even the oppressed of the Father, 162; all
entering the city-mound of the Mark dug the side chamber of
the Father, 162; all entering the Tel-City of thy Mark saw the
Rib of the Father, 166; cause you to see the Rib of the Father,
174; Father of the Shout, 177; the Corner mocked the
Instrument of the Father of the Shout, 177; the Father of the
Shout prophesies, 178; and the oppressed of the, they gazed at
the Lamb of Blood, 189; O the ravage of his Father's City; 191,
198; I the Father of Opulence shall awaken (Babylon), 197; the
Instrument of the, endured, 210; from My, ship He fed them to
be a lamp, 211; the flame of the Father of Hope, 212; the Hand
of my, is against the Tooth, 213; Instrument of the, 214; the
Instrument of the, was obedient, 216; the Instrument of the,
the Blood of His Shadow, showed obedience, 219; Hand of the,
220; O the quivering of the Father, O the quivering *lip*, 221;
the Instrument of the, showed obedience, 221; 223; 225; o the
quivering *lip* of the, 228; the, removed afar off the Shout, 232;
solace of the Father never wandered away, 249; Son of the
Father, 274.

מח	**fatling**, 14; 68; 74; 161; 179.
מוח	**fat thing**, 64.
של	**fault**, the Mark-of-All-of-Them bore thy, 136.
רצן	**favour**, 164; favour of the oppressed came, 170; and the Son, 178; has a sweet odour, 180; he shall shake the, of the oppressed and the Son, 183; now slumbers the, of the oppressed and the Son, 184; he fed them, 185; 187; the Favour of the Oppressed and the Son, 195; 209; 211; 212; 215; 217; 220; 222; 223; 225; 226; 227; 228; 231; 241; 259; of the oppressed My Son, 261.
חת	**fear** is a hook, 159.
ירא	**fear**, is thy, Me? 133.
מעט	**few**, 249.
פגה	**fig**, I am an **early**, to him, 131; **unripe**, 133.
רץ	**fierceness** of Sheol, 179.
בצא	**filth**, 234.

צאי   **filthy one**, 67.

אש   **fire** of wailing, 37; what is our fire? 39; of Desire, 61; fire of dew, 63; of My Desire, 107; the Head came but before fire proceeded, 117; 124; of Grace, 177; flickers, 184; 194; 195; gift of fire endureth, 197; 232; fragment of fire is dew, 242; fire of the lamp, 263.

Italic   *fire*, 121.

רשף   **firebolt**, 166; 169; 173; 193; firebolts, רשפות201; 204; 237; 240; 253.

רשפות   **firebolts**, shake thou the, 242.

איד\אד   **firebrand** of a whelp, 191; 199; 256.

ברך   **first born son**, His, 17.

דג\דגה   **fish** of a mountain, 61; 85; of Eminency, 102; was faint, 216; 222; 231.

דגה   **fisherman**, the tent of the, 77; 93; 99; 100.

דגתיו   **fishes, his own**, he talked wildly toward, 20.

אור   **flame**, a, he raised against thy necromancers, 166; My winepress at the flame of Ravage, 268.

להב   **flame**, 121; 143; 171; 194; of Y-H, 165; 243.

להבת   **flame of** the Father of Hope he made to flicker, 212; it shall feed them, 212.

להבי-תו   **flames of the Mark**, 14; of wine, 109; of Y-H, 176.

נוה   **flock, My**, is at the Constellation of the Great Bear, 115.

צאן   **flock**, 143.

ער   **foe**, 206.

גב\גבה   **food**, sufficient is his, 64; 107; 144; 211; 242.

אכל   **food**, 141; 145; 153; this is food, 173; 186; 208; 211; 216; 230; 243; storage tent, 244; 247; 248.

נבל   **fool**, bowels of the, 12-13.

אויל   **foolish** *man*, 253.

נבלתיו   **foolish ones, his**, 2.

כבש   **footstool**, 219; 222; 224; 226.

יער   **forest**, 109; 171.

לעד   **forever**, I shall feed them, 231.

פטשות   **forge hammers**, 16.

זנוה   **fornication**, 136; 254.

מעז   **fortress**, My Grace as a, 19.

חיל   **fortress**, knowledge of the, proceeded, 20; 98; 215.

חל   **fortress**, blood of thy, 15; of Siin, 72; the Mark brought low the fortress, 81; is the Mark of EL, 86; 156; of the coast of thy *harvest* heap shall increase, 261; of the region, 265; 269; 270; 271.

חל ארק   **Fortress Earth**, 259.

חלים   **fortresses**, 28.

שעל   **fox** is shattering all things, 45.

רץ   **fragment** of Sheol, 158; of the fire of dew, 194; 242.

פת   **fragment** of light, 218; 226.

החור   **free man**, Keith is a, 163.

חר   **free born**, a free born man smote them for thy ruin, 72; 267.

אב   **freshness**, who shall position his, 25.

ריע   **friend**, a, thrust away his hand, 191.

רעה   **friend** of His Sheep shall swallow *him* up, 17.

קל   **frivolity**, 249; 250.

ניב\וב   **fruit** of the sea, 1; belongs to Me, 53; fruit of the vessel, 69; house of, 87; he gave with its vigour, 96; 105; of appetite, 109; of Memphis, 132; 138; fruit of desire of Aeael came forth, 177; of fornication, 254; of perfection תם,260.

ניבים   **fruits** of My Robe, 23; fruits, 69.

מלאי   **fullness of** her son, 86.

מלא   **fullness**, Garden of, 140; I shall pour out a fullness by the injured one, 173; 269.

שדים   **furrows** of the Living Garden, 66.

תלם   **furrow**, 237; of thy hand, 244; 251; 252.

עד   **future**, 247.

G

לאירבג   **Gabriel** permitted loftiness, 70 (printed in reverse order).

עא   **Gae**, the wail of, 136.

אתקים   **galleries** of seed, 244.

גן\גנה   **garden**, in the, he wounded a seed, 17; in the, it came with him, 26; 28; 29; sufficient is the garden of its soothsayer, 31; in the, is the Mark exposed, 36; in the garden all is bitterness, 40; garden terraces flow, 40; the fullness of soothsayers in the garden, 45; 46; no door into the garden, 63; sufficiency of the, 65; the Living Garden, 66; Desire in the, 101; 106; wandered the garden, 125; garden of fullness, 140; Father of the, 140; the High Garden, 143; greatness of the, 145; 149; the abundance of My Garden, 154; leanness of My Garden, 170; garden of the

Bear of Ruin, 206; 207; 208; 210; 213; 214; 215; 218; 220; 221; 229.

מזו   **Garner**, the Perfect, is Prince, a Hand, 147.

שית   **garment** of trembling, 54.

מד   **garment**, he trod the, 270.

Italic   *garment*, 87.

דלי<u>ם</u>   **gates** of the Living One, 214.

בבה   **gate**, he shall shame the, 42.

שער   **Gate** of Ravage, 76.

שהם   **gem** of lust, sorrow is the, 245.

יחשי שד   **genealogists of the Demon**, 65.

יחשי תו   **genealogists of the Mark**, 91.

התיחשו   Hithpael verb, **genealogy, they themselves did**, but to cast it forth, 154; 253.

תיחשו   vb. genealogy, you shall do, 155.

דר   **generation** of profaneness set free, 59; a generation of wailing, 94; voice of his generation, 125; of So, 152.

זר   **Gentile**, toward the, is the Mouth of *the Jews'* judgment, 238; Gentiles of the regions of the profane, 240.

אט   **gentleness**, Mark of, 67; lodged for the night, 78; for the night, 81; 140; 187; 193.

גבן   **Gibbon** endured it, 180.

נת   **gift**, is My, 17; praise you My, 35.

שי   **gift** of knowledge, 26; the Father of the Gift, 26; his grace belongs to Me, 28; the Mountain is against the Gift, 28; magnified His Own, 31; disputed the, 33; My Will is a Gift, 34; gift of the noble ones, 60; of ruin, 64; Gift of the sea of time, 71; people of the Gift, 72; lamentation is the thinness of a, 76; abundance of the, 89; greatness of his G., 103; gift of lust, 113; a thin gift from a thin cloud glideth overhead, 116; Gift of the Veil is a Token, 119; who is the Gift from the Veil? 137; he is drowsy; he shall be smitten because of strength, 137; Gift of Desire, 144; I shall direct the Gift of the people of knowledge even the Mark, 146; the Gift was weakened even it became old, 158; I shall cast out the Gift of Knowledge; 162; this is dew the Gift of His Token, 174; the burden is a Gift of the Law, 182; he shall not remove the burden of the Gift of Knowledge, 188; the Man of Grace is a fine Gift but a friend surely why did he thrust away his hand? 191; thy posterity scattered the Gift of Y-H, 192; the fire of dew is in (the earth) from the Gift of the Thin One of the Isle. The Hand itself is judged. Surely My Son is the

Gift of the Veil, 194; a lament of the Gift of the Veil, 196; the Gift of Fire endureth even now, 197; Gift of the Veil, 199; the Wail of the Gift of the Veil, 202; My Son is the Gift of the Veil, 202; like the give of value he trampled, 206; a Gift shouted, 207; like a gift of value he trampled, 207; 208; whosoever is the Gift they of the abode of the flock are drowsy, 207; a gift of value he tread upon, 210; 213; 214; 215; My Booty is a gift of food from a jar, 216; as a gift of value he trampled, 218; rightly is My Booty the gift of the hand, 218; as a gift of value he trampled, 220; 221; gift of the Hand, the Tooth of EL, 222; Gift of the oppressed, 224; gift of value he trampled, 229; the gift of the Poor One is silent, 242; Tower of the Gift, 267; (the Revolter) is made low on account of the Gift even the Mark by name, 269.

יוהב   **Giver**, the, made them flow, 255.

מעף   **Gloom**, Cave of, 259.

כן   **gnat**, 224.

אקו   **goat, wild**, 227.

אל   **god**, this is the ruin of his, 38; he made thee a god, 46; the Moon his god, 46; 103; thy god is fattened, 148; 160; 161; 182.

אלה   **goddess**, 155.

אליך   **gods, thy**, the stumbling of, 73.

אל   **G-d** passed by His Bright One, 46; lament of his, 103; O G-d of my ruin, 107; God is with him, 107; 137; 141; 143; 145; 147; 148; 151; 152; 153; 154; 156; 157; of the region, 158; He was pleased with the Robe of the Pure One, 158; God rules, 160; G-d explored the *celestial* window, 160; thou shalt love the teeth of My Witness his G-d, 160; 161; the firebolt of Wailing is againt her as is G-d, 166; 173; maketh fat G-d, 174; a transgression God swallowed up, 175; Hand of thy, 176; Instrument of, 177; 178; G-d's Mist, 186; give thou O G-d all of us a plan, 193; give thou O G-d of all of us a Plan and a region, 200; I thy G-d shall lay bare the Stone Cutter, the Mark, 200; G-d lifted up an Alien to a Star, 202; 203; splitters of G-d, 208; Mouth of, 208; he shall be com-posed as G-d, 208; with the knowledge of, 209; terror of the G-d of Eminency, 209; maltreated *women* of G-d, 214; thy G-d Y-H, 216; for G-d the Instrument fed them, 216; wield thou power O G-d of Integrity, 219; Tranquility is before Us; as G-d wounded it, it praised G-d, 220; he quickly passed by G-d as G-d boasted of a few, 221; fish of his sheep is for the Mouth of G-d, 222; Mouth of G-d judged them, 225; Crown of G-d, 230; wailing is enough with G-d, 232; passage way of Time from G-d, 233; O G-d the tears of the oppressed, 233; the Pure One pulled along the people of G-d, 233; Hand of G-d, 235; the lament is for thy, 235; Thy Voice O G-d, 235; I shall reveal G-d as drinking ceases, 235; I shall expose G-d as a furrow, 237; the efficient Wisdom of G-d, 237; G-d shook the Window of Horon, 237; Now is the Passover of G-d, 238; wailing is sufficient with G-d, 238; it is the Passover even of G-d, 238; G-d loathes the proud ones of apostasy, 241; He shall not set the Mark 'Greatness' upon them, 241; thy G-d is Greatness, 245; he swallowed up the hater causing G-d pain, 252; there is no Pearl from G-d's Region, 265.;

כתם   **gold** of mourning, 76.

זהב   **gold**, 223; 224.

גד   **good fortune**, 124.

חן   **grace**, My, as a fortress, 19; My Grace sewn together, 34; who to Me is grace? 41; Adversary swallowed up, 64; twisted, 64; from the days it caused grace to be mocked, 88; My Grace, 134; My Grace is swallowing up, 171; fire of grace dripped, 177; Man of Grace, 191; O Grace of G-d thou dripped cassia-spice, 232; the rain of grace shall scatter about strength, 241.

זג   **grape skin**, 190; 196; 203.

עיש   **Great Bear, Constellation of the**, 115; 201. [*See also URSA Major*].

רב   **great one**, 211.

רוב   **greatness**, 245.

רב   **greatness** of terror, 31; 55; of Tooth, 102; of His Sheep, 112; 145; 149; 189; 212; 240; 241; 245.

נף   **Grief**, who is, 92.

ניר   **ground, tillable**, 211; 223.

חך   **gums**, set thou the, 140.

H

ניתי\נית   **habitation, My**, 57; of Ked, 73; of Moses, 73; at Jebus, 74; My Habitation is for ruin, 119.

תנא   **habitation**, 237.

נוה   **habitation**, 203; of the Shepherd, 214; of the Tablet, 237.

נוי   **habitations of** the Mark-of-All, 47.

התיב   **Hattib**, 207.

הוח   **Havach** became faint, 168.

הלאל	**Hallel**, 161.
חם	**Ham**, 237.
המש	**Hamas**, heart of, 169; howler of Hamas, 184.
אית	**hawk of** renown, 172.
חור יד	**hollow of the hand**, 167; 169.
רסן	**halter**, 155; 156.
יד	*(see also, Instrument, power, claw)*

hand of a species, 30; of Desire, 41; of destruction, 58; of Bel, 59; 87; 90; break into pieces the, 109; of the Adversary, 110; of His Pure Sign, 110; 111; of Iniquity, 111; swift, 112; set thou the, 114; vigour is the Hand and Terrible, 115; of knowledge leadeth to a watering hole its travelers, 115; of the wicked one; 117; grace of its hand healed, 117; it lengthened the Crown, 117; of his fathers, 124; bloody hand, 128; the terror of G-d is the Hand of the Mark-of-All-of-Them, 136; hand shook the door of the isle, 136; Hand of Y-H, 139; Who is the Hand? 140; The Hand of the Father shall behold the Vessel of its own flame, 143; he entered the High Garden and he vomited, he shook intensely; he repented; 143; at the time of judgment he allowed himself to be sick, 143; the Column of G-d is the Hand of Y-H, 143; The Hand of the Father is His Heap of Bitterness, 144; I shall consume the hand that mocked Him, 145; crush thou O G-d like the hand of the Seraph, 145; The Hand of the Father is the Mark, 146; the Perfect Gardner is Prince, a Hand, 147; be thou unwell O hand, 147; be thou drowsy O hand, 147; the Hand we shall support, 147; the hand of a Seraph and a hand of a man crushed the tel of Moab, 147; Hand of Integrity held dominion, 148; it extended godward; it fed them; it fed them a measure of My Nest, it raised up appetite, 148; the Pure One of the Nest is the Hand of the Father, 149; the Hand of a Seraph and the hand of a man crushed he who is forgetful toward my G-d, 151; Hand of Y-H, 158; above my strength a Seraph is faint and the hand, 159; of the region prominent, 161; Hand of Knowledge, 162; Babylon is bitterness of thy hand, 163; made white, 163; Hand of YAH, 163; hand of the region, 167; hollow of the hand, 167, 168; the Hand is His Sign, 168; Hand of the Shout, 176; Hand of thy G-d fed them, 176; Hand of My Light, 176; the hand of the Tabernacle is *against* Me, 177; Who judged the Hand? 180; an earthquake hath struck the Hand of Knowledge, 184; thou O Hand of Knowledge judged, 185; annihilation shall shake (haughtiness of Lust) because of the

Will of the Hand of His Token, 187; O Hand of Knowledge,
knead thou Knowledge, 189; and surely to whom I shall raise
up at the appointed time let him stretch forth from the hand,
190; he who is the hand of opinion scorched the Ambuscase of
the Mark, 190; the Hand shall be purified; he fed them Desire,
192; hand of sorrow the Pure One pushed away from Me, 193;
the Hand itself is judged, 194; A Lament of the Hand of the
Pure Turtledove, 196; the Hand kneaded the coast *as dough*,
196; the bowman of the firebolts shall thrust aside the hand
that would cut off the living and the pride of all, 201; for
counseling the hand engraved, 208; a hand disabled, 208; a
hand imprisoned a great region, 209; the Hand of my Father is
against the Tooth, 213; thy Hand stripped her, 213; pride of the
Hand makes a plan for her, 215; the Hand of the Father was
obedient...For G-d the Hand fed them, 216; he waved a hand;
he made us drowsy, 218; Gift of the Hand, 218 hand of sorrow
carried knowledge, 219; he waved a hand rightly so, 219; Hand
of the Father, 220; hand of a man is the sufficiency of the lord
of the afflicted, 221; hand of wailing, 221; he lapped up the
people of the Gift of the Hand the Tooth of EL, 222; a hand of
strength set up knowledge, 226; the hand of the Moel provided;
it swelled up. It fed them, 228; it fed the bare places...the Hand
silences the sufficiency of the lord of ruin, 229; Hand of the
King, 229; a hand has thrust away the Will of Thy Voice, 232;
His Hand on High circumcised all from the coast of Moses, 233;
the hand makes unsteady the mountains of desolation and
Hata-Hennom and the mouth of Keith, 233; pride of the hand,
235; the Hand of G-d, 235; hand of sorrow, 237; O people thy
palm is the Hand of Y-H, 239; the Hand of the remnant of
Mother scorns lust to unite a mountain and all by an utterance,
239; hand of Mother Nature, 242; her (bitterness) grasped to
establish thy sorrow, 242; he made lazy thy hand, 243; furrow
of thy hand, 244; strength of the hand, 244; the back of you is
the strength of the hand, 245; the strength of judgments is the
Hand of the Ram, 245; this is a loathsome thing: a hand
causing Desire to be twisted, 245; head of his seed, 246; food
from a hand, 248; hand of Jethea', 251; the Hand of
Knowledgeable things is known it pierced the blemish for us,
253; hand of Baal, 257; like a hand *cut off*, 264.

השם   **HaShem**, 1; 79.

הת-הנם   **Hata-Hennom**, 233.

שׂנא	**hater**, He swallowed up the hater *who* causes G-d pain, 252.
רם	**haughtiness** thou desired, 50; 85; 94; 103; 149; 168; 186; 187; 211; 215; 217; 230; of lust, 241; 242; 250; 253; 256; 258.
רמתיו	**haughty ones, his**, 103.
שׁד	**havoc**, 4; they liberated, 25; Who is, 91.
ראשׁ	**Head**, the, came but before fire proceeded, 117; the Head came but before Him the strength of the Pure One proceeded, 129.
שׁור	**head of cattle** spoke, 83; his, is lowly, 87.
שׁורים	**heads of cattle**, of the Mark, 66; circumcise thou, 74; 77; 86.
גל	**heap**, 130; 144; 151; 212.
נד	**heap** of the coast he heaped up for tears, 52; region of my heap, 56; 57; 63; 108; 109; of earrings, 111; 134; 141; 143; 144; 147; perfect heap, 149; 153; 156; 159; 160; 168; 169; 195; 205; 207; 210; 217; 229; 230; coastal heap, 231; 233; 237; 240; 241; 243; 246; 247; 250; 252; 259; 261; 265; 267; 270; 273..
לבב	**heart**, showed grief, 134; wounded the runner, 134; My Heart struggled, 174; the walls of thy heart, 174..
לב	**heart** divides in three parts, 63; voice and heart, 107; heart of oppression, 137; caused the voice to express grief, 151; heart of thy voice, 154; 157; 164; of thy voice, 169; and surely to circumcise them the heart the Voice is with all of them, 172; of the voice, 179; revolter of the heart, 194; emptiness of heart, 196; 204; 224; 232; 236; dual heart, 250.
לב המשׁ	**heart of Hamas**, 169.
Italic	*Heaven*, the levels of, 110
טיר	**hedged place**, 133.
על	**Height**, 268.
רם	**height** of an Island, 69; heaped up his height, 84; 212.
רום	**Height**, *the Father* made the, 97.
נף	**Height**, distresses of My, 53.
הקז	**Hekez**, 75.
איל	**help** is driven about, 14.
הנע	**Henna**, 168.
הנם	**Hennom**, 100; swallowed up, 121; 200; 272.
על	**High, on**, 231; 233.
רם	**High, on**, 154; 161; 209; 214; 247.
רם	**highness** of the Region, 259.
במים	**hills**, wine of the, 270.
הין	**Hin-measure**, 85; 222.
דבשׁ	**honey**, 191; 198.
סבר-ז	**hope, a certain**, 272.

מקוה   **Hope**, the Father of, 212.

חורן   **Horon**, window of, 237.

Italic   *horses*, my stamping, 188.

הבית יא   **house fair** is worthless, 211.

בית\בת   **House** of the Nile, 70; of fruit, 87; 105; **houses of** sorrow, 125; My House, 128; houses of oppression, 240.

צי   **Howler**, 10; 69; 118; 121; 162; 184; 189; 191; 196; 197.

אשן   **Humanity**, was not, wood to Him? 233.

מאיו   **hundred, his,** 148.

מאות\מאי   **hundreds** are for bitterness, 159; of the Veil shall shine, 213; 249.

צד   **hunter,** 100.

I

יכרס   **Icarus,** 152.

בדים   **idle talkers,** 20.

גלול   **idol**, turn you away the, 213.

פסל   **Idol,** 262.

תרף   **Idol** of Hennom, 272.

צקים   **idols,** put to death, 264.

צלם   **Image,** 263.

כלא   **imprisonment,** 220.

ירץ   **indignation** moves quickly by a word, 18.

זעמה   **indignation** is it not for them? 18.

נחל   **inheritance,** crush thou his, 161; 247.

ירשים   **inheritors of the Mark, 45.**

עון   **iniquity,** 19; hand of, 111.

עונים   **iniquities,** punishments of, 76.

עוה   **iniquity,** 23.

תך   **injury** of the poor, 79; is for them, 115.

עול   **injustice,** a god of, 20; 135; 261; 270.

תם   **innocence,** he took away his debt with, 173.

תם\תום   **Integrity,** Pure One of, 10; bristling of, 100; Chief of, 100; of His Bosom, 104; Integrity shall dull the tooth utterly, 132; hand of, 148; 216; 219; 221; 222; endured, 230; of Noah, 255.

יד   *(see also Hand, claw and power)*

     Instrument conquered Rohan the voice of his generation, 125; thy prince is the Instrument of My Knowledge, 127; Give you the dew which is the Instrument of Knowledge of the Father,

138; 160; of G-d, 177; O Ape of Distinction, the I. bringeth thee to an end and the Father of the Shout prophesies of it, 178; is not the Noble His In., 203; of the Father and his chamber endured, 210; 214; the In. of the Father, the Blood of His Shadow, showed obedience, 219; 221; 223; 225; out of the obedience of the In. I shall cut off the Shadow, 227; because of the obedience of the In. of the Mother, 227; 228; the In. prophesied, 232; was it not for the In. to discourse the mire; he would increase them, 234; the In. shall brood, 234; the In. of Y-H discoursed, 238; the In. prophesied of the Age of Brightness of the Instrument, 238; the In. of Distinction removed the Passover, 238; who is made a fool? The sojourner at the discourse of the In. of Y-H; so he sought for Grace, 238; Desire, Desire belongs to the In., 240; the In. fed them, 241; the In. shall be hidden, 244..

רי   irrigation, 167; of My Nest, 'The Son exists!", 171; he hated sufficiently the Instrument, 177; Instrument of the Father and the Shout, 177; the dispute with the Instrument of G-d, 178; of heart, 204; 244.

איר   **irradiation**, 198.

אי   **isle** for Keith, 57; of the heap, 63; height of an island, 69; 89; 136; 139; 140; 141; 144; 156;168; 213; 272.

אי"ם   **islands**, two, of secrecy, 182.

זב   **issue**, My, 29; his issue resembled a winding *staircase*, 29.

איתאאל   **Ithiel**, 207.

שי   **ivory** of G-d created, 58; burden of 122.

J

יחאש|ן   **Jachesahan** is not, 236.

אוחא   **jackal**, 243.

תן   **jackal** waveth at Me Terror, 71; shall be removed, 120; 142; 144; 150; 161; 164; the perfect jackal, 165; he fed them a measure of cold out of Lust; he did not waver; he caused Me to tremble, 165; 187; of Lust, 195; 221; 222; courage of the, 229; 240; from here made himself do genealogy and he separated thee hither, 253; of emptiness, 259; for the dividing into three the jackal, 274.

תנים   **jackals**, 148; 152; 212; 228.

יהן   **Jaihan**, 88.

The Linear Bible Code

ינת **Janet**, mouth of, 129.

ינתם **Janethom**, 61.

כד **jar** in Time, 73; perversity of a Jar is sorrow altogether, 116; 216; 236; a ringing cry overflowing a jar, 239.

ירב **Jareb**, 85.

יתיב **Jathib**, My daughter, 204.

יויז **Javeez**, 109.

Italic *jaw*, fear is a hook *in the*, 159.

רסני דאה **jaws of the kite**, 153.

יבס **Jebus**, habitations at, are thine, 74.

יח **Jeah**, 118; 136.

Italic *Jerusalem*, But the Garden of the Bear-of-Ruin as a gift of value he trampled for her *(Jerusalem)*, 220.

יתי **Jettite**, 103; 105.

יהוד **Jew** is lord of plunder, 208.

יוח **Joach**, 252.

יוחה **Jochah**, 247.

יויז **Joez**, 171.

דן **judgment**, the mouth of, 129.

דין **judgment** fulfilled, 135.

דן **judgment**, My, is with Me, 126; at the time of, 143; My Ju., 157; My sufficient, 219; 238; 245; 253.

דמע **juice**, he worked the orchard for, 96.

דמעים **juices** flow down, 270.

K

קב **Kab-measure**, 76; 80; 191; 198.

קי **Kai**, 42.

קד **Ked**, habitations of, 73.

קת **Keith**, 57; Keith and Janet, 129; is a free man, 163; mouth of, 233; 249.

אמלכם vb. **kings, I shall make them**, My sons, 272.

נמלך vb. **king, made**, 66.

מלך **king**, the Mark-of-All is, 35; Sheol and the Gate of Ravage even the king made for the punishments of iniquities of far away, 76; every king belongs to thee O Mark, 155; a delicacy to the king, 252; the pure king, 260.

מלכים   **kings,** all My kings the Wicked One swallowed up, 187; of strength have acted foolishly everyone of them; they murdered the light with its suffic-iency, the favour of the oppressed My Son, 261.

קיר   **Kir,** Mount, 53.

חלף   **knife,** you shall sharpen the, of Y-H, 109.

כנא   **knighthood,** 56.

דע   **knowledge,** journeyed, 64; was constrained, 64; k. of the Father, 104; Our, shall cover thee O people, 109; knowledge it learned because of the Son, 111; kn. Of the Token swallowed up, 118; kn. Of the Abode of the Shepherd, 123; a Hand of Strength set up Knowledge, 226; thy Prince is the Instrument of My Knowledge, 127; O the ruin of pure knowledge, 130; knowledge endeth the burden of the emptiness of the heart, 136; O Hand of Knowledge of the Father, 138; people of knowledge, 146; I shall cast out the Gift of, 162; sufficient is the Hand of Knowledge, 162; knowledge of the Mark-of-All-of-Them was put to death, 185; the burden of the Gift of Knowledge, 188; come thou to My Pen O Hand of Knowledge, knead thou knowledge; thou judged O Hand of Knowledge because We swallowed up the millstone, 189; knowledge is the Token for Man, 196; with the Knowledge of G-d, 209; and thou O hand of sorrow carried Knowledge, 219; My, 238; against which there is no knowledge, 245; sorrow is knowledge, 254.

L

לאית   **Laeth,** the mouth of weak, 56.

שרה   **Lady, Noble,** 48b.

סך   **lair,** 238.

כר   **lamb,** a, trembled, 169; Lamb of Blood, 189; he shall be brought low by the voice of the he-lamb, 195.

למך   **Lamech,** 148.

הי   **lament** of the Throne, 42.

נהי   **lamentation,** 265.

הי   **lamentation \ lament,** 5; 76; 83; 86; complete, 98; 102; 103; 111; 112; 115; 121; 130; 131; 133; 145; 156; 162; 164; 168; 181; 196; 199; 204; 205; 209; 214; 223; 236; 241; 244; 245; 269; 270; 273; 274.

נ׳ **lamentation \ lament**, 62; 74; 76; 77; 78; 79; 82; 83; 84; 111; 113; 115; 116; 132; 133; 148; 152; 160; 161; 168; 189; 196; 206; 209; 210; 217; 235; 245.

ניר **lamp**, of Shilo, 81; a lamp, thou shalt establish it, 175; empowered a lamp, 185; 189; is more than appetite, 222; 255.

נר **lamp**, a thousand of the lamp are idle talkers, 20; whosoever is a lamp of the Church of the Stout One is worthy of the knowledge of his Father, 104; thrust away the cold, 105; it shall scatter him the adversary of the Father, 105; who is the lamp? Voice and Heart, 107; Who is the lamp? He dimmed it, 107; region of the lamp, 113; this is the lamp I have been waiting for, 116; the Lamp of the Nest, 127; the Moon signaled the Lamp, 128; a lamp scattered the sufficiency of Y-H, 200; Lamp of Cheam, 232; fire of the lamp, 263.

רמח **lance**, 177.

ארץ **land**, of the Tamarisk-tree, 179; 265; 272.

דת **Law**, lights of the, 142; the Lights of the Law, 144; they snorted at the Law of YAH, 192; My Pure One promoted My Law, 193; My Noble removed afar off the Law of My Everlastingness, 202; and the courage of the jackals of blood is against Light and Law, 228; the Faint One shall consume a fullness of the Firebolts of the Law, 240.

רז **leanness**, 60, 170.

שאר **leaven**, 93; 117.

ליקת **Lekeith**, thou acted purely to obey, 159; 160.

נמר **leopard**, this is a, even Acco and he is among the Shout and also a lair, 238; the eggs of a leopard are more than Lust, 254; a leopard of the captivity of the Great Coast journeyed and with him the unclean one of the Nile, 263; here is a man alas the leopard of thy ravage, 266.

יבם **Levir,** 44; the Mark acts the, 91.

לוי **Levite,** He shall cause to come in a, 19; My Thine One the Levite, 186.

און vb. **life of plenty, he enjoyed a,** 153.

ברק **lightning,** 123.

אַור\אָר **light**, a weak, 10; is weak, 38; he who is their light has been made poor; he is made clean by washing, 54; let thou give the poor of mankind their light, 55; suppressed My Light, 55; light of Desire, 58; the light came, thou denied Desire, the Light of my G-d, 59; from window, 60; light of Thy Nest, 71; of the Nest, 73; a bit of light, 85; His Light is the Palate the Integrity

of His Bosom, 104; My Falcon is their Light the Spirit of the
Father, 106; Light of Desire, 107; Light of new Desire, 108;
Light shall outrun the mouth of Keith and Janet, 129; light of
My Token the Moon, 131; I shall feed them at the Light, 165;
light raised up toward the Father, 166; Light of the Nest, 175;
Hand of My Light, 176; lest there be the cloud and the light of
His Daughter, 192; seasoners of Light, *mankind* is bitter
because of light, 193; 198; a light thrust away thy flowing robe,
200; the Son of Light let him sctter it; let him shine, 200; light
of His Daughter, 200; Constellation of the Great Bear My
Light, 201; Lo, a light; how I shall salt it, 203; essence of My
Light, 204; thin ones of light, 210, 214, 222; 216; 218; fragment
of light, 218; mouth of light, 222; fragment of light, 226; 228;
chamber of light, 232; Light of His Beloved, 242; I shall
consume them at the Light, 243; they murdered the, 261; they
who cast down My Light, 264; light overflows, 264; the
Chamber of My Light he brandished, 266; now is My Light
toward the Region of the heap for them, 267.

אורה	**light** of, 264.
אורים	**lights**, the lights of the chamber, 59; of knowledge, 142; the lights of the Law, 144; cried shrilly, 272.
אורות	**lights**, 101.
קו	**line**, measure of a, 123; 167; 213; 220; 250.
התיחש	vb. Hithpael, **lineage, he shall make a, for himself**, 34.
לבי	**lion**, 130.
ליש	**lion** made to stretch out, 124.
אריות	**lionesses**, the blood of the sword of, 50.
אריותי	**lions, My,** and give thou *to*, 155.
לשכה	**Lishka**, secret of ruin is from the, 22.
חי	**living**, the hand that would cut off the living and the pride of all, 101.
חי	**Living One**, 23; 45; 46; 78; 91; 214; 253; 254.
חי פני	**Living Being of My Face**, 125; 150.
איד	**loac** of the Terrible One, 202.
זרא	**loathsome thing**, 245.
גב	**Locust**, 28; O the Day of the, 263; 264.
לוד	**Lod**, out of, is thy ruin, 20; 258; free born of, 267.
שיא	**loftiness**, 7; 83; 253.
בעל	**lord** of the afflicted, 221; lord of ruin, 229.
טעי תאי	**lost ones of My Chamber**, 152.
גי נב	**lowlands of Nob**, 168.

The Linear Bible Code

שח   **Lowly One,** with Me is the, 182; 235; this is the lowly one, the deflection of the Moon, 235; tongue tied, 244.

שחים   **lowly ones,** 29.

קדוַת   **lowly places,** 235.

לאשד   **lower region** of cold, 70.

לוד   **Lud** the proud, 14.

הלוק\לק   **Luke** slumbered, 59; voice of, 59.

מאר   **Luminary,** 262.

גש   **lump** *of earth,* 239.

או\אוה   **Lust,** 16; take you a measure of, 17; affliction of, 36; complete lust pushed Me, 48b; never exalted lust; he confined Lust. The timbrel shall blow *upon* lust, 52 thrust away, 54; 73; shall flee, 75; seeker of, 78; 85; Meni of, 88; at the Isle We shall judge, 89; 93; Gift of Lust, 113; 120; shall We judge Lust? 121; raised up the heap, 121; they wavered at lust, 127; Pit of Lust, 130; pride elevated Lust, 134; raised up, 139; haughty is L., 147; 161; to erase lust, 163; 165; 168;, root out lust, 177; 187; 191; 194; 195; 207; 215; every lust is for ruin, 216; 217; 230; lust of the Ram, 235; 239; 241; 242; 245; 250; 252; 253; 254; 256.

Italic   *lust,* 231.

לד   **Lydda,** is set free, 58; corner of Lydda swallowed up, 59; proud, 63.

M

גאוה   **majesty,** 244.

מת   **man** of blood, 42; he removed the, 89; sufficiency of, 97; 99; what is a, 144; hand of a, 147; 151; every man, 159; Man of Grace, 191; 215; 221; 266; (see Lekeith, 159; 160).

איש   **Man,** Knowledge is the Token for, 196; What is a man? 238; 241; 251.

אנוש   **mankind,** 55; is not seasoners of light, 193; is bitter because of Light, 193.

מלח   **mariner,** 204.

תו-כלם   **Mark of All of Them, the**

תו   **Mark, the:**
    loathes distress,1; works from the doubling of the Wonder, 1; Treasure of, 5; coverts of the Mark His Pure One, 16; is the Pure One, 16; *he* shall rise with difficulty against it, 16; of the Bosom of His Blood, 18; they shone upon, 20; causeth himself

to come, 30; magnified his own gift, 31; shall utterly hammer
the Adversary, 32; shook the Debt of the Mark, 32; revolted at
the sin, 33; the Pure One became the Mark for G-d, 34; The
Mark-of-All is King, 35; he is exposed in the Garden, 36; ran
with the rebellion, 36; I shall choose to beautify him, 39; out of
the inheritors of, 45; is above Seth, 46; is from the Greatness of
Seth, 46; the Seraph the Mark-of-All-of-Them is poor, 54; shall
never fall, 55; of blood, 56; hands of, 56; Spring of, 57; G-d
reproveth the Mark of Blood, 62; heads of cattle of the Mark,
66; of Gentleness, 67; Chamber of, 68; the Mark came, *Jebus*
trembled, 74; brought low the Fortress, 81; was quiet; he
grasped with a twist sackcloth, 86; lo, My Name, he hid the
Name toward the heads of cattle of the Pure Mark; the fortress
is the Mark of EL; the fullness of her son, 86; the Mark-of-All-
of-Them swallowed up all of them, 87; to order the genealogies
of the Mark-of-EL approach you even the Palate; come thou to
him and Wisdom he fashioned, 91; the Mark, Sufficiency of
Grace, acts the Levir, 92; he enabled them, 92; he moved out of
Time, 92; who is above a sheep? The Noble Mark, the
Passageway of G-d, 102; shall become wretched, 106; shifting
Reproach Sheol ran at the Mark-of-All, 108; is making it (the
word) increase, 110; the Mark traveled and swallowed up all of
them. The Mark-of-All-of-Them endures and he shall swallow
down the substances of the Veil, 110; the Mark of Terror is the
Mark-of-All-of-Them the Hand of His Pure Son, 110; the
wealth of dew resemble the, 110; O the city-mound of, 113;
from Cain the Wicked One shall wound the, 113; the Sheep
Raiser waited for, 114; lo, the Council of, 114; is sick, 118;
created Jeah, 118; the bird of prey of pureness My Mark
created, 120; with the Terror of G-d the Mark threw down all of
them, 122; the knowledgeable ones of G-d he silenced
swallowing up the burden of a sheep, the burden of ivory, 122;
the Mark fell *earthward*; he shall be swaddled, 124; the Lamp of
the Nest is above the city-mound of, 127; the Son shall ascend;
the Mark grew great, 132; descended with battle spoils, 135; he
was made to show grief, 135; the Terror of G-d is the Hand of
the, 136; *he* bore thy fault, 136; they shall see the Mark is
brought low; 136; our G-d of the Shout and of the Mark, 143;
the Hand of the Father is the Mark, 146; I shall direct the Gift
of the people of knowledge even the Mark, 146; *he* darted
through the cloud-mass, 146; I shall hide his mother, 146; he
shall empty the Tel of the Dragon, 146; every king belongs to

thee O Mark, 155; *he* explored the dwellings of the Teeth of the
Eagle, 157; O his sobs; it wounded the heart, 157; the Mark
came, 158; for thou acted purely O Lekeith having circumcised
a sheep even the likes of the Mark. He confounded the
Tabernacle, 159; if only the Mark could change all of them, 162;
he came; he swallowed up the Tabernacle, 162; he knew alas My
Thin One even the Mark-of-All-of-Them, 163; *he* pushed away
Beren; he humbled him, 164; the dew of the Chamber of the
Mark languished, 166; all entering the city-mound of the Mark
dug the side-chamber of the Father, 166; They cried shrilly:
'The Son exists!' the Instrument of My Nest. Is not the Mark-
of-All-of-Them to be pounded to powder? The Pure One is
among the valleys; he is becoming sorrowful, 171; all of them
are against Me of the city-mound of the Mark, 174; wailing
shall bring down the Mark; it wounded My Thin One for itself,
181; *he* even is swallowing up the burden of a sheep, 182; the
burden of the sheep is the Law, 182; have thou dominion and
let thou become inventive, 182; I shall change, 185; I shall
magnify, 185; they were drowsy as knowledge of the Mark-of-
All-of-Them was put to death; he fed them the favour of the
oppressed and the Son, 185; the Mark for Shiloh dug out the
Lust of the Jackal, 187; Go thou, 188; I shall change the, 189;
he (the Terrible One) removed afar off the Greatness of the
Mark, 189; he who is the hand of opinion scorched the
Ambuscade of the Mark, 190; let thou O Death turn aside the
knee of the Pure Mark and thou shalt totter the Mark, 192; I
shall lay bare everything of the Mark *whom* they pushed away,
193; where does Gentleness from Y-H rule? The Mark changed
it; My Pure One promoted My Law, 193; (the howler) shall
judge the one hating the, 196; I thy G-d shall lay bare the
Stone Cutter, the Mark, 200; whosoever is the Changeling even
he shook the Mark, 201; and the Mark-of-All-of-Them wounded
(the burden) because the Abyss he caused to totter, 205; *he*
refused the booty he shall plunder, 217; Our Mark made a split
for a fragment of Light, 226; the Lamp of Cheam is above the
Mark, 232; the Chamber of the Mark-of-All-of-Them thou
pressed upon, 234; *he* brought low Somnolence, 235; *he* took
hold of sorrow; *he* scraped clean the coast of Moses in regards to
the Calamity of the coast, 236; *his* posterity is the wandering
ones of Noah, 255; The Mark is the Mark-of-Salt, 259; the Son
is the Mark-of-All. He cut off the Wicked One, 259; The Mark-
of-All, the Pure King, he crashed them into ruins. He shall

spring about *as a calf*. Ah! Above the Sea of Burden he traveled through Time itself. 260; the Mark is salt, 262; (the Revolter) is made low on account of the Gift even the Mark by name, 269; the Mark-of-All-of-Them is for the dividing into three the Jackal, 274.

מוח   **marrow** ruled, 180.

מש   **Mash**, 63; 64; 97.

שלט   **master**, the Terrible One is, of them, 189.

מיעבש   **Meabesh**, 61; 62.

מד   **measure** of His Seed, 43; of ruin-ations, 62; poured out a, 95; measure of EL I shall make fruitful, 96; of the Nest, 113; of a line, 123; of the Nest, 125; measure of cinnamon, 136; 141; 143; 148; 149; 157; 160; 161; 168; 203; 207; 211; 220; 237; 242; 243; 246; 248; 253.

לג   **measure**, 230.

מיבל   **Mebal**, 15.

מבבל   **Mebabel**, 28; 58.

מידבש   **Medebesh**, 61.

ממש   **Memesh**, 1.

נף   **Memphis**, 33; 127; 132; 186.

Italic   *men*, I shall feed *the*, 156; 162; 237.

מני   **Meni** of Lust, 88; 248.

מירז   **Meraz**, 15.

שוכר   **mercenary**, 29.

מישה   **Meshach**, 15.

לאך   vb, **messenger, he sent a**, 48b; I will send a, 95; G-d sent a messenger and food, 173; 209.

מלאך   **messenger** of the Assembly, 83.

משיח   **Messiah**, Noah shall make abundant the Region of, 134.

מיתייה   **Metai-yah**, 63.

ג   **middle**, 244.

דחן   **millet**, 144.

פלח   **millstone**, 185; 189; 190; 196.

משרתו   **minister**, the oppression of **his**, 151.

בץ   **mire**, 99; 234; 235.

אד   **mist**, thin one of the, 175; 186; 222.

אדי   **mists of**, 160.

מאב   **Moab**, 147.

אוטט   **moaner**, 180.

מוקי   **mockers of Y-H**, 125.

מַזָל **Moel**, they removed afar off the, 10; the Moel met the heads of cattle of the pasture of the people; he beat fine the fatling and he subdued sorrow, 74; secrecy shall remove the Moel here, 184.

לח **moisture**, 204; the hand of the Moel provided…, 228-229.

רי **moisture**, 239.

ירח **month**, who twisted the, 14.

ירי **Moon**, thou hast removed afar off the, 4; I set the Window of the Moon a god, his god., 46; and the Moon abideth above it, 113; light of My Token, 131.

ירחא **Moon**, who resembles the people of the, 9; the Moon shall say:, 53; the Moon shriveled, 65; the Moon died with him, 92; Barque of the, 108; the Moon and the leaven are in the hand of the Wicked One, 117; the Moon signaled the Lamp, 128; thou caused the Moon to endure, 132; moon of desire, 231; 235; I shall uncover the, 236; 240.

ברם **morose noise**, 28.

פת **morsel** of vigour, 77; 233; 234.

בג **morsel**, 220.

משה\מושה **Moses**, waters of, 5; and from, a severe commandment, 24; habitations of, 73; trouble is from, 73; waters of, 77; coast of, 233; scraped clean the coast of, 236; region of, 245.

אם-לח **Mother Nature**, 242; the bear is alongside of the bowmen of Mother Nature; they (the posterity of the wandering ones of Noah) inflamed Mother Nature, 255-256.

אם **mother**, the Mark divided into three, 1; poverty of a, 6; 7; mother of My people; 18; poor one of a, 56; of a people, 82; poverty of a, 83; it swallowed up Knowledge and Mother, 118; 134; I shall hide (the Mark's) mother, 146; 157; of the Table, 195; he exalted a, even the mother of the winepress, 196; the High Mother belongs to Him, 214; 215; 218; because of the obedience of the Instrument of the Mother, 227; 228; mother of Zellah of Ham, 237; remnant of, 239; of the scorner, 239; for her favour, 253; poverty of the, 266..

אמי בר **mothers of purity**, 72; the poverty of the mothers of My Door, 266; the desire of the, 272.

הר\הור **mountain**, cold pure, 10; was veiled, 24; against the Gift, 28; of My Altar Shovels, 47; Mount Ker, 53; Mount Ravage, 59; fish of a, 61; Mount of Devastation and Distress, 82; Seraph parted, 93; mountain *stream*, 102; the sweat of a, 105; thou mocketh the, 128; Mount Put, 183; Mount Shaphan, 231; Neglect ran into the, 161; deliver thou the, 162; unite a, 239; of Bacah, 247; of blood, 251; desirable thing of the, 251.

הרי   **mountains of** Azum-Toah, 101; of desolation, 233.

הריות   **mountains of** YAH are for Unity, 118.

חך   **mouth** of a sheep, 149.

Italic   *mouth*, 263.

פם   **mouth**, 71; is for Me, 73.

פה   **mouth**, the Father made the Mouth, 97; it died...was with his G-d; 92; mouth of Dan, 129; 232; of Keith, 233.

פי   **mouth of** Noah, 23; of G-d, 208; 217; of G-d fed them; judged them, 225.

שפי   **mouth of** His Beloved, 242.

מור   **myrrh**, 218; 228.

פרד   **mule**, no lowly mule of desire, 152; 153; 155; 156; of sorrow, 156; of G-d, 157; of sorrow, 210; 228; of God, 228.

רב   **multitude**, 66; 78; 79; he shall mark the, 108; 213; 214; 215; 246; 264.

המת   vb. Hophal, **murdered the Light...My Son**, 261.

מלני נף   **murmurers of Memphis**, 33.

לט   **mystery** of the measuring line, 213.

לטה   **mystery** of Y-H, 200.

N

שם   **name**, he hid My Name 'Pure One' toward Tirab, 64; it withdrew My Name, 65; It removed My Name, 66; He shall conceal a name, 68; Lo, My Name, he hid the Name in regards to the heads of cattle of the Pure Mark, 86; lo, and a Name He established, 125; by the name of the Favour of the Oppressed and the Son lo, I shall make thee tremble, 180; a name for him "Rama-Yad", 188.

הער   **naked, the**, 272.

נתן   **Nathan**, 99.

נתי   **Natai**, 265.

גוי   **nation**, 139.

נעה   **Neah**, 254.

נבו   **Nebo**, mouth of, 37; I killed, 41.

נבן   **Nebon**, valleys of, 242.

אוב\אב   **necromancer**, 40; 95.

אבות	**necromancers** (fem.), A bolt of lightning and a flame he raised against thy necromancers, 166.
של	**Neglect**, rain into the mountain, 161.
נל	**Nel**, 265.
נם	**Nem**, 265.
קן	**Nest**, remnant of the, 63; Light of Thy, 71; Light of the, 73; measure of the, 113; 125; 127; 148; 149; 160; Instrument of My Nest, 171; Light of My Nest, 175; 202; 219; 230; 246; 247..
הלח	**New Thing**, 70; 197.
ליל	**night** has departed, 240.
טל	**night mist**, 229.
יאר	**Nile**, judge the falcon of the, 9; regions of the, 59; House of the, 70; the blood of the ruinationsof the Nile, 104; with him the unclean one of the Nile, 263.
תשע	**nine**, is Distinction, 19; surely the waters of Moses are for thee instead of the Nine of Thebes, 77.
נוח\נח	**Noah**, the mouth of Noah he loosened among My altar shovels, he ruled them. 23; Noah caused the burning to be removed by the blood of ruin of G-d, 51; Who is for Me? The Mouth and Noah. They restrained the habitations of Ked the stumbling of thy gods. 73; I shall cause Noah to be circumcised. He shall make abundant the Region of Messiah, 134; the splitters of G-d and Noah, at the Mouth of G-d they shall be judged. 208; the wandering ones of; the Integrity of Noah endured, 255.
נב	**Nob**, 52; 95; 96; valleys of, 147; 163.
השע	**Noble One**, O that his Noble One had caused bluntness to be shamed, 71.
חור\חר	**Noble**, nobleman, 14; noble, 101; Noble Mark, 102; Ah! The Noble of Desire of My Will, 132; thou hast walked o Noble of G-d the *celestial* Window, 160; The Noble One caused Me to tremble. He caused himself distress to feed them the favour of the oppressed and the Son. He swallowed the Gentleness from G-d; thus the Mark for Shiloh dug out the Lust of the Jackal. 187; My Noble, 202; is not he Noble his Instrument? 203; noble one, 262..
שרה	**Noble Lady**, and O, Noble Lady of thy Chamber give thou birth to a proud *son*, 48b.
נד	**Nod**, coast of, 153.
קול\קל	**noise**, O the distress of, 139.

O

אלותי   **oaths**, My Own, 57.

מיקהם   **obedience, their**, 245.

מיקיו   **obedient one, Our**, Wailing! His Hand on High circumcised all from the coast of Moses, the Reconciler, **Our obedient one. 233.**

ימי כח   **Oceans of Strength, 241.**

רית   vb. **odour, he perceived an odour of Emptiness**, 17.

בשם   vb. **odour, a sweet**, 180.

סחי   **offscouring**, 119.

נינת   **offspring of** the Moon, 132.

שגרה   **offspring, her**, 149; (see, 'young').

עג   **Og**, throat of, 52.

ישן   **Old One**, praise you My Gift because of the, 35.

אן   **On**, the vapour of Rottenness, I am hating *it*, 127; 132; Caleph of On, 216; 217.

רקי   **only one, My**, she is, 236.

הרקי   **Only One, My**, prophesied, 18.

דע   **opinion**, erred, 3; error of, 10; erred, 12-13; erred, 29; abundant, 98; ceaseth, 110; caused an increase in the cloud of emptiness, 185; 189; 190; 196.

דך   **oppressed, the**, belongs to the Pure One, 34; great is the oppressed, 50; but a few he caused to shine even the oppressed of the Father, 162; for wailing; the firebolt is at the windows of My oppressed. 166.

אצי   **oppressed one, My**, 101.

תך   **oppressed** of the Father gazed at the Lamb of Blood, 189; 211; 212; 215; 217; 220; 224; 225; 227; 228; 231; 233; 241; 259; 261; 274.

דך   **oppression**, waters of, 25; it derided Desire, 88; 270.

איד   **oppression**, 240.

ינת   **oppression of**, 242.

תך   **oppression**, 48b; 61; 77; heart of, 137; 151; 183; 184; 239; 240.

דך   **oppressor, My**, 53.

טלמי   **oppressors, My**, 11.

שע\השע   **Opulence**, 23; Opulent One, 30; at the Opulent One they refused, 42; 197.

גנה\וג   **orchard**, 37; he worked the orchard for juice, 96.

צו	**ordinance**, and proud Lydda is in the Ordinance, 63; out of Mash from the waters of the Ordinance he lured thy face, 64; The Father established the Ordinance of the Veil, 97.
מזי-נזל	**overflowing** of the *celestial* window, 218; 222; 224;226.
עו\עוה.	**overturning**, 123, 191; 197.

P

זג	**pair**, 232.
היכלים	**palaces** of His Obedient One, 273; 274.
חך	**Palate**, of excess is Zael, 52; pierceth itself? 57; created Ivory of G-d and this Chamber, 58; approach you the Palate; come thou to him and Wisdom he fashioned, 91; the P. was with his G-d, 92; the blood of the children of the Father of the Palate, 103; His Light is the Palate the Integrity of His Bosom, 104; 141; 153; 154; 155; of the Poor One, 271.
מוצב	**palisade**, a kind of, 86.
פס	**palm**, My, 51; 180; 239.
עבר	**Passage**, Sea of, 69.
עבר	**passageway** of G-d, the Noble Mark, 102.
מעבר	**Passageway** of Time from G-d, the Passover is the, 233.
פסח	**Passover** shall come the Passageway of Time from G-d, 233; the Passover of the Abode of the Shepherd was drowsy, 234; I shall cause the Passover to dangle with the Pure One of the people of G-d, 234; The Passover of the Abode of the Shepherd was drowsy, 234; Now is the Passover of G-d, 238; it is the Passover even of G-d, 238; the Instrument of the Abode of the Flock removed the Passover; they slumbered, 238.
עד	**Past**, from the past is the food, 145.
נוה	**pasture**, 137; 156; 203; 269.
כרי	**pastures of** the people, 74.
שך	**Pavilion**, 37; 57; 257.
סך	**pavilion**, 177; 265.
דר	**Pearl** of My habitations, 57.
קאתי	**Pelicans of** Kur, 219; 222; 224; 226.
עט	**pen**, the blood of the, 136; pure pen, 179; come thou to My Pen, 189; slumbered, 189; My Pen is with the Ram, 196; 207; of Integrity silenced, 222.
פנאל	**Penuel**, 231.

עם **people** of emptiness, 14; mother of My, 18; deceitful is My, 18; dealt violently with, 24; this is the measure of his, 28; bill of divorcement of a, 31; quarreled, 33; acted crafty, 33; on account of My people his poor ones, 35; a profane people despised him, 39; slumbered, 42; and the Shatterer of all of them is against a People with its Father. 43; turned aside, 48a; of profaneness, 49; double is the people of Thy Tooth O Y-H, 55; a people fall, 57; exterminated, 66; I shall establish a, 71; people of the Gift, 72; are not a people a sheep? 73; pasture of the, 74; shall propagate by it, 77; a poor people, 82; mother of a people, 82; people of Ravage and the Fortress, 98; a people shall Passover, lo, from the Father, 105; Our Knowledge shall cover thee O people, 109; this is a Terrible Thing for a people, 118; of ruin, 123; I shall direct the Gift of the people of knowledge even the Mark, 146; draw near O people of the ravaged tel-city, 146; for a people is Sheol, 147; thin people of Edom, 149; all of them for a people preserve Emptiness, 157; people of Sheol, 161; at the time of a people a sheep was wanted, 166; O the exclusive root of the mighty people of Y-H, 191; A Lament for a People, 196; O the Prince of the vine tendrils of the mighty people of Y-H, 198; people of the pasture, 203; he lapped up the people of the Gift of the Hand, 222; We lapped up a people, 226; the Pure One pulled along the people of G-d, 233; 234; 239; poor of the, 260; light overflows he who is a people, 264; increase for a people, 265.

Italic ***people***, My Only One prophesied against him, 18; to the fishes he shall go for ruin, 19; he fished, 105; are unwell, are drowsy, 168; a sleeping, 196; 210; sleeping, 228.

תם\תום **perfection** of Desire, 63; perfection from Dignity, 64; of strength, 171.

עד **perpetual**, 245.

עוו **perversity** of a jar, 116.

חג **pilgrim feast** is My Gift, 17.

פתם **Pithom**, 71.

חור **Pit** of Lust, 130 is more than its darkness, 257.

באר **Pit**, 209.

גב **Pit**, 211.

יזם vb. **plan, he makes a**, 215.

זמ\זמם **Plan**, give Thou O G-d of all of us a, 193; 200; shineth out, 266.

נעם **pleasantness**, 76; 80.

אוֹהַ **pleasure**, 145.

את   **ploughshare**, 102; 225.

שלל   **plunder**, spoils of, 142.

רמן   **pomegranate** is as the Moon, 131.

רשי   **poor**, he shall be made poor, 48b.

עני רח   **poor in spirit**, 203.

עני   **poor one**, 229.

דל   **poor**, the Son shall see enough of the poor, 236; they are rolled up as the heart, 236; the Gift of the Poor One is silent, 242; great of strength is thy Poor One, 260.

רש   **poor**, 54; of mankind, 55; Poor One given a Knighthood, 56; Poor One of his people, 61; of G-d, 63; injured of the, 77; the tent of the fisherman belongs to the , 77; injury of the, 79; poor people, 82; poor one journeyed, 83; 87; sorrow of the, 89; the House of the Nile caused the Poor One of EL to be swallowed up, 93; I shall make exceedingly white the Poor One, 99; poor of the Affliction, 128; with Me, 131; Poor One of quivering *lips*, 133; he caused a daughter to show grief; this My Thin One maketh fat G-d, 174; give thou O poor My ringing cry, 184; poor of the people, 260; light of the Poor One, 264; poor of the land, 265; What is in the Palate of the Poor One? The Desire of the Eternities, 271; My Poor One shall bear fruit, 272.

רשיו   **poor ones, his**, 35.

שער   **Porter** of My Salvation, 47.

מן   **portion**, he measured a, 127; 160; My portion, 173; 176; 230; 232; 247.

נן\נין   **posterity**, 192; 255.

עני   **poverty** of desire, 14.

רש   **poverty**, of a mother, 6; 7; makes them filthy, 54; 77; of a mother, 83; poverty of the mothers of My Door, 266; of the mother, 266.

יד   **power**, ravage of, 60; The Instrument prophesied of the Age of Brightness of Power *and* My Knowledge, 238; day of, 270.

גס   vb. **power, wield**, 219; 221.

כח   **power**, what shall the Power permit? 1; days of power, 173; 195; 204; 246.

צ   **Precept**, he is, the wine of desire, 48b.

הריה   vb. **pregnancy, caused a**, 180.

גא\גאי   **pride**, 162; **proud**, 213, 184; **proud ones** of apostasy, 214.

זח   **pride**, go and circumcise thy, 47; lap up, 48a; 48b; My proud suck *the breast*, 51; 53; 67; 70; 102; 116; 121; 123; 124; 130; 131; 176; 200; 201; 209; 215; 235; 240; 245.

נשא **prince**, 133.

אר **prince**, he exposed the prince when he shaved the pubis of thy daughter, 176.

סר **prince**, thy Prince I shall prepare, 126; is the Instrument of My Knowledge, 127.

שר **prince**, the Seraph is, 135; the perfect Garner is Prince, a Hand, 147; Who is the Prince? He knowls enough; he shall pound at the region of his heap, 150; waters of the, 160; Prince of the vine tendrils of the mighty people of Y-H...he circumcised His Hundreds; he united them, 198; of the Region, 207; Whomsover Thou appointed has returned; the Prince comprehended them, 259; Tower of the Prince, 267..

חל **profane**, regions of the, 240.

חל **profaneness**, 10; 19; of heart, 49; generation of, 59; demon of, 61; 62; 67; 183; the, of all rained down, 252.

נין **progeny**, from the desire of the, of the affliction, 211.

נבא vb. **prophesied**, 18; 161; he shall, 178; Father of the Shout prophesied, 178; 232.

קלן **pubis**, when he shaved the pubis of thy daughter, 176.

בר **Pure One, the**: of Integrity, 10; Who is the Pure One? 10; The Mark, His Pure One, 16; the Mark is the Pure One, 16; Who is the Pure One? 17; he wept, 17; made tender, 17; slow to anger, 17; made hast against him; he pledged a dwelling., 22; Who is the, 23; 34; he became the Mark for G-d, 34; the tears of G-d, 34; who is the, 38; Our Pure One was made to slumber, 38; We gave Our Pure One, 39; Who is the, 41; on account of the, 45; is to devastate to save, 47; Pure One of the Appointed Time, 70; Pure One of separation grasped with a twist a species of vapour, 70 he presented desire, 80; Who is the, 89; 90; they swallowed up the, 90; the Chamber of the Shovels of the Pure One, 114; and each hundred of the Shovels of the Pure One is His Sign, 114; the pride of the explorer testing because of the Pure One, 116; the PO purified himself, 116; he grasped with a twist them of Memphis, 116; he praised Me, 116; Kaid refused the Hand of the PO, the PO of strength, 124; the measure of the Nest is with the PO even His Son, 125; the ruin of the PO, 130; Jacha' is the PO of Desire the Valiant One, 133; the PO of the Nest is the Hand of the Father, 149; *G-d* was pleased with the Robe of the PO, 158; His Pure One purified himself, 161; the PO is among the valleys; he is becoming sorrowful, 171; the PO purified himself, 172; the PO volunteered and they of the

Affliction shall become his debt; he shall take it away with Innocence, 173; where was he strengthened? Come forth Error when he feedeth My Portion. This is food: the Utterance of the Witness. 173; the PO is here, the PO purified himself and he fed them; 177; the Abode of the Flock is with him, 177; the PO purified himself and he fed them, 178; the PO purified himself; he exalted the world; he sought thee against the fierceness of Sheol; Transgression trembled; he boasted of Thee O Y-H, 179; he staggered with the pure wine of the PO, 181; the PO even he shall confine the shining one, 181; Alas, the bird of prey of the Pure One of Heart is at the Island of G-d's Mist, 186; My PO promoted My Law, 193; the calamity of the Terrible One is the burden of the PO, 202; O the lament of the PO their PO is like YAH, 205; a lament for the PO, 209; and the Son the PO of My nest, PO cast a spear at the coast of ruin, 211; they shall turn away the lamentation of the PO, 214; His PO overthrew the courage of the Jackal, 229; the PO purified himself, 230; the PO of the Appointed Time is a vessel; he shall discourse. The PO pulled along the people of G-d, 233; PO of the people of G-d, 234; the PO shall boast with Me, 273; he fined the Adversary, 273.;

בר   **pure, the,** 231.

בר   **purity,** mothers of, 72; vessel of, 143.

בר   **pureness,** he hid My Name "Pureness", 64; the bird of prey of pureness, 120.

פוט   **Put,** 28; Mount, 183.

Q

רעש   **quaking,** he left behind, 209.

ניד   **Quivering** *of lips,* 133; 143; O the quivering of the Father; O the quivering *lip,* 221; 228.

ניחח   **quietness,** 231.

R

איל   **Ram,** My, is Mine, 130; My Pen is with the, 196; 234; 235; 245.

שא   **Ravage,** of thy threshing-floor, 53; of power, 60; prince of Ravage, 78; 88; 98; 169; 191; 198.

שוא   **ravage**, 144; 192; 262.

מרי   **rebellion**, who is in, 6.

מורתי   **rebellious ones, My**, 20.

רבדג   **Rabedag**, region of, 227; 228.

רבתד   **Rabethad**, region of, 227; 228.

מטר   **rain** of Grace shall scatter about strength, 241.

איל   **Ram**, where is the Ram of the worshipper? 190.

רמא-יד   **Rama-Yad**, a name for him:, 188; *lit. 'bowman at hand'*.

חל   **rampart**, 177; 178.

שוא\שא   **ravage**, o people of the ravage of the Tel-City, draw near, 146; bosom of, 177; 206; 222; 266; 268.

רזגר   **Razegar**, region of, 227; 228.

לאם   **Reconciler**, 233.

אבה   **reed**, 258.

רגח   **Regech**, 61.

חו   **Register**, the core of the, 191.

אי   **region**, 8; of My Witness, 23; of Nob, 52; 55; 56; 59; 94; 95; 96; 97; 98; 108; 109; of the Lamp, 113; 120; Thin One of the, 127; 128; 134; 141; 142; 145; 147; 149; 156; 166; 186; 193; 194; 206; 209; 211; 221; 223; 227; 229; 230; 239; 240; 241; 258; 259; 261; 265; 267; 270.

אי"   **regions of**, (favourable) 222.

אית יאר   **regions of the Nile**, 59.

גל   **rejoicing**, their, becomes bitter, 137; 149; 154; 156; 161; 162; 167; 168; 171; 175; 183; 200; 206; 207; 214; 218; 222; 225.

שאר   **remnant**, 10; thy remnant a chamber exists for it, 25; of the Nest, 63; My remnant spoke rashly, 134; 200; 236; 240; of faithfulness, 265.

נוזח   **Remover**, The R. poured out of thy water courses a measure. He leaped toward Nob; he removed afar off the greatness of its region. He moved to and fro; he spoke rashly toward here...95; is against the Light of Desire, 107; is against the Light of New Desire thou carry *My Words* away; 108; the Barque is removed afar off *by* the R. 108; the Remover is against Thee, 262.

שם   **renown**, Hawk of, 172.

רפה- קדץ   **Rephah-Kedez**, 187.

כלמה   **reproach**, 20; 88; 113; 164; 258 he shall cast down, 261; 264; 270.

שם   **reputation**, words of, 17; 244.

צק   **restraint**, 199.

שט   **Revolter**, of the heart, 194; 269.

צלע	**Rib** of the Father, 158; he made a loving jesture surely; but they denied his strength, 158; all entering the Tel-City of Thy Mark saw the Rib of the Father, 166; cause you to see the Rib of the Father, 174.
עשר	**rich**, who is, 2.
רן	**ringing cry**, 184.
דוח	vb. **rinsed clean**, 238.
טומו	vb. **ritually stained**, Shem and the lights, 272.
שבל	**robe**, flowing, 200.
מעילי	**Robe**, My, 23.
של	**robe** of the Pure One, 158.
כף	**Rock** hither I shall exalt with Me, 52.
רהן	**Rohan**, 125.
תא	**room** of fruit, 63.
שרש	**root**, of Desire, 78; 150; and exclusive root, 188; 191.
מק	**rottenness**, all, he shall remove, 32; 78.
נירם	**rows of untilled earth**, 131.
עי	**ruin**, has regarded him, 2; catch fire, 10; tarries, 10; blood of, 12-13; 19; 20; 24; blood of, 37; 48b; blood of, 51; 53; the blood of, 70; 72; 89; 94; complete, 94; 97; 103; My Ruin, 107; 118; 119; 130; his ruin is the pride of My Daughter, 134; 182; 200; 211; 216; 229; 261.
עו	**ruin**, 19; secret of ruin, 22; two is thy ruin from upn thy ruin, 27; 44; 70; Gift of Ruin, 64; my cold is above, 68; doube is the ruin, 71; spoil the ruin, 90; raised up ruin, 91; a people of ruin, 126; 146; G-d of Ruin, 156; 163; 206; 207; 208; 210; 213; 214; 215; 218; 220; 221; 229; 245; 268.
שד	**ruin**, 259.
עוה	**ruin**, 19.
הותי	**ruin, my engulfing**, 107.
צהוה	**ruins**, make it, 99.
Italic	*ruins*, heap of, 142.
עות	**ruination of**, 161.
עית	**ruinations**, of Mount Ravage, 59; 62; of the Nile, 104..
עייו	**ruinations, his**, the blood of, 92.
רץ	**runner** permitted error, 12-13; wounded the runner, 134; 202.
חלאת	**rust of**, 227; 228.

S

שק   **sackcloth**, 86.

כון   **sacrificial cake**, 182.

מלח   *vb.* **Salt** the watering-hole, 253.

מלח   **salt** of the coast, 134; inflamed them, 169; 240; Mark of Salt, 259; Son of Salt, 259.

חול   **sand** of the coast, 249.

חולי   **sands of** strength, 246.

השעי   **saved ones, My**, 31; His saved ones, 36.

ילף   *vb.* **Scab, form a**, 234.

תלמיד   **scholar**, because of a scholar has fed them Somnolence he is brought low, 213.

לץ   **scorner**, 207.

ביזים   **scorners of** the White Washer, 135; they fasted, 135; of the Gift of Desire, 144..

ים   **sea**, fruit of the, 1; look to the, 6; 7; inaccessible, 14; brings Seth, 21; waited on the blood of ruin, 12-13; who thrust from the sea, 33; from the sea a messenger, 48b; 53; of passage, 69; Sea of Time, 71; it divided the, 132; Sea of the Veil, 203; of Burden, 260; they have disguised themselves from the, 265; 267; wail of the, 270; 272.

סא   **seah-measure**, 191; 198.

מולח   **seasoning, the one**, the Chamber, 257; salting reproach he weakened haughtiness, 258.

מלחים   **seasoners of** light, Mankind is not, 193.

לט   **secrecy**, 184.

שלי   **secrecy**, two islands of, 182.

Italic   *secrecy*, 132.

Italic   *secret, works in*, 201.

רז   **secret**, the secret of ruin is from the Lishka among him, 22; the secret is in the guiding to a watering-station, 233; of injustice, 261; the blood of ruin and wailing *which is* the secret of injustice, 262; 265; 269; 270.

Italic   *seed*, he shall scatter, 183.

מעא   **seed**, 244.

מעה   **seed**, 12-13; his own seed, 32; 33; 36; 37; 38; 39; 43; he teaches the **seeds** מעהם; his, 74; 233; 246; 264.

דרש   **seeker** of Lust, 78.

תר   **seeker**, made smooth wealth, 93.

סנב	**Seneb**, measuring line of, 250.
סנה	**Seneh**, 140.
שרף	**Seraph**, who is the Seraph with Him? 17; he chose a Seraph to teach the seeds, 47.
סרף	**Seraph**, a, inscribed, 49; they abhoreth My, 54; is the Mark, 54; bedecked all of them a prince, 63; parted a mountain, 93; is Prince, 135; 160.
סרף	**serpent**, the hand of the, 145; hand of a serpent, 147; 151; in comparison to My Strength the serpent is weak and the hand, 159.
חוה	**serpent**, from the Veil I shall cut off the, 202.
גה	vb. **set free** a generation of profaneness, 59.
שת	**Seth**, 1; the Mark is above Seth, 46; the Mark is from the Greatness of Seth, 46; made king, 66; 99; 232.
צל	**shadow**, bow down *beneath* the, 75; strengthen then the, 112; 216; 218; 219; 221; 222; 223; 225; 227; 238.
שהנאל	**Shahanael**, 154.
בש	**shame** of My Kinsfolk, 28; strength is his shame, 87.
בשה	**shame**, I have confined, 34.
בשים	**shamed ones**, 40.
שפם	**Shapham**, 166.
שפן	**Shaphan**, Mount, 231.
שרון	**Sharon**, 75.
חד	**sharp** sharp one, 136.
חד	**sharpness**, devastation of, 82.
נופץ	**Shatterer**...is his Father, 37; how sufficient is a seed but the Shatterer of all of them shamed *the Distresser*, 38; and the Shatterer wounded His Own seed on account of a profane people the ones having despised Him, 39; and the Shatterer obscured more than the measure of the bowels, 42; the Shatterer of all of them is against a people with its father; He brightened not its father. And *the people* smote the Upright One who is the favour of the measure of His seed, 43.
קוצב	**Shearer**, who is calamity? The, 66.
שה	**sheep, a**, a friend of His Sheep, 17; who is willing and shall move to and fro among His Sheep (flock of sheep), 34; 35 among the sheep, 64; concealed a sheep, 68; 69; are not a people a sheep, 73; 75; he hid a, 79; a species of, 87; everyone heaped up a, 99; what is above a sheep, 102; the Adverary of Desire prevailed over His Sheep, 103; blood of a species is for us knowledge, 110; greatness of, 112; 149; Palate of a sheep, 153;

Sheep of G-d, 154; Palate of a sheep, 154; 155; *jaw* of a sheep, 159; circumcised, 159; 160; scarcely was the Sheep of G-d destroyed, 161; thou at the time of a people a Sheep was wanted, 166; thou tarried O Sheep, 167; thou make praise to YAH because of His Strength, 167; thou tarried O Sheep, 169, 170; 229; dew of the sheep, 236; swallowed up, 246; as a sheep 262; he pruned the people of sheep, 264; Tower of the Sheep, 265; Bel's sheep, 268; He causes the chastening of the Tower of Shemah for them His Sheep, 269.

נקד **sheepraiser**, waited for the Mark, 114.

שם **Shem**, the sea brings, 21; a hand of a species from Shem, 30; city mound of, 45; was made to weep, 134; the scorners of Shem fasted, 135; Shem wept, 240; species of, 270; howled at thee, 272.

שמה **Shemah**, Tower of, 269.

שם-אוה **Shem-Avah**, dominion of, 146.

שאול **Sheol**, and to protect Sheol he made thee a god, 46; Sheol and the Gate of Ravage even the King made for the punishments of iniquities of far away, 76; he trembled from Sheol, 84; shifting reproach Sheol ran at the Mark-of-All, 108; for a people is Sheol, 147; fragment of, 158; people of, 161; the Pure One...sought Thee against the fierceness of Sheol, 179; he betook himself to the Error of the Pit and the Burden of Sheol, 209; he fed them as they of Sheol spoke incoherently, 221..

רעה **shepherd**, by a, he made them shine, 89.

שלט **shield**, 191.

שלו\שלוה **Shilo\Shiloh**, Lamp of, 81; the Mark for Shiloh dug out the Lust of the Jackal, 187; he shall judge Shiloh, 207.

אוהל **Shining One**, 61.

הילַל **Shining One**, 85.

צי **ship**, 14; burn thy ship, 76.

תא צי **ship's hold**, 69.

שאה **Shoah**, 49; 107; (*see 'Devastating Storm'*).

חף **shore**, 152.

ריע **shout** *of war*, 71.

הד **shout**, 71; 79; 132; our G-d of the Shout, 143; 161; 163; 176; 177; 228; 232; 238; 239; 243; 253; 270.

קל **shout**, 149.

עבשי **shriveled ones, My**, 5.

שוריַת **Shurioth**, 66.

צד **side**, 228.

אות\את **Sign**, and Distress was against him, 15; marches with the lowly ones, 28; as a Sign and a Token, 114; His Pure Sign, 110; each hundred of the Pure One is His Sign, 114; 124; His Sign, 138; 141; 142; 143; 144; 147; 148; 151; 152; 155; the Hand is His Sign, 168; 227; 242; 248.

סין **Siin**, Fortress of, 72.

יחשיה vb. **silence, he causes**, 90.

שג **sin**, 33.

פש **sin** of lust, 252.

יתע **skin sore** was contagious, 44.

שול **skirt**, 63.

שובל **skirt, flowing**, of a daughter, 126.

Italic *sky* wander the, 167.

אבחה **slaughter**, among him is of My Sword, 59.

שן vb. **sleep**, 19.

נוך **smiter**, 253.

סא **So**, the generation of, 152.

בכאות **sobs**, O his, *they* wounded the heart, 157.

בכות **sobs**, 160.

תשב **sojourner**, 252.

גר **sojourner**, 96; dung of the, 126; 132; 166; 174; 199; 234; sought for Grace, 238.

פס **sole** *of foot*, 159.

ניד **solace**, 249.

נמה\נם **Somnolence**, 213; 229; 235.

בן **son**, Sufficiency of the Son, 39; decked out, 56; a son was made perpetual, 66; I shall raise up a son among them, 68; he shall bedeck My Son, 68; the Fortress is the Mark of EL; the fullness of her son, 86; the Hand of Iniquity was perplexed; knowledge it learned because of the Son, 111; A Son shall ascend; the Mark grew great, 132; I G-d shall awaken the Son; he shall see his sufficiency; he shall sweep it away *and* the region, 137; each king is His son, 157; My Son abideth, 161; the favour of the oppressed, the Son of Will came, 164; with a thumb the Spirit of G-d he made a writing: "Thou shalt despise His Son." 165; he came; he fed them, 168; and the favour of the oppressed came; the Son fed them and the daughter, 170; they cried shrilly: "The Son exists!" the Instrument of My Nest, 171; He shall prophesy:...the Son abideth and his efficient Wisdom, 178; the favour of the oppressed came and the Son, 178; the Bear of thy trouble...said: Marrow ruled! The favour of the oppressed has a sweet odour; but the Son, lo, I shall make thee tremble, 180;

but have I caused a pregnancy? Then His Son thou shalt suckle. 180; for a basket he shall rule; he shall shake the favour of the oppressed and the Son. 183; now slumbers the favour of the oppressed and the Son. 184; he caused himself distress to feed them the favour of the oppressed and the Son. 187; the Sonof Lighthe spread it *(light)* about; it shineth forth. 193; Surely My Son is the Gift of the Veil, 194; the Son of Light let him scatter it; let him shine, 200; Aa-Og, a son of Mine, 201; a leading man, 201; My Son is the Gift of the Veil, 202; and the Son, lo, I shall send him down. "Descend thou O Seed! 205; Alas the Chamber I shall approach. It is smitten in front of Ravage the Foe. I shall send a Son; he shall see enough of this. 206; What is the Terrible Thing? All faithlessness! He fed them the favour of the oppressed and the Son of Heart. 206; Alas, He sent a Messenger. He shall increase on High Desire for the favour of the oppressed and the Son. 209; I shall awaken the city-mound *to feed them* the favour of the oppressed and the Son, the Pure One of My Nest. 211; the flame of the Father of Hope he made to flicker; and it shall feed them the favour of the oppressed and the Son. 212; the fortress of Man is the favour of the oppressed and the Son. 215; Give thou rest I pray. O the tranquility of Chael! I shall feed them the favour of the oppressed and the Son at the lamentation of the haughtiness of Lust. 217; the Son caused a trembling, 220; the City of the Sojourner is against the favour of the oppressed and the Son. 220; I shall feed them the favour of the oppressed and the Son, for the Lamp is more than Appetite. 222; the Thin One by Thy Voice fed them the favour of the oppressed and the Son on account the Instrument of the Father was obedient. 223; ...it fed them the favour of the oppressed and the Son because of the Instrument of the Father was obedient *even* the Blood of the Wandering Shadow. 225; The Thin One has hidden at his own time a Delicacy even the favour of the oppressed and the Son. 226; Out of the obedience of the Instrument I shall cut off the Shadow by an utterance. O the wailing from a wild goat! I shall feed them the favour of the oppressed and the Son. 227; I shall feed them the favour of the oppressed and the Son. 228; And Penuel is on High lest He feed them the favour of the oppressed and the Son. 231; I shall feed them the favour of the oppressed and the Son for a witness and a sufficiency. 241; Set you in place the Mark-of-Salt, the favour of the oppressed; the Son-of-Salt is the favour of the oppressed. The Son is the Mark-

of-All. He cut off the Wicked One. 259; they murdered the
Light with its sufficiency the favour of the oppressed My Son,
261; He cut off the walls of thy heart to make sick the strength
of the oppressed and the Son of the Father. 274.

בן	**son** of the Bear of Ruin. 268.
בר	**son**, the Pure One even His Son, 125; Pure Son, 129; Our Son purified himself, 133.
בני	**sons of** Behala shall retreat, 262; I shall make kings My sons, 272.
Italic	*son*, a proud, a Noble Lady gave birth to, 48b.
שיר	**song**, 192; 200.
אובות	**soothsayers**, the fullness of, in the Garden, 45.
ענים	**soothsayers** of Irradiation, 198.
מג	**soothsayer**, Garden of its, 31; thee shall be no, 42.
נחם	**sorrow**, 187.
אן\און	**sorrow**, 73; 74; 85; exterminate, 115; pasture of, 124; House of, 125; 134; 156; 160; 170; 193; 201; 212; 213; 216; 224; 226; 236; 237; 242; 243; 244; 254; is the Gem of Lust, 245.
אט	**gentle** *sound*, 71.
קין	**spear**, the, is the spirit of wickedness, 113.
קינים	**spears**, thy, are drowsy, 120.
מין	**species**, a hand of a species from Shem, 30; of renown, 38; lustful, 51; Father of Species, 54; of vanity, 65; 66; of vapour, 70; of sheep, 87; wounded the Thin One, 93; abundant, 254; 270.
סם	**spice**, 97.
קדה	**spice**, they fainted *for* spice, 137.
קר\קור	**spider's web**, 157; 166.
רח\רח	**spirit**, 25; for a spirit art thou, 71; Spirit of the Father, 106; of wickedness, 113; of G-d, 165; spirit of the tent of Ithiel, 207.
שד	**spirit, protective**, 26.
רקיו	**spitters, his** wounded the burden of the captive, 122.
הוד	**splendour**, 239.
גסי	**splitters of** G-d and Noah, at the Mouth of G-d they shall be judged, 208.
בז	**spoils**, 142.
עין\ען	**spring** of the Mark is empty, 57; 94; spring *waters*, 245..
פט	**stalemate**, 65.
קוע	**Stallion** of the Chamber, 127.
תכן	**standard-measure**, 227; 228.
כוכב\ככב	**star**, voice of a Star, 161; God lifted up an Alien to Star, 201.

אבן	**stone**, to enter a, 48b; 139.
פוסל	**Stone Cutter**, the Mark is the, 200.
שאוה	**storm, devastating**, (Shoah) 158.
עבל	**Stout One**, the Church of the, 104.
זר	**stranger**, 158; 161; 246.
כח	**strength**, 167; perfection of, 171; waters of, 229; 241; 243; 245; 250; 260.
לש	**strength**, 137.
אן	**strength**, exclusive, of My oppressed ones, 101; I shall awaken strength, 120; 129; 158; 159; 191; 223; 241; 244; 245; 246; 265; 274.
חל	**strength**, 160.
איל	**strength**, see you! My Strength is My Own, 123; 223.
אצם	**strong**, he is, 260; kings of strength, 261..
אמצי-אל	**strong ones of G-d**, 33.
טם	**stupid one**, 232.
עט	**stylus**, My, 14; come thou to My Stylus; strengthen thou knowledge, 185; slumbered, 185; it empowers the Lamp and the oppressed, 185.
קש	**stubble**, 86.
שי	**substance** of the hand, 110; of the swift hand, 112; of My Flame, 121.
הון	**sufficiency**, 241.
די	**sufficiency** of the Garden, 65; of Man, 97; the Son shall see this sufficiency, 137; of Terror, 163; of Y-H, 200; Sufficiency of G-d is His Distinction, 216; 257.
Italic	**sufficiencies**, He gave the, a boy, 204.
שמש	**Sun**, the Tower of the, he caused to chasten, 268.
סוני\סני	**Sunni**, the, waveth! A Banner fluttered!, 222; 226.
שרץ	**swarm**, 205.
יזע	**sweat**, of a mountain, 105.
חבר	**sword**, blood of the, of lionesses, 50; the slaughter among him is of My Sword and O how *the sword* swallows up to the corner of Lydda, 59.

T

לח	**tablet**, he raised them up toward his, 24; Habitation of the Tablet the efficient wisdom of G-d, 237.

אהל	**Tabernacle** is Mine, 103; confounded, 159; swallowed up, 162; 177.
לח	**table**, 153; Mother of the table of the *harvest* heap, 195.
תיאאר	**Tae'er** turned away from the poor, 251.
תיהו	**Taihu**, nation of, 139.
תי	**Tai**, 183.
תיא	**Tai**, valley of, 222.
תיי	**Taii** shall jest, 181; he shall refuse them gold, 181.
אשל	**tamarisk-tree**, land of the, 179.
דמע	**tear**, cut off My, 48a; heaped up for tears, 52; winked back a, 87.
דמעי	**tears of** EL/G-d, 28; he will make soft the distress with his, 35; 36; 44; of G-d fell down, 106; 258.
דמעת	**tears of** G-d, 34.
זרפות	**tears**, O the, 233; 234.
זרפים	**tears of** the oppressed, 233.
תד	**Ted** became faint, 141.
שני	**teeth of** Thebes, 58; of the Eagle, 157; 160.
תקז	**Tekez** of the darkness even Tekez of the cloud mass ate food, 144.
תל	**tel-city**, 127; 146; 148; 150; 152; 158; 166; 172; 177; 178; 186; 211; 212; 213; 214; 230; 254.
ביתה	**Temple, toward the**, 249.
רך	**tender one**, thou ravaged My, 65.
אהל	**tent** of the fisher, 77; thy tent, 82; of the terrible one, 205; 207; 210; 244.
אהלי	**tents of** My Bosom, 214; the father of the tents of astonishment, 241.
אים	**terrible**, 149.
אים	**Terrible Thing**, 118; 122; 123; 137; 164; 206; 226; 236.
אים	**Terrible One**, 131; 135; 171; 186; 189; 191; 197; 199; 200; 201; 202; 203; 205; 224; 232; 246.
אימי כח	**terrible ones of strength**, 167.
עורגת	**terraces**, Garden, 40
תלמי	**terraces of**, 247.
חת	**terror**, greatness of, 31; chief of terror of the sea, 45; is set apart, 50; 71; 72; 73; of the Mark-of-All-of-Them, 110; terror of the G-d of Eminency, 209.
חתת	**terror** 69; with the terror of G-d, 122; the terror of G-d, 136; of EL, 232.
רט	**terror**, a sufficiency, is Babylon, 163.

בעתא   **terror**, war of, 265.

טת   **Teth**, 143.

תוד   **thanksgiving** I emptied it, 111.

תדה   **thanksgiving**, 248.

נא   **Thebes**, blow thou on, 48b; teeth of, 58; bloods of, 71; Nine of, 77; captivity of, 107; 254.

שך   **thicket**, 157.

סך   **thicket**, 240.

עב   **thicket**, he caused the destruction of, 38; My, 148; 150; 152; 155.

תאוה   **thing desired** broke forth, 213.

דק   **thinness** of a gift, 76; 254.

דק'ן   **thinness** (pl.) 255.

דל   **Thin One**: of Y-H, 44; shall be magnified, 57; lo, the T.O. of the region fled, 156; of the Mist, 175; the fire of dew is in (the earth) from the Gift of the Thin One of the Isle, 194; did not My Noble, the Thin One cause the Jackal to be scorched? 195; I shall thresh the likes of tillable ground when he pierceth the Thin One of Strength because of gold, 223; O the greatness of the TO, 240; who is My Thin One? 263; the multitude of the Thin One raved, 264; who is the Thin One of Y-H? Shall I raise him up or wailing? 264.

דל   **thin one**, and he fed them a thin measure *till* there was not a thin one *left* of the affliction, 242.

דלים   **thin ones** of light, 210; 214; 216; 218; 222; 224; 272.

רק   **Thin One**: wounded by a species, 93; the Thin One with perpetual pureness, 97; My TO even the Mark-of-All-of-Them, 163; My TO was made to descend and his pure Token with him, 164; the Poor One is here...this My TO maketh fat G-d, 174; it wounded My TO for itself, 181; on what account did My TO the Levite descend? The pure banner's shaft was with him, 186; the to withdrew, 199; Kur refused the TO of the Nest, 219; 222; 223; 224; 226; the TO has hidden at his own time a Delicacy, 226.

דק   **Thin One**: on account of the TO an Ape was drowsy, 125; I shall perfect the TO of the region, 127; because of the TO I shall judge exceedingly, 133; so the TO slumbered not, 163.

שך   **thorn**, 87.

סיר   **thorn**, a, in the sole of the foot, 159.

אלף   **thousand**, 196.

תא   **threshing-floor**, 53; 55.

לע   **throat** of Og, 52; 150.

Italic   **Throne-Room** תא, 79.

כס\כסא   **throne**, lament of the, 42; for a cup, 62; 231.

כשי   **thrones of** fullness, 269.

בהן   **thumb**, 165.

תיבל   **Tibal**, 150.

תיבץ   **Tibaz**, 118.

תף   **timbrel**, 28; shall blow upon Lust, 52; 163; 212; 213; 214; 268; 270.

עת   **time**, the blood of His, 1; of G-d has run out, 44; the sufficiency of the Garden is sep-arate from, 65; of the appointed, 70; sea of, 71; time of emptiness, 73; a jar in time, 73; his own time, 75; who squeezed time? 91; the Mark moved out of, 92; time makes afraid, 120; increaseth the flame, 121; who is the Beloved of My Time? 133; of judgment, 143; at the time of a people a sheep was wanted, 166; extreme 184; reserved for a time, 188; appointed time, 190; at the time, 205; appointed time, 207; passageway of Time, 233; appointed time, 233; wandering in time, 255; he traveled through time itself, 260.

אזו   **time, his own**, 226.

תירב   **Tirab**, 64.

תח   **Toah**, 101; food of Toah, 107; 242.

את\אות   **token**, as a sign and a, 114; knowledge of the token swallowed up, 118; the Gift of the Veil is a Token, 119; window of His Token, 156; slumber, 156; His Pure Token, 164; 174; His Token, 187; 191; 196; 197; 198; 201; 232; 255.

מחר   **tomorrow** and future, 247.

שן   **tooth**, 55; greatness of, 102; dull the, 132; knoweth appetite, 148, 152; 186; 191; 199; 213; of EL, 222; 228.

תפת   **Tophet**, region of, 227; 228.

נחל   **torrent-valley**, 27.

סהר   **Tower** of Shem, he shall chasten the, My enemy, 261; of the Sheep, he causeth to chasten the, 265; of the Prince, he caused to chasten the, because of his region, 267; of the Sun, he caused to chasten, 268; of Shemah, he causes the chastening of the, 269.

ניח   **tranquility of** Chael, 217; is before US, 220.

פש   **transgression** G-d swallowed up, 175; trembled, 179.

שט   **transgressor**, come forth, the heart of Hamas, from thy ravage, 169.

צמי   **traps of** creeping things, 84.

הלכיו   **travelers, his**, 115.

מעל   **treachery** of Acath, 68; double is the ruin as the treachery, 71; thy treacherous act, 137; 141; 164.

תרמא   **treachery**, 172.

צפן   **treasure** of the Mark, 5.

הנתי   **treasures, My**, 268.

אנתי   **treasures, My**, with Me is the heap of, 273.

שלכת   vb. **tree, fell of a**, 110.

נע   **trembling**, 166.

מדה   **tribute**, 255.

עמל   **trouble**, 73.

עוכר   **troublemaker**, 71.

תר   **turtledove**, his, shall cry shrilly, 77; boiled, 79; 196.

תאום   **twin**, 266.

דו   **two** islands of secrecy, 182.

U

טמא   **unclean**, they are sucked out, 115.

טמה   **unclean one**, 263.

מעל   **unfaithful** are in distress, 83; 224; Y-H journeyed he separated the unfaithful, 271.

יחד   vb. **unite, to**, the hand of the remnant of Mother scorns Lust to unite a mountain and all by an utterance, 239.

יחד   **unity**, 118.

ישר   **Upright One**, he smote the, who is the favour of the measure of His seed, 43.

עש   **URSA MAJOR** is the Mouth, 68.

משא   **usury**, tear you away his, 96.

קל   **utterance**, 214; 227; 239; 254.

מלה   **utterance** of the Witness, 173.

V

אבר   **Valiant One, the**, Jacha' is the Pure One of Desire the, 133.

גי   **valleys, my**, hanging down of the hand of, 90; his **valley** was touched, 94; of Nob, 147; **valley** of Tia, 222; of Nebon, 242.

שוה   **vanity**, O species of, 65; 66; 111; 153.

שואות   **vanities**, burden of, 130.

אד   **vapour**, species of, 70; of Rotten On, 127.

דק   **Veil**, the Father established the Ordinance of the, 97; the Gift of the Veil is a Token, 119; He shall be silent if perchance fire together with My Veil is to return, 124; Gift from the, 137; My Veil is thinned by thy voice, 141; O Hand I shall feed them from the Veil, 147; perfect heap of the Veil measured, 149; Gift of the Veil, 194; A Lament of the Gift of the Veil, 196; thou favourest the Terrible One of Tooth above the Gift of the Veil and his companion, 199; The Wail of the Gift of the Veil, 202; from the Veil I shall cut off the Serpent, 202; the Sea of the Veil, 203; Hundreds of the Veil shall shine, 213; rebuke the Veil, 214; he has fed them from the Veil at the region of the *harvest* heap, 241.

כוכבת   **Venus** was made to wander *the sky*, 167.

כלי   **vessel**, the fruit of the, 69.

קב   **vessel**, he fashioned a, 143.

גלה   **vessel** of purity, 143.

חרש   **vessel** of My Wealth, 81.

השע   vb. **victory, worketh**, the Watcher over thee, 20.

פך   **vial**, nor the hands of the Mark his, 56; shaking a vial, 67.

שרק   **vine tendrils**, 198.

ענביו   **vineyards**, they showed comtempt over *their* own, 25.

פרצתיו   **violent ones, his**, 2.

א   **vigour** is the Hand and terrible, 115.

און   **vigour**, morsel of, 77; 96.

ראי   **vision**, I shall give a, 201.

ראה   **vision**, the Dragon caused not to weaken Error by vision, 263.

קול\קל   **voice** of Luke, 59; voice and heart, 107; voice of his generation, 125; of Desire, 128; by thy voice, 141; the shall become the measure of a voice, 143; the heart caused the voice to express grief, 151; heart of thy, 154; 169; 172; the voice of the poor in spirit, 203, 207; 223; 224; 232; 234; 235.

קא\י דם   pt. **vomiting, those, blood**, of Emptiness are bringing down the Calamity of the Thicket, 157.

קא   **vomitus**, 158; 165; 169; 228; 253.

נדר   **vow**, against him is a, 80; pride of the Vow, 130; 131.

W

הי   **wail** of its bowels, 50.

מי שר **waters of the Prince**, 160.

מי רפס **waters of Rephes**, 87.

מי כח **waters of strength**, 229; waters of his strength, 249.

מי מחר **waters of tomorrow** were veiled, 81.

פש **weak of** thy G-d, 272.

חלש **weak one** of YAH, 141.

חלשים **weak ones**, his, 15.

רקי **weak ones of**, 167.

חמש **wealth**, 67.

און\און **wealth**, My, 73; possess thou My, 75; My wealth, 81; of Dew, 110; to establish them, 114; 199..

הוני **wealth, My**, 81; made smooth, 93; spit upon, 93; makes bitter a defect, 99.

נטל **weight**, bloods of, 227; blood of, 228.

גר **whelp**, 191.

בצי **White One, My**, 162.

בוץ vb. **white, make**, 163.

אבץ **whiteness**, My, judgeth them for him, 185.

שיד **white washer**, 135.

תמד **wholeness** of G-d the Father return thou gardenward, 41.

רשע **wicked**, 264.

און **wickedness**, 4.

זמה **wickedness**, 128.

רשע **wicked one**, 47; and from Cain the wicked wounded the Mark-of-All-of-Them. The W.O. made drowsy the region of the lamp, 113; the hand of the, 117; swallowed up all My Kings, 187; 259; who is the Adversary?...the, 265.

רשעי **wicked ones of** Dagon, 54.

לבללבב **will**, My, is a Gift, 34; community of will, 34; Ah! The Noble of Desire of My Will, 132; Son of Will came, 164; 187; 229; 232; 243; 249; 269.

רוח **wind**, billowing, 126.

ללַל **winding** *staircase*, 29.

כ **window** of His Token, 155; *celestial* w. 170; 199; 224.

כוא **window**, 235.

כוה **window**, 218; 222; 226; 237.

כויך **window, Thy**, O G-d, 51; windows of plenty hang low, 59; *celestial*, 60.

כויתי **windows, My**, 60; windows of My oppressed, 166.

כות **window of** the Moon, I set the, a god, his god, 46.

יין	**wine** of desire, 48b; wine he refresheth, 77; flame of, 109; he staggered with the pure wine of the Pure One, 181; 270.
זג	**wine, cheap,** 241.
גת	**winepress,** *the Father,* begat a, 101; My w. made unclean, 138; 217; 268.
יקב	**wine vat,** 233.
חכם	**wisdom,** the Palate fashioned, 91.
תשה	**wisdom, efficient,** 178; 237.
רית	**wish** of Y-H, 213.
דק	**withered thing,** 14.
עד	**witness,** My, 5; 23; thy w. belonged to the rebellion, 36; 160; for a w. 241; they increased the Witness and the Chamber, 256; *the Witness* shall speak, 257; *the Witness* shall be salted, 258.
Italic	*women,* I shall diminish *the,* 156; 162; 204; 210; 214; 216.
פלא	**wonder,** the Mark works from the doubling of the, 1; who worked a, 97; wonder of Y-H, 125; 179.
אע	**wood,** 233.
מל	**word** of the witness, they have flung away the, 110.
מלות	**words,** 161.
מלי	**words, My,** 106; 107.
מלים	**words,** all the, 82.
מליך	**words, thy,** they knew, were from strength, 94; words of G-d, 102.
חלד	**world,** he exalted the, 179.
לען vb.	**wormwood, shall become,** 109.
לען	**wormwood,** 185.
עתר	**worshipper,** 190.
יאהת	**worthies** to be circumcised, 106.
אלל	**worthlessness** hath gotten thee by greed, 140.
חמת	**wrath of,** 67.
חם	**wrath,** he raised not up, 179; My W. cometh, 182.
הלה	**wreath,** 249.
הליהו	**wreath, his,** 249.

Y

יה	**Y-H,** wailing from, 1; consecrated the chamber, 15; striking against Y-H, 16; Le thou come Y-H not for ruin, 19; the Thin One of, 44; Witness of, 49; at thy Window O Y-H, 51; double is

the people of Thy Tooth O Y-H, 55; enough, I Y-H have ascended, 61; your Living One Y-H, 78; Y-H Thou hast made Lust ill, 85; Y-H held back, 86; YAH shall confine it, 86; you shall sharpen the knife of Y-H, 109; against the Bear is Y-H, 110; Mountains of Y-H, 118; passed by, 122; praise you Y-H, 123; mockers of Y-H, 125; he shall work extraordinarily a wonder of, 125; The Hand of Y-H waved not about, 139; Y-H waved not toward it or toward the bowman, 140; weak one of Y-H, 141; Y-H journeyed to feed them, 143; The Column of G-d is the Hand of Y-H, 143; Y-H urged the thin people of Edom, 149; This is Y-H, 154; Hand of, 158; the burden on High is for the ruination of the Witness of Y-H, 161; Y-H is with the howler in the desert. My White One obeyed Y-H, 162; thou made praise to Y-H because of His Strength, 167; let Thou lead on O Y-H, 172; Y-H established the Sabbath, 173; flames of, 176; they laid bare Y-H and they swallowed up his debt, 176; Y-H is against his god 'the Bosom of Ravage', 177; draw Thou near O Y-H, 177 and 178; is made drowsy, 178; a wonder of, 179; he boasted of Thee o Y-H, 179; he sought Thee, 179; O the exclusive root of the mighty people of Y-H, 191; they snorted at the Law of Y-H, 192; thy posterity scattered the Gift of Y-H, 192; where does Gentleness from Y-H rule? The Mark changed it; My Pure One promoted My Law, 193; the flame of Y-H caused wailing to shake, 194; the skin of the grape is with Y-H, 196; the mighty people of, 198; lest the soothsayers of Irradiation should break asunder Y-H even he circumcised His Hundreds, 198; the chamber of Y-H openeth; a Lamp scattered the sufficiency of Y-H, 200; the Mystery of Y-H, 200; a runner I shall send to the Daughter, the Bowman of Y-H, 202; O YAH the people of the pasture give thou dew among her, 203; their Pure One is like Y-H, 205; he is sick of food more than their breaking with Y-H, 208; Y-H acted the kinsman for her, 212; Wish of Y-H, 213; thy G-d Y-H, 216; the fish of the basket of the coastal heap belongs to Him *even* Y-H, 231; Chamber of Y-H, 232; the Instrument of Y-H discoursed, 238; who is made a fool? The sojourner at the discourse of the Instrument of Y-H, 238; the oppression spewed moisture even Y-H and o people thy palm is the Hand of Y-H, 239; what is the city of Y-H but a ringing cry overflowing a jar, 239; Mountain of Blood Y-H shall judge, 251; and smiter, thou art thrusting away Y-H of the Shout, 253; Neah and Chaan inflamed, 254; Day of Y-H, 262; as is Bel, as is a sheep, so he reckoned them because of Y-

H, 262; *the Dragon* caused not to measure for Y-H, 262; is the
Enabler, 263; who is the Thin One of Y-H, 264; Y-H is the
Enabler, 270; Y-H journeyed He separated the unfaithful, 271;
on account of Y-H, 273.

ישע   **Yeshua**, the Assembly of, from the, I shall feed them, 155.

שגרה   **young of her *herd***, 145; 153. (see Offspring).

נער   **youth**, who is the, of the Plan against the Dragon, 263.

Z

זבי   **Zabai** tottered, 142.

צעאל   **Zael**, palate of excess is, 52.

זהם   **Zaham**, 75.

צלת חם   **Zillah of Ham**, 237.

Bibliography

The following resources were used in the translation of The SEALED BOOK of DANIEL REVEALED.

BIBLIA HEBRAICA STUTTGARTENSIA, Deutsche Bibelgesellschaft, Stuttgart, copyrights 1967-1977, 1984.

English/Hebrew Hebrew/English DICTIONARY, Ehud Ben-Yehuda/David Weinstein, Washington Square Press, 13th printing, May 1971.

THE BROWN-DRIVER-BRIGGS HEBREW AND ENGLISH LEXICON: With An Appendix Containing The Biblical Aramaic, Hendrickson Publishers, Inc., fifth printing, March 2000.

William Gesenius, HEBREW/CHALDEE LEXICON TO THE OLD TESTAMENT, Translated into English by Samuel P. Tregelles, With An Exhaustive English Index of More Than 12,000 Entries, WM. B. Eerdmans Publishing Company, Grand Rapids, Michigan; this edition first published September 1949, 14th printing, November 1980.
Reuben Sivan/ Edward A. Levenston, compilors, THE MEGIDDO MODERN DICTIONARY, Megiddo Publishing Company LTD, Tel Aviv 1965, 2nd edition 1967.

Allen P. Ross, INTRODUCING BIBLICAL HEBREW, Baker Academic, A Division of Baker Book House Co, Grand Rapids, Michigan 49516, copyright 2001 by Allen P. Ross.

THE NEW ENGLISH BIBLE WITH THE APOCRYPHA, Oxford University Press, Cambridge University Press, 1970.

J. Weingreen, M.A., Ph.D., A PRACTICAL GRAMMAR FOR CLASSIC HEBREW, Oxford At The Clarendon Press, First Edition 1939, copyright Oxford University Press, 1959, Second Edition 1959, reprint of 1969.

Michael Drosnin, THE BIBLE CODE, Simon & Schuster, New York, New York, 1997.

"And thou Daniel shut up סתם the words and fasten up by sealing חתם until Time's end." Daniel 12.4a

The CODE is activated!

'the last shall be first and the first last'
Matthew 20.16

Forward Text

בשנתשלושלמכ \ לגרלכלקצזהימין

Daniel 12.13......................Daniel 1.1

Reversed becomes...

נימיהצקלכללרגל \ כלמלשולשתנשב

Daniel 1.1......................Daniel 12.13

...The Back Text

The <u>end</u> of the Book of Daniel is the <u>beginning</u> Of the hidden book of Daniel.

"One jot or one tittle shall in no wise pass from the Law, till all be fulfilled." Matthew 5.18

After more than 2400 years, God is again speaking to mankind, through the reading of His original Hebrew Scriptures in *reverse!*